The Life of the Mind

Willing

Books by Hannah Arendt

The Origins of Totalitarianism

The Human Condition

Between Past and Future

On Revolution

Eichmann in Jerusalem

Men in Dark Times

On Violence

Crises of the Republic

Rahel Varnhagen

The Life of the Mind:

One / Thinking
Two / Willing

The Life of the Mind

One / Thinking

Two / Willing

Hannah Arendt

Willing

Harcourt Brace Jovanovich

 New York and London

Printed in the United States of America

The quotation from Rainer Maria Rilke is from *Duino Elegies,* by Rainer
Maria Rilke, translated by J. B. Leishman and Stephen Spender, copyright
1939 by W. W. Norton & Company, Inc., copyright renewed 1967 by
Stephen Spender and J. B. Leishman, and is reprinted with the permission of W. W. Norton & Company, Inc., and The Hogarth Press.

Library of Congress Cataloging in Publication Data
Arendt, Hannah.
   Willing.

   (Her The life of the mind; v. 2)
   Includes bibliographical references and index.
   1. Will.   2. Liberty.   I. Title.
B29.A73   vol. 2   [BJ1461]   108s [123]   77–74801
ISBN 0–15–151896–3

First edition

B C D E

Contents

Contents

Editor's Note

As Hannah Arendt's friend and literary executor, I have prepared *The Life of the Mind* for publication. In 1973 *Thinking* was delivered in briefer form as Gifford Lectures at the University of Aberdeen, and in 1974 the opening part of *Willing* as well. Both *Thinking* and *Willing*, again in briefer form, were given as lecture courses at the New School for Social Research in New York in 1974–5 and 1975. The history of the work and of its editorial preparation will be related in the editor's postface to be found at the end of each volume. The second volume contains an appendix on Judging, drawn from a lecture course on Kant's political philosophy given in 1970 at the New School.

On Hannah Arendt's behalf, thanks are extended to Professor Archibald Wernham and Professor Robert Cross of the University of Aberdeen, and to Mrs. Wernham and Mrs. Cross, for their kindness and hospitality during the periods she spent there as Gifford Lecturer. Thanks are due, too, to the Senatus Academicus of the University, which was responsible for the invitation.

My own thanks, as editor, are extended, above all, to Jerome Kohn, Dr. Arendt's teaching assistant at the New School for his continuing helpfulness in resolving some difficult textual questions and for his industry and care in hunting down and checking references. And I am grateful to him and to Larry May for preparing the index. My particular thanks go also to Margo Viscusi for her saintly patience in retyping a heavily worked-over manuscript, with many insertions and interlineations in different handwritings, and for her searching editorial questions. I thank her husband, Anthony Viscusi, for the loan of his college textbooks, which much facilitated the checking of some elusive quotations. I thank my own husband, James West, for the windfall of *his* college textbooks in philosophy and for his readiness to discuss the manuscript and its occasional perplexities, and I thank him also for his decisiveness in cutting several Gordian knots in the general plan and lay-out of these volumes. I am grateful to Lotte Köhler, my co-executor, for making the relevant books from Hannah Arendt's library available to the publisher's editors, and for her overall helpfulness and devotion. Great appreciation is due Roberta Leighton and her staff at Harcourt Brace Jovanovich for the enormous pains and the intelligence they have brought to bear on the manuscript, far surpassing normal editorial practice. I warmly thank William Jovanovich for the personal interest he has always taken in *The Life of the Mind*, already evident in his presence in Aberdeen at three of the Gifford Lectures. Hannah Arendt was much more than an "author" to him, and she, on her side, valued not only his friendship but also his comments on and critical insights into her text. Since her death, he has encouraged and fortified me by his attentive reading of the edited text and by his suggestions for handling the Judgment material from the Kant lectures. Over and above that, there has been his willingness to share the burdens of decision on some minute points as well as on larger ones. I must thank too my friends Stanley Geist and Joseph Frank for being available for consultation on linguistic problems raised by the manuscript. And, for giving a hand with the German, my friend Werner Stemans of the Goethe Institute in Paris. Acknowledgments are due *The New Yorker*, which has published *Thinking* with a few slight changes; I feel gratitude to William Shawn for his enthusiastic response to the manuscript—a reaction that would have been very satisfying to the author. Finally, and most of all, I thank Hannah Arendt for the privilege of working on her book.

MARY MCCARTHY

Introduction

The second volume of *The Life of the Mind* will be devoted to the faculty of the Will and, by implication, to the problem of Freedom, which, as Bergson said, "has been to the moderns what the paradoxes of the Eleatics were to the ancients." The phenomena we have to deal with are overlaid to an extraordinary extent by a coat of argumentative reasoning, by no means arbitrary and hence not to be neglected but which parts company with the actual experiences of the willing ego in favor of doctrines and theories that are not necessarily interested in "saving the phenomena."

One reason for these difficulties is very simple: the faculty of the Will was unknown to Greek antiquity and was discovered as a result of experiences about which we hear next to nothing before the first century of the Christian era. The problem for later centuries was to reconcile this faculty with the main tenets of Greek philosophy: men of thought were no longer willing to abandon philosophy altogether and say, with Paul, "we preach Christ crucified, a stumbling-block to Jews and folly to Gentiles," and let it go at that. This, as we shall see, only Paul himself was ever prepared to do.

But the end of the Christian era by no means spells the end of these difficulties. The main strictly Christian difficulty, viz., how to reconcile faith in an all-powerful and omniscient God with the claims of free will, survives in various ways deep into the modern age, where we often meet almost the same kind of argumentation as before. Either free will is found to clash with the law of causality or, later, it can hardly be reconciled with the laws of History, whose meaningfulness depends on progress or a *necessary* development of the World Spirit. These difficulties even persist when all strictly traditional—metaphysical or theological—interests have withered away. John

3

Stuart Mill, for instance, sums up an oft-repeated argument when he says: "Our *internal* consciousness tells us that we have a power, which the whole outward experience of the human race tells us that we never use." Or, to use the most extreme example, Nietzsche calls "the entire doctrine of the Will the most fateful *falsification* in psychology hitherto . . . essentially invented for the sake of punishment."

The greatest difficulty faced by every discussion of the Will is the simple fact that there is no other capacity of the mind whose very existence has been so consistently doubted and refuted by so eminent a series of philosophers. The latest is Gilbert Ryle, to whom the Will is an "artificial concept" corresponding to nothing that has ever existed and creating useless riddles like so many of the metaphysical fallacies. Unaware, apparently, of his distinguished predecessors, he sets out to refute "the doctrine that there exists a Faculty . . . of the 'Will,' and, accordingly, that there occur processes, or operations, corresponding to what it describes as volitions." He is aware of "the fact that Plato and Aristotle never mentioned [volitions] in their frequent and elaborate discussions of the nature of the soul and the springs of conduct," because they were still unacquainted with this "special hypothesis [of later times] the acceptance of which rests not on the discovery but on the postulation of [certain] ghostly thrusts."

It is in the nature of every critical examination of the faculty of the Will that it should be undertaken by "professional thinkers" (Kant's *Denker von Gewerbe*), and this gives rise to the suspicion that the denunciations of the Will as a mere illusion of consciousness and the refutations of its very existence, which we find supported by almost identical arguments in philosophers of widely differing assumptions, might be due to a basic conflict between the experiences of the thinking ego and those of the willing ego.

Although it is always the same mind that thinks and wills, as it is the same self that unites body, soul, and mind, it is by no means a matter of course that the thinking ego's evaluation can be trusted to remain unbiased and "objective" when it comes to other mental activities. For the truth of the matter is that the notion of free will serves not only as a necessary postulate of every ethics and every system of laws but is no less an "immediate datum of consciousness" (in the words of Bergson) than the I-think in Kant or the *cogito* in Descartes, whose existence was hardly ever doubted by traditional philosophy. To anticipate: what aroused the philosophers' distrust of this faculty was its inevitable connection with Freedom: "If I must necessarily will, why need I speak of will at all?" as Augustine put it. The touchstone of a free act is always our awareness that we could also have left undone what we actually did—something not at all true of mere desire or of the appetites, where bodily needs, the necessities of the life process, or the sheer force of wanting something close at hand may override any considerations of either Will or Reason. Willing, it appears, has an infinitely greater freedom than thinking, which even in its freest, most speculative form cannot escape the law of non-contradiction. This undeniable fact has never been felt to be an unmixed blessing. By men of thought, more often than not, it has been felt to be a curse.

In what follows, I shall take the internal evidence of an I-will as sufficient testimony to the reality of the phenomenon, and since I agree with Ryle—and many others—that this phenomenon and all the problems connected with it were unknown in Greek antiquity, I must accept what Ryle rejects, namely, that this faculty was indeed "discovered" and can be dated. In brief, I shall analyze the Will in terms of its history, and this in itself has its difficulties.

Are not the human faculties, as distinct from the conditions and circumstances of human life, coeval with the appearance of man on earth? If this were not the case, how could we ever understand the literature and thoughts of bygone ages? To be sure, there is a "history of ideas," and it would be rather easy to trace the idea of Freedom historically: how it changed from being a word indicating a political status—that of a free citizen and not a slave—and a physical fact—that of a healthy man, whose body was not paralyzed but able to obey his mind—into a word indicating an *inner* disposition by virtue of which a man could *feel* free when he actually was a slave or unable to move his limbs. Ideas are mental artifacts, and their history presupposes the unchanging identity of man the artificer. We shall return to this problem later. In any event, the fact is that prior to the rise of Christianity we nowhere find any notion of a mental faculty corresponding to the "idea" of Freedom, as the faculty of the Intellect corresponds to truth and the faculty of Reason to things beyond human knowledge, or, as we said here, to Meaning.

We shall begin our examination of the nature of the willing capability and its function in the life of the mind by investigating the post-classical and pre-modern literature testifying to the mental experiences that caused its discovery as well as to those that the discovery itself caused—a literature covering the period from Paul's Letter to the Romans to Duns Scotus' questioning of Thomas Aquinas' position. But first I shall deal briefly with Aristotle, partly because of "the philosopher" 's decisive influence on medieval thought, and partly because his notion of *proairesis,* in my opinion a kind of forerunner of the Will, can serve as a paradigmatic example of how certain problems of the soul were raised and answered before the discovery of the Will.

However, this section—embracing chapters II and III—will be preceded by a rather lengthy preliminary consideration of the arguments and theories which, since the revival of philosophy in the seventeenth century, have overlaid but also reinterpreted many of these authentic experiences. After all, it is with these theories, doctrines, and arguments in mind that we approach our subject.

The final section will begin with an examination of Nietzsche's and Heidegger's "conversion" to the philosophy of antiquity as a consequence of their re-evaluation and repudiation of the willing faculty. We then shall ask ourselves whether men of action were not perhaps in a better position to come to terms with the problems of the Will than the men of thought dealt with in the first volume of this study. What will be at stake here is the Will as the spring of action, that is, as a "power of *spontaneously* beginning a series of successive things or states" (Kant). No doubt every man, by virtue of his birth, is a new beginning, and his power of beginning may well correspond to this fact of the human condition. It is in line with these Augustinian reflections that the Will has sometimes, and not only by Augustine, been considered to be the actualization of the *principium individuationis*. The question is how this faculty of being able to bring about something new and hence to "change the world" can function in the world of appearances, namely, in an environment of factuality which is old by definition and which relentlessly transforms all the spontaneity of its newcomers into the "has been" of facts—*fieri; factus sum.*

The Philosophers and the Will   I

1 *Time and mental activities*

I concluded the first volume of *The Life of the Mind* with certain time speculations. This was an attempt to clarify a very old question, first raised by Plato but never answered by him: Where is the *topos noētos,* the region of the mind in which the philosopher dwells?[1] I reformulated it in the course of the inquiry as: Where are we when we think? To what do we withdraw when we withdraw from the world of appearances, stop all ordinary activities, and start what Parmenides, at the beginning of our philosophical tradition, had so emphatically urged on us: "Look at what, though absent [from the senses], is so reliably present to the mind."[2]

Framed in spatial terms, the question received a negative answer. Though known to us only in inseparable union with a body that is at home in the world of appearances by virtue of having arrived one day and knowing that one day it will depart, the invisible thinking ego is, strictly speaking, Nowhere. It has withdrawn from the world of appearances, including its own body, and therefore also from the self, of which it is no longer aware. This to the point that Plato can ironically call the philosopher a man in love with death, and Valéry can say *"Tantôt je pense et tantôt je suis,"* implying that the thinking ego loses all sense of reality and that the real, appearing self does not think. From this it follows that our question—Where are we when we think?—was asked outside the thinking experience, hence was inappropriate.

When we then decided to inquire into the time experience of the thinking ego, we found our question no longer out of place. Memory, the mind's power of having present what is irrevocably past and thus absent from the senses, has always been the most plausible paradigmatic example of the mind's power to make invisibles present. By virtue of this power, the

1. Notes are on pages 219–239.

11

mind seems to be even stronger than reality; it pits its strength against the inherent futility of everything that is subject to change; it collects and re-collects what otherwise would be doomed to ruin and oblivion. The time region in which this salvage takes place is the Present of the thinking ego, a kind of lasting "todayness" (*hodiernus*, "of this day," Augustine called God's eternity),[3] the "standing now" (*nunc stans*) of medieval meditation, an "enduring present" (Bergson's *présent qui dure*),[4] or "the gap between past and future," as we called it in explicating Kafka's time parable. But only if we accept the medieval interpretation of that time experience as an intimation of divine eternity are we forced to conclude that not just spatiality but also temporality is provisionally suspended in mental activities. Such an interpretation shrouds our whole mental life in an aura of mysticism and strangely overlooks the very ordinariness of the experience itself. The constitution of an "enduring present" is "the habitual, normal, banal act of our intellect,"[5] performed in every kind of reflection, whether its subject matter is ordinary day-to-day occurrences or whether the attention is focused on things forever invisible and outside the sphere of human power. The activity of the mind always creates for itself *un présent qui dure*, a "gap between past and future."

(Aristotle, it seems, was the first to mention this suspension of time's motion in an enduring present, and this, interestingly enough, in his discussion of pleasure, *hēdonē*, in the tenth book of the *Nicomachean Ethics*. "Pleasure," he says, "is not in time. For what takes place in a Now is a whole"—there is no motion. And since according to him the activity of thinking, "marvelous in purity and certainty," was the "most pleasant" of all activities, clearly he was talking about the motionless Now,[6] the later *nunc stans*. For him, the most sober of the great thinkers, this seems to have been no less a moment of rapture than it was for the medieval mystics except, of course, that Aristotle would have been the last to indulge in hysterical extravagances.)

I have said before that mental activities, and especially the activity of thinking, are always "out of order" when seen from the perspective of the unbroken continuity of our business in the world of appearances. There the chain of "nows" rolls on relentlessly, so that the present is understood as precariously binding past and future together: the moment we try to pin it down, it is either a "no more" or a "not yet." From that perspective, the enduring present looks like an extended "now"— a contradiction in terms—as though the thinking ego were capable of stretching the moment out and thus producing a kind of spatial habitat for itself. But this seeming spatiality of a temporal phenomenon is an error, caused by the metaphors we traditionally use in terminology dealing with the phenomenon of Time. As Bergson first discovered, they are all terms "borrowed from spatial language. If we want to reflect on time, it is space that responds." Thus "duration is always expressed as extension,"[7] and the past is understood as something lying behind us, the future as lying somewhere ahead of us. The reason for preferring the spatial metaphor is obvious: for our everyday business in the world, on which the thinking ego may reflect but in which it is not involved, we need time measurements, and we can measure time only by measuring spatial distances. Even the common distinction between spatial juxtaposition and temporal succession presupposes an extended space through which the succession must occur.

Such preliminary and by no means satisfactory considerations of the time concept seem to me necessary for our discussion of the willing ego because the Will, if it exists at all—and an uncomfortably large number of great philosophers who never doubted the existence of reason or mind held that the Will was nothing but an illusion—is as obviously our mental organ for the future as memory is our mental organ for the past. (The strange ambivalence of the English language, in which "will" as an auxiliary designates the future whereas the verb "to will" indicates volitions, properly speaking, testifies to our uncertainties in these matters.) In our context, the basic trouble with the Will is that it deals not merely with things that are absent from the senses and need to be made present through the mind's power of re-presentation, but with things, visibles and invisibles, that have never existed at all.

The moment we turn our mind to the future, we are no

longer concerned with "objects" but with *projects,* and it is not decisive whether they are formed spontaneously or as anticipated reactions to future circumstances. And just as the past always presents itself to the mind in the guise of certainty, the future's main characteristic is its basic uncertainty, no matter how high a degree of probability prediction may attain. In other words, we are dealing with matters that never were, that are not yet, and that may well never be. Our Last Will and Testament, providing for the only future of which we can be reasonably certain, namely our own death, shows that the Will's need to will is no less strong than Reason's need to think; in both instances the mind transcends its own natural limitations, either by asking unanswerable questions or by projecting itself into a future which, for the willing subject, will never be.

Aristotle laid the foundations for philosophy's attitude toward the Will, and throughout the centuries their resiliency has withstood the most momentous tests and challenges. According to Aristotle,[8] all matters that may be or may not be, that have happened but may not have happened, are by chance, *kata symbēbekos*—or, in the Latin translation, accidental or contingent—as distinguished from what necessarily is as it is, what *is* and cannot not be. This second, which he called the *"hypokeimenon,"* lies below what is added by chance, i.e., whatever does not belong to the very essence—as color is added to objects whose essence is independent of these "secondary qualities." Attributes that may or may not attach to what underlies them—their *substratum* or *substance* (the Latin translations of *hypokeimenon*)—are accidental.

There can hardly be anything more contingent than willed acts, which—on the assumption of free will—could all be defined as acts about which I know that I could as well have left them undone. A will that is not free is a contradiction in terms—unless one understands the faculty of volition as a mere auxiliary executive organ for whatever either desire or reason has proposed. In the framework of these categories, everything that happens in the realm of human affairs is accidental or contingent (*"prakton d'esti to endechomenon kai allōs echein,"* "what is brought into being by action is that which could also be otherwise"⁹): Aristotle's very words already indicate the realm's low ontological status—a status never seriously challenged till Hegel's discovery of Meaning and Necessity in History.

Within the sphere of human activities, Aristotle admitted one important exception to this rule, namely, making or fabrication—*poiein,* as distinct from *prattein,* acting or praxis. To use Aristotle's example, the craftsman who makes a "brazen sphere" joins together matter and form, brass and sphere, both of which existed before he began his work, and produces a *new* object to be added to a world consisting of man-made things and of things that have come into being independent of human doings. The human product, this "compound of matter and form"—for instance, a house made of wood according to a form pre-existing in the craftsman's mind (*nous*)—clearly was not made out of nothing, and so was understood by Aristotle to pre-exist "potentially" before it was actualized by human hands. This notion was derived from the mode of being peculiar to the nature of living things, where everything that appears grows out of something that contains the finished product potentially, as the oak exists potentially in the acorn and the animal in the semen.

The view that everything real must be preceded by a potentiality as one of its causes implicitly denies the future as an authentic tense: the future is nothing but a consequence of the past, and the difference between natural and man-made things is merely between those whose potentialities necessarily grow into actualities and those that may or may not be actualized. Under these circumstances, any notion of the Will as an organ for the future, as memory is an organ for the past, was entirely superfluous; Aristotle did not have to be aware of the Will's existence; the Greeks "do not even have a word for" what we consider to be "the mainspring of action." (*Thelein* means "to be ready, to be prepared for something," *boulesthai* is "to view something as [more] desirable," and Aristotle's own newly coined word, which comes closer than these to our notion of some mental state that must precede action, is *pro-airesis,* the "choice" between two possibilities, or, rather, the preference that makes me choose one action instead of another.)¹⁰

Authors well read in Greek literature have always been aware of this lacuna. Thus Gilson notices as a well-known fact "that Aristotle speaks neither of liberty nor of free will . . . the term itself is lacking,"[11] and Hobbes is already quite explicit on the point.[12] It is still somewhat difficult to spot, because the Greek language of course knows the distinction between intentional and unintentional acts, between the voluntary (*hekōn*) and the involuntary (*akōn*), that is, legally speaking, between murder and manslaughter, and Aristotle is careful to point out that only voluntary acts are subject to blame and praise,[13] but what he understands by voluntary means no more than that the act was not haphazard but was performed by the agent in full possession of his physical and mental strength—"the source of motion was in the agent"[14]—and the distinction covers no more than injuries committed in ignorance or as mishaps. An act in which I am under the threat of violence but am not physically coerced—as when I give my money, pulling it out with my own hands, to the man who threatens me with a gun—would have qualified as voluntary.

It is of some importance to note that this curious lacuna in Greek philosophy—"the fact that Plato and Aristotle never mentioned [volitions] in their frequent and elaborate discussions of the nature of the soul and the springs of conduct"[15] and that therefore it cannot be "seriously maintained that the problem of freedom ever became the subject of debate in the philosophy of Socrates, Plato, and Aristotle"[16]—is in perfect accord with the time concept of antiquity, which identified temporality with the circular movements of the heavenly bodies and with the no less cyclical nature of life on earth: the ever-repeated change of day and night, summer and winter, the constant renewal of animal species through birth and death. When Aristotle holds that "coming-into-being necessarily implies the pre-existence of something which is potentially but is not actually,"[17] he is applying the cyclical movement in which everything that is alive swings—where indeed every end is a beginning and every beginning an end, so that "coming-to-be continues though things are constantly being destroyed"[18]—to the realm of human affairs, and this to the point that he can say that not only events but even opinions (*doxai*) "as they occur among men, revolve not only once or a few times but infinitely often."[19] This strange view of human affairs was not peculiar to philosophic speculation. Thucydides' claim to leave to posterity a *ktēma es aei*—a sempiternally useful paradigm of how to inquire into the future by virtue of a clear knowledge of the greatest event yet known in history—rested implicitly on the same conviction of a recurrent movement of human affairs.

To us, who think in terms of a rectilinear time concept, with its emphasis on the uniqueness of the "historical moment," the Greek pre-philosophical praise of greatness and stress on the extraordinary, which, "whether for evil or for good" (Thucydides), beyond all moral considerations, deserves to be saved from oblivion, first by the bards and then by the historians, seems to be incompatible with their cyclical time concept. But until the philosophers discovered Being as everlasting, birthless as well as deathless, time and change in time constituted no problem. Homer's "circling years" provided no more than the background against which the noteworthy story had appeared and was being told. Traces of this earlier nonspeculative view can be found throughout Greek literature; thus Aristotle himself, in his discussion of *eudaimonia* (in the *Nicomachean Ethics*), is thinking in Homeric terms when he points to the ups and downs, the accidental circumstances (*tychai*) that "revolve many times in one person's lifetime," whereas his *eudaimonia* is more durable because it resides in certain activities (*energeiai kat' aretēn*) worth remembering because of their excellence and about which therefore "oblivion does not grow" (*genesthai*).[20]

No matter what historical origins and influences—Babylonian, Persian, Egyptian—we may be able to trace for the cyclical time concept, its emergence was logically almost inevitable once the philosophers had discovered an everlasting Being, birthless and deathless, within whose framework they then had to explain movement, change, the constant coming and going of living beings. Aristotle was quite explicit about the primacy of the assumption "that the whole heaven was not generated and cannot be destroyed, as some allege, but is single and forever, having no beginning and no end of its whole existence, containing and embracing in itself infinite time."[21] "That everything returns" is indeed, as Nietzsche observed, "the closest [possible] approximation of a world of Becoming to a world of Being."[22] Hence it is not surprising that the Greeks had no notion of the faculty of the Will, our mental organ for a future that in principle is indeterminable and therefore a possible harbinger of novelty. What is so very surprising is to find such a strong inclination to denounce the Will as an illusion or an entirely superfluous hypothesis after the Hebrew-Christian credo of a divine beginning—"In the beginning God created the heavens and the earth"—had become a dogmatic assumption of philosophy. Especially as this new creed also stated that man was the only creature made in God's own image, hence endowed with a like faculty of beginning. Yet of all the Christian thinkers, only Augustine, it seems, drew the consequence: "*[Initium] ut esset, creatus est homo*" ("That a beginning be made man was created").[23]

The reluctance to recognize the Will as a separate, autonomous mental faculty finally ceded during the long centuries of Christian philosophy, which we shall be examining later in greater detail. Whatever its indebtedness to Greek philosophy and especially to Aristotle, it was bound to break with the cyclical time concept of antiquity and its notion of everlasting recurrence. The story that begins with Adam's expulsion from Paradise and ends with Christ's death and resurrection is a story of unique, unrepeatable events: "Once Christ died for our sins; and rising from the dead, He dieth no more."[24] The story's sequence presupposes a rectilinear time concept; it has a definite beginning, a turning-point—the year One of our calendar[25]—and a definite end. And it was a story of supreme importance to the Christian, although it hardly touched the course of ordinary secular events: empires could be expected to rise and fall as in the past. Moreover, since the Christian's after-life was decided while he was still a "pilgrim on earth," he himself had a future beyond the determined, necessary end of his life, and it was in close connection with the preparation for a future life that the Will and its necessary Freedom in all their complexity were first discovered by Paul.

Hence one of the difficulties of our topic is that the problems we are dealing with have their "historical origin" in theology rather than in an unbroken tradition of philosophical thought.[26] For whatever may be the merits of post-antique assumptions about the location of human freedom in the I-will, it is certain that in the frame of pre-Christian thought freedom was localized in the I-can; freedom was an objective state of the body, not a datum of consciousness or of the mind. Freedom meant that one could do as one pleased, forced neither by the bidding of a master nor by some physical necessity that demanded laboring for wages in order to sustain the body nor by some somatic handicap such as ill health or the paralysis of one's members. According to Greek etymology, that is, according to Greek self-interpretation, the root of the word for freedom, *eleutheria,* is *eleuthein hopōs erō,* to go as I wish,[27] and there is no doubt that the basic freedom was understood as freedom of movement. A person was free who could move as he wished; the I-can, not the I-will, was the criterion.

2   *The Will and the modern age*

In the context of these preliminary considerations, we may be permitted to skip the complexities of the medieval era and try to have a brief look at the next important turning-point in our intellectual history, the rise of the modern age. Here we are entitled to expect an even stronger interest in a mental organ for the future than in the medieval period, because the modern age's main and entirely new concept, the notion of *Progress* as the ruling force in human history, placed an unprecedented emphasis on the future. Yet medieval speculations on the subject still exerted a strong influence at least in the sixteenth and seventeenth centuries. And, so strong was the suspicion of the willing faculty, so sharp the reluctance to grant human beings, unprotected by any divine Providence or guidance, absolute power over their own destinies and thus burden them with a formidable responsibility for things whose very existence would depend exclusively on themselves, so great, in Kant's words, was the embarrassment of "speculative reason in dealing with the question of the freedom of the will . . . [namely with] a power of *spontaneously* beginning a series of successive things or states"[28]—as distinguished from the faculty of choice between two or more given objects (the *liberum arbitrium*, strictly speaking)—that it was not till the last stage of the modern age that the Will began to be substituted for Reason as man's highest mental faculty. This coincided with the last era of authentic metaphysical thought; at the turn of the nineteenth century, still in the vein of the metaphysics that had started with Parmenides' equation of Being and Thinking (*to gar auto esti noein te kai einai*), suddenly, right after Kant, it became fashionable to equate Willing and Being.

Thus Schiller declared that "there is no other power in man but his Will," and Will as "the ground of reality has power over both, Reason and Sensuality," whose opposition—the opposition of two necessities, Truth and Passion—provides for the origin of freedom.[29] Thus Schopenhauer decided that the Kantian thing-in-itself, the Being behind the appearances, the world's "inmost nature," its "core," of which "the objective world . . . [is] merely the outward side," is Will,[30] while Schelling on a much higher level of speculation apodictically stated: "In the final and highest instance there is no other Being than Will."[31] This development, however, reached its culmination in Hegel's philosophy of history (which for that reason I prefer to treat separately) and came to a surprisingly rapid end at the close of the same century.

Nietzsche's philosophy, centered on the Will to Power, seems at first glance to constitute the climax of the Will's ascendancy in theoretical reflection. I think that this interpretation of Nietzsche is a misunderstanding caused partly by the rather unfortunate circumstances surrounding the first uncritical editions of his posthumously published writings. We owe to Nietzsche a number of decisive insights into the nature of the willing faculty and the willing ego, to which we shall return later, but most of the passages about the Will in his work testify to an outspoken hostility toward the "theory of 'freedom of the Will,' a hundred times refuted, [which] owes its permanence" precisely to its being "refutable": "Somebody always comes along who feels strong enough to refute it once more."[32]

Nietzsche's own final refutation is contained in his "thought of Eternal Return," the "basic concept of the *Zarathustra*," which expresses "the highest possible formula of affirmation."[33] As such, it stands historically in the series of "theodicies," those strange justifications of God or of Being which, ever since the seventeenth century, philosophers felt were needed to reconcile man's mind to the world in which he was to spend his life. The "thought of Eternal Return" implies an unconditional denial of the modern rectilinear time concept and its progressing course; it is nothing less than an explicit reversion to the cyclical time concept of antiquity. What makes it modern is the pathetic tone in which it is expressed, indicating the amount of willful intensity needed by modern man to regain the simple admiring and affirming wonder, *thaumazein,* which once, for Plato, was the beginning of philosophy. Modern philosophy, on the contrary, had originated in the Cartesian and Leibnizian doubt that Being—"Why is there something and not, rather, nothing?"—could be justified at all. Nietzsche speaks of Eternal Recurrence in the tone of a religious convert, and it *was* a conversion that brought him to it, though not a religious one. With this thought he tried to convert himself to the ancient concept of Being and deny the entire philosophical creed of the modern age, which he was the first to diagnose as the "Age of Suspicion." Ascribing his thought to an "inspiration," he does not doubt that "one must go back thousands of years to find somebody who would have the right to tell [him], 'this is also my experience.' "[34]

Although in the early decades of our century Nietzsche was read and misread by almost everybody in the European intellectual community, his influence on philosophy properly speaking was minimal; to this day, there are no Nietzscheans in the sense that there are still Kantians and Hegelians. His first recognition as a philosopher came with the very influential rebellion of thinkers against academic philosophy that, unhappily, goes under the name of "existentialism." No serious study of Nietzsche's thought existed before Jaspers' and Heidegger's books about him;[35] yet that does not mean that either Jaspers or Heidegger can be understood as a belated founder of a Nietzsche school. More important in the present context, neither Jaspers nor Heidegger in his own philosophy put the Will at the center of the human faculties.

For Jaspers, human freedom is guaranteed by our not having *the* truth; truth compels, and man can be free only because he does not know the answer to the ultimate questions: "I must will because I do *not* know. The Being which is inaccessible to knowledge can be revealed only to my volition. Not-knowing is the root of having to will."[36]

Heidegger in his early work had shared the modern age's emphasis on the future as the decisive temporal entity—"the future is the primary phenomenon of an original and authentic temporality"—and had introduced *Sorge* (a German word that appeared for the first time as a philosophical term in *Being and Time* and that means "a caring for," as well as "worry about the future") as the key existential fact of human existence. Ten years later he broke with the whole modern age's philosophy (in the second volume of his book about Nietzsche), precisely because he had discovered to what an extent the age itself, and not just its theoretical products, was based on the domination of the Will. He concluded his later philosophy with the seemingly paradoxical proposition of "willing not-to-will."[37]

To be sure, in his early philosophy Heidegger did not share the modern age's belief in Progress, and his proposition "to will not-to-will" has nothing in common with Nietzsche's overcoming of the Will by restricting it to willing that whatever happens shall happen again and again. But Heidegger's famous *Kehre*, the turning-about of his late philosophy, nevertheless somewhat resembles Nietzsche's conversion; in the first place, it *was* a kind of conversion, and secondly, it had the identical consequence of leading him back to the earliest Greek thinkers. It is as though at the very end, the thinkers of the modern age escaped into a "land of thought" (Kant)[38] where their own specifically modern preoccupations—with the future, with the Will as the mental organ for it, and with freedom as a problem—had been non-existent, where, in other words, there was no notion of a mental faculty that might correspond to freedom as the faculty of thinking corresponded to truth.

3   The main objections to the Will
in post-medieval philosophy

The purpose of these preliminary remarks is to facilitate our approach to the complexities of the willing ego, and in our methodological concern we can hardly afford to overlook the simple fact that every philosophy of the Will is the product of the thinking rather than the willing ego. Though of course it is always the same mind that thinks and wills, we have seen that it cannot be taken for granted that the thinking ego's evaluation of the other mental activities will remain unbiased; and to find thinkers with widely different general philosophies raising identical arguments against the Will is bound to arouse our mistrust. I shall briefly outline the main objections as we find them in post-medieval philosophy before I enter into a discussion of Hegel's position.

There is, first, the ever-recurring disbelief in the very existence of the faculty. The Will is suspected of being a mere illusion, a phantasm of consciousness, a kind of delusion inherent in consciousness' very structure. "A wooden top," in Hobbes's words, ". . . lashed by the boys . . . sometimes spinning, sometimes hitting men on the shin, if it were sensible of its own motion, would think it proceeded from its own will, unless it felt what lashed it."[39] And Spinoza thought along the same lines: a stone set in motion by some external force "would believe itself to be completely free and would think that it continued in motion solely because of its own wish," provided that it was "conscious of its own endeavor" and "capable of thinking."[40] In other words, "men believe themselves to be free, simply because they are conscious of their actions, and unconscious of the causes whereby those actions are determined." Thus men are subjectively free, objectively necessitated. Spinoza's correspondents raise the obvious objection: "If this were granted, all wickedness would be excusable," which disturbs Spinoza not in the least. He answers: "Wicked men are not less to be feared, and not less harmful, when they are wicked from necessity."[41]

Hobbes and Spinoza admit the existence of the Will as a subjectively felt faculty and deny only its freedom: "I acknowledge this liberty, that I can do if I will; but to say I can will if I will, I take to be an absurd speech." For "Liberty or Freedom, signifieth properly the absence of . . . external impediments of motion. . . . But when the impediment of motion is in the constitution of the thing itself, we use not to say: it wants the liberty, but the power to move; as when a stone lieth still or a man is fastened to his bed by sickness." These reflections are entirely in accordance with the Greek position on the matter. What is no longer in line with classical philosophy is Hobbes's conclusion that "Liberty and necessity are consistent: as in the water, that hath not only liberty, but a necessity of descending by the channel; so likewise in the actions which men voluntarily do: which because they proceed from their will, proceed from liberty; and yet, because every act of man's will . . . proceedeth from some cause and that from another cause, in a continual chain . . . proceed from necessity. So that to him that could see the connection of those causes, the necessity of all men's voluntary actions would appear manifest."[42]

With both Hobbes and Spinoza the negation of the Will is firmly grounded in their respective philosophies. But we find virtually the same argument in Schopenhauer, whose general philosophy was very nearly the opposite and for whom consciousness or subjectivity was the very essence of Being: like Hobbes, he does not deny Will but denies that Will is free: there is an illusory feeling of freedom when I experience volition; when I deliberate about what to do next, and, rejecting a number of possibilities, finally come to some definite decision, it is "with just as free a will . . . as if water spoke to itself: 'I can make high waves . . . I can rush down hill . . . I can plunge down foaming and gushing . . . I can rise freely as a stream of water into the air (. . . in the fountain) . . . but I

am doing none of these things now, and am voluntarily remaining quiet and clear water in the reflecting pond."⁴³ This kind of
argument is best summed up by John Stuart Mill in the passage
already quoted: "Our *internal* consciousness tells us that we
have a power, which the whole outward experience of the
human race tells us that we never use" (italics added).⁴⁴

What is so striking in these objections raised against the
very existence of the faculty is, first of all, that they are invari-
ably raised in terms of the modern notion of consciousness—a
notion just as unknown to ancient philosophy as the notion of
the Will. The Greek *synesis*—that I can share knowledge with
myself (*syniēmi*) about things to which no one else can testify
—is the predecessor more of conscience than of consciousness,⁴⁵ as is seen when Plato mentions how the memory of
the bloody deed haunts the homicide.⁴⁶

Next, the same objections could easily be raised, but hardly
ever were, against the existence of the faculty of thought. To
be sure, Hobbes's reckoning with consequences, if that is to be
understood as thinking, is not open to such suspicions, but this
power of figuring and calculating ahead coincides, rather, with
the willing ego's deliberations about means to an end or with
the capacity used in solving riddles and mathematical problems. (Some such equation, clearly, is behind Ryle's refutation
of "the doctrine that there exists a Faculty . . . of the 'Will'
and, accordingly, that there occur processes, or operations,
corresponding to what it describes as 'volitions.' " In Ryle's own
words: "No one ever says such things as that . . . he performed five quick and easy volitions and two slow and difficult
volitions between midday and lunch-time."⁴⁷ It cannot be
seriously maintained that enduring thought-products, such as
Kant's *Critique of Pure Reason* or Hegel's *Phenomenology of
Mind,* could ever be understood in these terms.) The only
philosophers I know of who dared doubt the existence of the
faculty of thought were Nietzsche and Wittgenstein. The latter
in his early thought-experiments held that the thinking ego
(what he called the *"vorstellendes Subjekt,"* deriving his
terminology from Schopenhauer) could "in the last resort be
mere superstition," probably an "empty delusion, but the willing subject exists." In justification of his thesis Wittgenstein

reiterates the arguments commonly raised in the seventeenth century against Spinoza's denial of the Will, to wit, "If the Will did not exist, neither would there be . . . the bearer of ethics."[48] As for Nietzsche, it must be said that he had his doubts about both willing and thinking.

The disturbing fact that even the so-called voluntarists among the philosophers, those entirely convinced, like Hobbes, of the *power* of the will, could so easily glide to doubting its very existence may be somewhat clarified by examining the second of our ever-recurring difficulties. What aroused the philosophers' distrust was precisely the inevitable connection with Freedom—to repeat, the notion of an unfree will is a contradiction in terms: "If I must necessarily will, why need I speak of will at all? . . . Our will would not be will unless it were in our power. Because it is in our power it is free."[49] To quote Descartes, whom one may count among the voluntarists: "No one, when he considers himself alone, fails to experience the fact that to will and to be free are the same thing."[50]

As I have said more than once, the touchstone of a free act—from the decision to get out of bed in the morning or take a walk in the afternoon to the highest resolutions by which we bind ourselves for the future—is always that we know that we could also have left undone what we actually did. Willing, it appears, is characterized by an infinitely greater freedom than thinking, and—again to repeat—this undeniable fact has never been felt to be an unmixed blessing. Thus we hear from Descartes: "I am conscious of a will so extended as to be subject to no limits. . . . It is free will alone . . . which I find to be so great in me that I can conceive no other idea to be more great; it is . . . this will that causes me to know that . . . I bear the image and similitude of God," and he immediately adds that this experience "consists solely in the fact that . . . we act in such a way that we are not in the least conscious that any outside force constrains us [in] the power of choosing to do a thing or choosing not to do it."[51]

In so saying, he leaves the door wide open on the one hand to the doubts of his successors and on the other to the attempts of his contemporaries "to make [God's] pre-ordinances harmonize with the freedom of our will."[52] Descartes himself, unwilling to become "involved in the great difficulties [that would ensue] if we undertook to reconcile God's foresight and omnipotence with human freedom," explicitly appeals to the beneficial limitations of "our thought [which] is finite" and therefore subject to certain rules, for instance, the axiom of non-contradiction, and the compelling "necessities" of self-evident truth.[53]

It is precisely the "lawless" freedom the will seems to enjoy that made even Kant occasionally talk of freedom as perhaps being no more than "a mere thought entity, a phantom of the brain."[54] Others, like Schopenhauer, found it easier to reconcile Freedom and Necessity and thus escape the dilemma inherent in the simple fact that man is at the same time a thinking and a willing being—a coincidence fraught with the most serious consequences—by simply declaring: "man does at all times only what he wills, and yet he does this necessarily. But this is due to the fact that he . . . *is* what he wills. . . . Subjectively . . . everyone feels that he always does only what he wills. But this merely means that his activity is a pure expression of his very own being. Every natural being, even the lowest, would feel the same, if it *could* feel."[55]

Our third difficulty is linked with that dilemma. In the eyes of philosophers who spoke in the name of the thinking ego, it had always been the curse of *contingency* that condemned the realm of merely human affairs to a rather low status in the ontological hierarchy. But before the modern age, there had existed—not many but a few—well-trodden escape routes, at least for philosophers. In antiquity, there was the *bios theōrētikos:* the thinker dwelt in the neighborhood of things necessary and everlasting, partaking in their Being to the extent that this is possible for mortals. In the era of Christian philosophy, there was the *vita contemplativa* of the monasteries and the universities, but also the consoling thought of divine Providence, joined to the expectation of an after-life when what had seemed contingent and meaningless in this world would become crystal clear, the soul seeing "face to face" instead of "though a glass, darkly," no longer knowing "in part"—for he shall "know even as also [he is] known." Without such hope for a Hereafter, even Kant still deemed human life too miserable, devoid of meaning, to be borne.

It is obvious that the advancing secularization, or, rather, de-Christianization, of the modern world, coupled, as it was, with an entirely new emphasis on the future, on progress, and therefore on things neither necessary nor sempiternal, would expose men of thought to the contingency of all things human more radically and more mercilessly than ever before. What had been ever since the end of antiquity the "problem of freedom" was now incorporated, as it were, in the haphazardness of history, "full of sound and fury," "a tale told by an idiot . . . signifying nothing," to which there corresponded the random character of personal decisions originating in a free will that was guided neither by reason nor by desire. And this old problem reappearing in the dress of the new age, the Age of Progress, which is reaching its end only now in our own time (as Progress rapidly nears the limits given by the human condition on earth), found its pseudo-solution in the nineteenth-century *philosophy of history,* whose greatest representative worked out an ingenious theory of a hidden Reason and Meaning in the course of world events, directing men's wills in all their contingency toward an ultimate goal they never intended. Once this story is complete—and Hegel seems to have believed that the beginning of the end of the story was coeval with the French Revolution—the backward-directed glance of the philosopher, through the sheer effort of the thinking ego, can internalize and recollect (*er-innern*) the meaningfulness and necessity of the unfolding movement, so that again he can dwell with what is and cannot not-be. Finally, in other words, the process of thinking coincides once more with authentic Being: thought has purified reality of the merely accidental.

4   *The problem of the new*

If we reconsider the objections raised by philosophers against the Will—against the faculty's existence, against the notion of human freedom implicit in it, and against the contingency adhering to free will, that is, to an act that by definition can also be left undone—it becomes obvious that they apply much less to what tradition knows as *liberum arbitrium,* the freedom of choice between two or more desirable objects or ways of conduct, than to the Will as an organ for the future and identical with the power of beginning something new. The *liberum arbitrium* decides between things equally possible and given to us, as it were, in *statu nascendi* as mere potentialities, whereas a power to begin something really new could not very well be preceded by any potentiality, which then would figure as one of the causes of the accomplished act.

I have previously mentioned Kant's embarrassment "in dealing with . . . a power of *spontaneously* beginning a series of successive things or states"—for instance, if "I at this moment arise from my chair . . . a new series . . . has its *absolute* beginning in this event, although [he adds] as regards time this event is only the continuation of a preceding series."[56] What is so very troublesome is the notion of an *absolute* beginning, for "a series occurring in the world can have only a relatively first beginning, being always preceded by some other state of things," and this is, of course, also true for the person of the thinker inasmuch as I who think never cease to be an appearance among appearances, no matter how successfully I may have withdrawn from them mentally. No doubt the very hypothesis of an absolute beginning goes back to the Biblical doctrine of Creation, as distinct from the Oriental theories of "emanation," according to which pre-existing forces developed and unfolded into a world. But this doctrine is a sufficient reason in our context only if one adds that God's creation is *ex nihilo,* and of such a creation the Hebrew Bible knows nothing; it is an addition of later speculations.[57]

These speculations arose when the Fathers of the Church had already begun to account for the Christian faith in terms of Greek philosophy, that is, when they were confronted with *Being,* for which the Hebrew language has no word. Logically speaking, it seems rather obvious that an equation of the universe with Being ought to imply "nothingness" as its opposite;

still, the transition from Nothing to Something is logically so difficult that one may tentatively suspect that it was the new willing ego which, regardless of doctrines and credos, found the idea of an absolute beginning appropriate to its experience of forming projects. For there is something fundamentally wrong with Kant's example. Only if he, arising from his chair, has something in mind he wishes to do, does this "event" start a "new series"; if this is not the case, if he habitually gets up at this time or if he gets up in order to fetch something he needs for his present occupation, this event is itself "the continuation of a preceding series."

But let us suppose that this was an oversight and that Kant had clearly in mind the "power of spontaneously beginning" and therefore was concerned about a possible reconciliation of a "new series of acts and states" with the time continuum that this "new series" interrupts: the traditional solution of the problem even at that date would still have been the Aristotelian distinction between potentiality and actuality, as saving the unity of the time concept by assuming that the "new series" was potentially contained in the "preceding series." But the insufficiency of the Aristotelian explanation is evident: Can anybody seriously maintain that the symphony produced by a composer was "possible before it was actual"?[58]—unless one means by "possible" no more than that it was clearly not impossible, which of course is entirely different from its having existed in a state of potentiality, waiting for some musician who would take the trouble to make it actual.

Yet, as Bergson very well knew, there is another side to the matter. In the perspective of memory, that is, looked at retrospectively, a freely performed act loses its air of contingency under the impact of now being an accomplished fact, of having become part and parcel of the reality in which we live. The impact of reality is overwhelming to the point that we are unable to "think it away"; the act appears to us now in the guise of necessity, a necessity that is by no means a mere delusion of consciousness or due only to our limited ability to imagine possible alternatives. This is most obvious in the realm of action, where no deed can be safely undone, but it is also true, though perhaps in a less compelling way, of the countless new objects that human fabrication constantly adds to the world and its civilization, art objects as well as use objects; it is almost as impossible to think away the great art works of our cultural inheritance as to think away the outbreak of the two World Wars or any other events that have decided the very structure of our reality. In Bergson's own words: "By virtue of its sheer factuality, reality throws its shadow behind it into an infinitely distant past; thus it appears to have existed in the mode of potentiality in advance of its own actualization." (*"Par le seul fait de s'accomplir, la réalité projette derrière son ombre dans le passé indéfiniment lointain; elle paraît ainsi avoir préexisté, sous forme de possible à sa propre réalisation."*)[59]

Seen in this perspective, which is the perspective of the willing ego, it is not freedom but necessity that appears as a delusion of consciousness. Bergson's insight seems to me both elementary and highly significant, but may there not be significance, too, in the fact that this observation, despite its simple plausibility, never played any role in the endless discussions of necessity versus freedom? As far as I know, the point was made only once before Bergson. That was by Duns Scotus, the lonely defender of the primacy of the Will over the Intellect and—more than that—of the factor of contingency in everything that is. If there is such a thing as Christian philosophy, then Duns Scotus would have to be recognized not only as "the most important thinker of the Christian Middle Ages"[60] but perhaps also as the unique one who did not seek a compromise between the Christian faith and Greek philosophy, and who dared, therefore, to make it a badge of true "Christians [to say] that God acts contingently." "Those who deny that some being is contingent," said Scotus, "should be exposed to torments until they concede that it is possible for them not to be tormented."[61]

Whether contingency, for classical philosophy the ultimate of meaninglessness, burst as a reality upon the early centuries of the common era because of Biblical doctrine—which "pitted contingency against necessity, particularity against universality, will against intellect," thus securing "a place for the 'contingent' within philosophy against the latter's original bias"[62]— or whether the shattering political experiences of these early centuries had forced wide open the truisms and plausibilities of ancient thinking may be open to doubt. What is not open to doubt is that the original bias against contingency, particularity, and Will—and the predominance accorded to necessity, universality, and Intellect—survived the challenge deep into the modern age. Religious and medieval as well as secular and modern philosophy found many different ways of assimilating the Will, the organ of freedom and the future, to the older order of things. For however we may look at these matters, *factually* Bergson is quite right when he asserts: "Most philosophers . . . are unable . . . to conceive of radical novelty and unpredictability. . . . Even those very few who believed in the *liberum arbitrium* have reduced it to a simple 'choice' between two or several options, as though these options were 'possibilities' . . . and the Will was restricted to 'realizing' one of them. Hence, they still admitted . . . that everything is given. They seem never to have had the slightest notion of an entirely new activity. . . . And such an activity is after all free action."[63] No doubt, even today if we listen to a dispute between two philosophers one of whom argues for determinism and the other for freedom, "it will always be the determinist who appears to be right. . . . [The audience] will always agree that he is simple, clear, and true."[64]

Theoretically, the trouble has always been that free will— whether understood as freedom of choice or as the freedom to start something unpredictably new—seems utterly incompatible, not just with divine Providence, but with the law of causality; the Will's freedom can be assumed on the strength, or, rather, the weakness, of interior experience, but it cannot be proved. The implausibility of the assumption or Postulate of Freedom is due to our outward experiences in the world of appearances, where as a matter of fact, Kant notwithstanding, we seldom start a new series. Even Bergson, whose whole philosophy rests on the conviction that "each of us has the immediate knowledge . . . of his free spontaneity,"[65] admits that "although we are free whenever we are willing to get back into ourselves, it seldom happens that we are willing." And

"Free acts are exceptional."[66] (Most of our acts are taken care of by habits, just as many of our everyday judgments are taken care of by prejudices.)

The first to refuse consciously and deliberately to come to grips with the implausibility of free will was Descartes: "It would be absurd to doubt that of which we inwardly experience and perceive as existing within ourselves, just because we do not comprehend a matter which from its nature we know to be incomprehensible."[67] For "these matters are such that anyone ought to experience them in himself rather than be convinced by ratiocination; but you . . . appear not to pay heed to what the mind transacts within itself. Refuse then to be free, *if freedom does not please you*" (italics added).[68] To which one is tempted to reply that the Cartesian *Cogito* is certainly nothing but a "transaction of the mind within itself," but it never occurred either to Descartes or to those who objected to his philosophy to speak of thinking or *cogitare* as something assumed without proof, a mere datum of consciousness. What, then, is it that gives the *cogito me cogitare* its ascendancy over the *volo me velle*—even in Descartes, who was a "voluntarist"? *Could it be that professional thinkers, basing their speculations on the experience of the thinking ego, were less "pleased" with freedom than with necessity?* This suspicion appears inevitable when we consider the strange assembly of theories on record, theories trying either to deny outright the experience of freedom "within ourselves" or to weaken freedom by reconciling it with necessity by means of dialectical speculations that are entirely "speculative" in that they cannot appeal to any experience whatsoever. The suspicion is strengthened when one considers how closely all free-will theories are tied to the problem of evil. Thus Augustine begins his treatise *De libero arbitrio voluntatis* (*The Free Choice of the Will*) with the question: "Tell me, please, whether God is not the cause of evil?" It was a question first raised in all its complexity by Paul (in the Letter to the Romans) and then generalized into What is the cause of evil? with many variations concerning the existence both of physical harm caused by destructive nature and of deliberate malice caused by men.

The whole problem has haunted philosophers, and their

attempts at solving it have never been very successful; as a rule their arguments evade the issue in its stark simplicity. Evil is either denied true reality (it exists only as a deficient mode of the good) or is explained away as a kind of optical illusion (the fault is with our limited intellect, which fails to fit some particular properly into the encompassing whole that would justify it), all this on the unargued assumption that "only the whole is actually real" (*"nur das Ganze hat eigentliche Wirklichkeit"*), in the words of Hegel. Evil, not unlike freedom, seems to belong to those "things about which the most learned and ingenious men can know almost nothing."[69]

5 *The clash between thinking and willing: the tonality of mental activities*

If one looks at this record with eyes unclouded by theories and traditions, religious or secular, it is certainly hard to escape the conclusion that philosophers seem genetically unable to come to terms with certain phenomena of the mind and its position in the world, that we can no more trust men of thought to arrive at a fair estimate of the Will than we could trust them to arrive at a fair estimate of the body. But the philosophers' hostility to the body is well known and a matter of record ever since Plato at least. It is not motivated primarily by the unreliability of sense experience—for these errors can be corrected—or by the famous unruliness of the passions— for these can be tamed by reason—but by the simple and incorrigible nature of our bodily needs and wants. The body, as Plato rightly stresses, always "wants to be taken care of" and even under the best of circumstances—health and leisure on one hand, a well-regulated commonwealth on the other—it will interrupt with its ever-recurring claims the activity of the thinking ego; in terms of the Cave parable, it will compel the philosopher to return from the sky of Ideas to the Cave of human affairs. (It is usual to blame this hostility on the Christian antagonism toward the flesh. Not only is the hostility much older; one could even argue that one of the crucial Christian dogmas, the resurrection of the flesh, as distinguished from older speculations about the immortality of the soul, stood in sharp contrast not only to common gnostic beliefs but also to the common notions of classical philosophy.)

The antagonism of the thinking ego toward the Will is of course of a very different kind. The clash here is between two *mental* activities that seem unable to co-exist. When we form a volition, that is, when we focus our attention on some future project, we have no less withdrawn from the world of appearances than when we are following a train of thought. Thinking and willing are antagonists only insofar as they affect our psychic states; both, it is true, make present to our mind what is actually absent, but thinking draws into its enduring present what either is or at least has been, whereas willing, stretching out into the future, moves in a region where no such certainties exist. Our psychic apparatus—the soul as distinguished from the mind—is equipped to deal with what comes toward it from this region of the unknown by means of expectation, whose chief modes are hope and fear. The two modes of feeling are intimately connected in that each of them is prone to veer to its seeming opposite, and because of the uncertainties of the region these shiftings are almost automatic. Every hope carries within itself a fear, and every fear cures itself by turning to the corresponding hope. It is because of their shifting, unstable, and disquieting nature that classical antiquity counted both among the evil gifts of Pandora's box.

What the soul demands of the mind in this uncomfortable situation is not so much a prophetic gift that can foretell the future and thus confirm either hope or fear; far more soothing than the fraudulent games of the soothsayers—augurs, astrologists, and the like—is the no less fraudulent theory that claims to prove that whatever is or will be "was to be," in the felicitous phrase of Gilbert Ryle.[70] Fatalism, which indeed "no philosopher of the first or second rank has defended . . . or been at great pains to attack," has nevertheless had an astoundingly successful career in popular thinking throughout the centuries; "we do all have our fatalist moments," as Ryle says,[71] and the reason is that no other theory can lull so effectively any urge to act, any impulse to make a project, in short, any form of the I-will. These existential advantages of fatalism are clearly outlined in Cicero's treatise *On Fate,* still the classical argumentation of the case. For the proposition "Everything is foreordained," he uses the following example: When you get sick, "it is foreordained that you will recover or not recover, whether you call a doctor or do not call a doctor,"[72] and of course whether you call in a doctor or not would also be foreordained. Hence the argument leads into "infinite regress."[73] Under the name of "idle argument," it is rejected because it would obviously "lead to the entire abolition of action from life." Its great attraction is that through it "the mind is released from all necessity of motion."[74] In our context, the interest of the proposition lies in the fact that it succeeds in totally abolishing the future tense by assimilating it to the past. What *will* or may be *"was* to be," for "everything that will be, *if it will actually be,* cannot be conceived not to be" (*"quicquid futurum est, id intelligi non potest,* si futurum sit, *non futurum esse"*), as Leibniz put it.[75] The formula's soothing quality is borrowed from what Hegel called "the quiet of the past" (*"die Ruhe der Vergangenheit"*),[76] a quiet guaranteed by the fact that what is past cannot be undone and that the Will "cannot will backwards."[77]

It is not the future as such but the future as the Will's *project* that *negates* the given. In Hegel and Marx, the power of negation, whose motor drives History forward, is derived from the Will's ability to actualize a project: the project negates the now as well as the past and thus threatens the thinking ego's enduring present. Inasmuch as the mind, withdrawn from the world of appearances, draws the absent—what is no more as well as what is not yet—into its own presence, it looks as though past and future could be united under a common denominator and thus be saved together from the flux of time. But the *nunc stans,* the gap between past and future where we localized the thinking ego, while it can absorb what is no more without any disturbance from the outside world, cannot react with the same equanimity to projects formed by the will for the future. Every volition, although a mental activity, relates to the world of appearances in which its project is to be realized; in flagrant contrast to thinking, no willing is ever done for its own sake or finds its fulfillment in the act itself. Every volition not only concerns particulars but—and this is of great importance—looks forward to its own end, when willing-something will have changed into doing-it. In other words, the normal mood of the willing ego is impatience, disquiet, and worry (*Sorge*), not merely because of the soul's reacting to the future in fear and hope, but also because the will's project pre-supposes an I-can that is by no means guaranteed. The will's worrying disquiet can be stilled only by the I-can-and-I-do, that is, by a cessation of its own activity and release of the mind from its dominance.

In short, the will always wills to *do* something and thus implicitly holds in contempt sheer thinking, whose whole activity depends on "doing nothing." We shall see when we examine the history of the Will that no theologian or philos-opher has ever praised the "sweetness" of the willing ego's experience, as philosophers were wont to praise that of the thinking ego. (There are two important exceptions: Duns Scotus and Nietzsche, both of whom understood the Will as a kind of power—"*voluntas est potentia quia ipsa aliquid potest.*" That is, the willing ego is delighted with itself—"*condelectari sibi*"—to the extent that the I-will anticipates an I-can; the I-will-*and*-I-can is the Will's delight.[78])

In this respect—let me call it the "tonality" of mental activ-ities—the Will's ability to have present the not-yet is the very opposite of remembrance. Remembrance has a natural affinity to thought; all thoughts, as I have said, are after-thoughts. Thought-trains rise naturally, almost automatically, out of re-remembering, without any break. This is why *anamnēsis*, in Plato, could become such a plausible hypothesis for the human capacity for learning, and why Augustine could so very plaus-ibly equate mind and *memoria*. Remembrance may affect the soul with longing for the past, but this nostalgia, while it may hold grief and sorrow, does not upset the mind's equanimity, because it concerns things which are beyond our power to change. On the contrary, the willing ego, looking forward and not backward, deals with things which are in our power but whose accomplishment is by no means certain. The resulting tension, unlike the rather stimulating excitement that may accompany problem-solving activities, causes a kind of disquiet in the soul easily bordering on turmoil, a mixture of fear and hope that becomes unbearable when it is discovered that, in Augustine's formula, to will and to be able to perform, *velle* and *posse*, are not the same. The tension can be overcome only by doing, that is, by giving up the mental activity altogether; a switch from willing to thinking produces no more than a temporary paralysis of the will, just as a switch from thinking to willing is felt by the thinking ego to be a temporary paralysis of the thinking activity.

Speaking in terms of tonality—that is, in terms of the way the mind affects the soul and produces its *moods,* regardless of outside events, thus creating a kind of *life* of the mind—the predominant mood of the thinking ego is *serenity,* the mere enjoyment of an activity that never has to overcome the resistance of matter. To the extent that this activity is closely connected with remembrance, its mood inclines to melancholy— according to Kant and Aristotle, the mood characteristic of the philosopher. The predominant mood of the Will is *tenseness,* which brings ruin to the "mind's tranquillity," Leibniz's "*animi tranquillitas,*" which, according to him, all "serious philosophers" insist on[79] and which he himself found in thought-trains proving that this is the "best of all possible worlds." In this perspective, the only task left for the Will is indeed to "will not to will," since every willed act can only interfere with the "universal harmony" of the world, in which "everything that is, looked at from the viewpoint of the Whole, is the best."[80]

Thus Leibniz, with admirable consistency, finds that the sin of Judas lies not in his betrayal of Jesus but in his suicide: in condemning himself, he implicitly condemned the whole of God's creation; by hating himself, he hated the Creator.[81] We find the same thought in its most radical version in one of Master Eckhart's condemned sentences: "Should a man have committed a thousand mortal sins, were he rightly dis-

posed he ought not to will not to have committed them"
("*Wenn jemand tausend Todsünden begangen hätte, dürfte
er, wäre es recht um ihn bestellt, nicht wollen, sie nicht begangen zu haben*").[82] We may be permitted to conjecture that
this startling rejection of repentance on the part of two Christian thinkers in Eckhart was motivated by a superabundance of
faith, which demanded, Jesus-like, that the sinner forgive himself as he was asked to forgive others, "seven times a day," because the alternative would be to declare that it would have
been better—not only for him but also for the whole of Creation
—never to be born ("that a millstone were hanged about his
neck, and he cast into the sea"), whereas in Leibniz we may
see it as an ultimate victory of the thinking ego over the willing ego, because of the latter's futile attempt at willing backward which, if successful, could only end in the annihilation of
everything that is.

6   *Hegel's solution: the philosophy of History*

No philosopher has described the willing ego in its clash
with the thinking ego with greater sympathy, insight, and consequence for the history of thought than Hegel. This is a
somewhat complex business, not only because of Hegel's eso-
teric and highly idiosyncratic terminology, but also because he
treats the whole problem in the course of his time speculations
and not in the rather meager though by no means insignificant
passages—in the *Phenomenology of Mind*, the *Philosophy
of Right*, the *Encyclopedia*, and the *Philosophy of History*—
that deal directly with the Will. These passages have been
assembled and interpreted by Alexandre Koyré in a little-
known and very important essay (published in 1934 under the
misleading title *Hegel à Iéna*),[83] devoted to Hegel's crucial
texts on Time—from the early *Jenenser Logik* and the *Jenenser Realphilosophie* to the *Phenomenology*, the *Encyclopedia*,
and the various manuscripts belonging to the *Philosophy of
History*. Koyré's translation and commentaries became "the

source and basis" of Alexandre Kojève's highly influential interpretation of the *Phenomenology*.[84] In the following I shall closely follow Koyré's argumentation.

His central thesis is that Hegel's "greatest originality" resides in his "insistence on the future, the primacy ascribed to the future over the past."[85] We would not find this surprising if it were not said about Hegel. Why should not a nineteenth-century thinker, sharing the confidence in Progress of his predecessors of the seventeenth and eighteenth centuries and of his contemporaries, too, draw the proper inference and ascribe to the future primacy over the past? After all, Hegel himself said that "everyone is the son of his own time, and therefore philosophy is *its time comprehended in thought.*" But he also said in the same context that "to understand what exists is the task of philosophy, for what exists is reason," or "what is *thought* is, and what is exists only insofar as it is thought" (*"Was* gedacht *ist, ist; und was* ist, ist *nur, insofern es* Gedanke *ist"*).[86] And it is on this premise that Hegel's most important and most influential contribution to philosophy is based. For Hegel is, above all, the first thinker to conceive of a philosophy of history, that is, of the past: re-collected by the backward-directed glance of the thinking and remembering ego, it is "internalized" (*er-innert*), becomes part and parcel of the mind through "the effort of the concept" (*"die Anstrengung des Begriffs"*), and in this internalizing way achieves the *"reconciliation"* of Mind and World. Was there ever a greater triumph of the thinking ego than is represented in this scenario? In its withdrawal from the world of appearances, the thinking ego no longer has to pay the price of "absent-mindedness" and alienation from the world. According to Hegel, the mind, by sheer force of reflection, can assimilate to itself—suck into itself, as it were—not, to be sure, all the appearances but whatever has been meaningful in them, leaving aside everything not assimilable as irrelevant accident, without consequence for either the course of History or the train of discursive thought.

The primacy of the past, however—as Koyré discovered—disappears entirely when Hegel comes to discuss Time, for him, above all, "human time"[87] whose flux man first, as it were, unthinkingly experiences as sheer motion, until he happens to reflect on the meaning of outside events. It then turns out that the mind's attention is primarily directed toward the future, namely, toward the time that is in the process of coming toward us (indicated, as I have said, in the German *Zukunft*, from *zu kommen,* like the French *avenir* from *à venir*), and this anticipated future negates the mind's "enduring present," which it transforms into an anticipated "no-more." In this context, "the dominant dimension of time is the future, which takes priority over the past." "Time finds its truth in the future since it is the future that will finish and accomplish Being. But Being, finished and accomplished, belongs as such to the Past."[88] This reversal of the ordinary time sequence—past-present-future—is caused by man's denying his present: he "says *no* to his Now" and thus creates his own future.[89] Hegel himself does not mention the Will in this context, nor does Koyré, but it seems obvious that the faculty behind the Mind's negation is not thinking but willing, and that Hegel's description of experienced human time relates to the time sequence appropriate to the willing ego.

It is appropriate because the willing ego when it forms its projects does indeed live for the future. In Hegel's famous words, the reason "the present [the Now] cannot resist the future" is by no means the inexorability with which every today is followed by a tomorrow (for this tomorrow, if not projected and mastered by the Will, could just as well be a mere repetition of what went before—as indeed it frequently is); the today in its very essence is threatened only by the mind's interference, which negates it and, by virtue of the Will, summons up the absent not-yet, mentally canceling the present, or, rather, looking upon the present as that ephemeral time span whose essence is not to be: "The Now is empty . . . it fulfills itself in the future. The future is its reality."[90] From the perspective of the willing ego, "the future is directly within the present, for it is contained as its negative fact. The Now is just as much the being that disappears as it is also the non-being [that] . . . is converted into Being."[91]

To the extent that the self identifies itself with the willing ego—and we shall see that this identification is proposed by some of the voluntarists who derive the *principium individua-tionis* from the willing faculty—it exists "in a continual trans-formation of [its own] future into a Now, and it ceases to be the day when there is no future left, when there is nothing still outstanding [*le jour où il n'y a plus d'avenir, où rien n'est plus à venir*], when everything has arrived and when everything is 'accomplished.' "[92] Seen from the perspective of the Will, old age consists in the shrinkage of the future dimension, and man's death signifies less his disappearance from the world of appearances than his final loss of a future. This loss, however, coincides with the ultimate accomplishment of the individual's life, which at its end, having escaped the incessant change of time and the uncertainty of its own future, opens itself to the "tranquillity of the past" and thereby to inspection, reflection, and the backward glance of the thinking ego in its search for meaning. Hence, from the viewpoint of the thinking ego, old age, in Heidegger's words, is the time of meditation or, in the words of Sophocles, it is the time of "peace and freedom"[93]— release from bondage, not only to the passions of the body, but to the all-consuming passion the mind inflicts on the soul, the passion of the will called "ambition."

In other words, the past begins with disappearance of the future, and, in that tranquillity, the thinking ego asserts itself. But this happens only when everything has reached its end, when Becoming, in whose process Being unfolds and de-velops, has been arrested. For "restlessness is the ground of Being";[94] it is the price paid for Life, as death, or, rather, the anticipation of death, is the price paid for tranquillity. And the restlessness of the living does not come from contemplating either the cosmos or history; it is not the effect of external motion—the incessant movement of natural things or the in-cessant ups and downs of human destinies; it is localized in and engendered by the mind of man. What in later existential thought became the notion of the auto-production of man's mind we find in Hegel as the "auto-constitution of Time":[95] man is not just temporal; he *is* Time.

Without him there might be movement and motion, but there would not be Time. Nor could there be, if man's mind were equipped only for thinking, for reflecting on the given, on what is as it is and could not be otherwise; in that case man would live mentally in an everlasting present. He would be unable to realize that he himself once was not and that one day he will be no more, that is, he would be unable to understand what it means for him to exist. (It is because of Hegel's view that the human mind produces time that his other, more obvious, identification of logic and history comes about, and this identification is indeed, as Léon Brunschvicg pointed out long ago, "one of the essential pillars of his system."[96])

But in Hegel the mind produces time only by virtue of the will, its organ for the future, and the future in this perspective is also the source of the past, insofar as that is mentally engendered by the mind's anticipation of a second future, when the immediate I-shall-be will have become an I-shall-have-been. In this schema, the past is produced by the future, and thinking, which contemplates the past, is the result of the Will. For the will, in the last resort, anticipates the ultimate frustration of the will's projects, which is death; they too, one day, will have been. (It may be interesting to note that Heidegger, too, says *"Die Gewesenheit entspringt in gewisser Weise der Zukunft"*—the past, the "having-been," has its origin in a certain sense in the future.[97])

In Hegel, man is not distinguished from other animal species by being an *animal rationale* but by being the only living creature that knows about his own death. It is at this ultimate point of the willing ego's anticipation that the thinking ego constitutes itself. In the anticipation of death, the will's projects take on the appearance of an anticipated past and as such can become the object of reflection; and it is in this sense that Hegel maintains that only the mind that "does not ignore death" enables man to "dominate death," to "endure it and to maintain itself within it."[98] To put it in Koyré's words: at the moment in which the mind confronts its own end "the incessant motion of the temporal dialectics is arrested and time has 'fulfilled' itself; this 'fulfilled' time falls naturally and in its entirety into the past," which means that the "future has lost its power over it" and it has become ready for the enduring present of the thinking ego. Thus it turns out that "the [future's] true Being is to be the Now."[99] But in Hegel this *nunc stans* is no longer temporal; it is a *"nunc aeternitatis,"* as eternity for Hegel is also the quintessential nature of Time, the Platonic "image of eternity," seen as the "eternal movement of the mind."[100] Time itself is eternal in "the union of Present, Future and Past."[101]

To oversimplify: That there exists such a thing as the *Life* of the mind is due to the mind's organ for the future and its resulting "restlessness"; that there exists such a thing as the life of the *Mind* is due to death, which, foreseen as an absolute end, halts the will and transforms the future into an antici- pated past, the will's projects into objects of thought, and the soul's expectation into an anticipated remembrance. Thus summarized and oversimplified, the doctrine of Hegel sounds so modern, the primacy of the future in its time speculations so well attuned to his century's dogmatic faith in Progress, and its shift from thinking to willing and back again to think- ing so ingenious a solution of the modern philosopher's problem of how to come to terms with the tradition in a mode acceptable to the modern age, that one is inclined to dismiss the Hegelian construct as an authentic contribution to the problems of the willing ego. Yet in his time speculations Hegel has a strange predecessor to whom nothing could have been more alien than the notion of Progress nor anything of less interest than discovering a law that ruled over historical events.

That is Plotinus. He, too, holds that the human mind, man's "soul" (*psychē*), is the originator of time. Time is gener- ated by the soul's "over-active" nature (*polypragmōn,* a term suggesting busybodiness); longing for its own future immor- tality, it "seeks for more than its present stage" and thus al- ways "moves on to a 'next' and an 'after' and to what is not the same but is something else and then else again. So moving, we made a long stretch of our journey [toward our future eter- nity] and constructed time, the image of eternity." Thus, "time is the life of the soul"; since "the spreading out of life involves time," the soul "produces the succession [of time] along with its activity" in the form of "discursive thought," whose discursiveness corresponds to the "soul's movement of passing from one way of being to another"; hence time is "not an accompaniment of Soul . . . but something which . . . is in it and with it."[102] In other words, for Plotinus as for Hegel, time is generated by the mind's innate restlessness, its stretching out to the future, its projects, and its negation of "the present state." And in both cases the true fulfillment of time is eternity, or, in secular terms, existentially speaking, the mind's switch from willing to thinking.

However that may be, there are many passages in Hegel that indicate that his philosophy is less inspired by the works of his predecessors, less a reaction to their opinions, less an attempt to "solve" problems of metaphysics, less bookish, in brief, than the systems of almost all post-ancient philosophers, not only those who came before him but those who came after, too. In recent times this peculiarity has been often recognized.[103] It was Hegel who, by constructing a sequential history of philosophy that corresponded to factual, political history—something quite unknown before him—actually broke with the tradition, because he was the first great thinker to take history seriously, that is, as yielding truth.

The realm of human affairs, in which everything that is has been brought into being by man or men, had never been so looked on by a philosopher. And the change was due to an event—the French Revolution. "The revolution," Hegel admits, "may have got its first impulse from philosophy," but its "world-historical significance" consists in that, for the first time, man dared to turn himself upside down, "to stand on his head and on thought, and to build reality according to it." "Never since the sun had stood in the firmament and the planets revolved around him had it been perceived that man's existence centers in his head, that is, in thought. . . . This was a glorious mental dawn. All thinking beings shared in the jubilation of this epoch . . . a spiritual enthusiasm thrilled through the world, as if the reconciliation between the Divine and the Secular was now first accomplished."[104] What the event had shown amounted to a new dignity of man; "making public the ideas of how something ought to be [will cause] the lethargy of smugly sedate people [*die gesetzten Leute*], who always accept everything as it is, to disappear."[105]

Hegel never forgot that early experience. As late as 1829/30, he told his students: "In such times of political turnabout philosophy finds its place; this is when thought precedes and shapes reality. For when one form of the Spirit no longer gives satisfaction, philosophy sharply takes note of it in order to understand the dissatisfaction."[106] In short, he almost explicitly contradicted his famous statement about the owl of Minerva in the Preface to the *Philosophy of Right*. The "glorious mental dawn" of his youth inspired and informed all of his writing up to the end. In the French Revolution, principles and thoughts had been *realized;* a *reconciliation* had occurred between the "Divine," with which man spends his time while thinking, and the "secular," the affairs of men.

This reconciliation is at the center of the whole Hegelian system. If it was possible to understand *World History*—and not just the histories of particular epochs and nations—as a single succession of events whose eventual outcome would be the moment when the "Spiritual Kingdom . . . manifests itself in outward existence," becomes "embodied" in "secular life,"[107] then the course of history would no longer be haphazard and the realm of human affairs no longer devoid of meaning. The French Revolution had proved that "Truth in its living form [could be] exhibited in the affairs of the world."[108] Now one could indeed consider every moment in the world's historical sequence as an "it was to be" and assign to philosophy the task of "comprehending this plan" from its beginning, its "concealed fount" or "nascent principle . . . in the womb of time," up to its "phenomenal, present existence."[109] Hegel identifies this "Spiritual Kingdom" with the "Kingdom of the Will"[110] because the wills of men are necessary to bring the spiritual realm about, and for this reason he asserts that "the Freedom of the Will *per se* [that is, the freedom the Will necessarily wills] . . . is itself absolute . . . it is . . . that by which Man becomes Man, and is therefore the fundamental principle of the Mind."[111] As a matter of fact, the only guarantee—if such it is—that the ultimate goal of the unfolding of the World Spirit in the world's affairs must be Freedom is implicit in the freedom that is implicit in the Will.

"The insight then to which . . . philosophy is to lead us, is, that the real world is as it ought to be,"[112] and since for Hegel philosophy is concerned with "what is true eternally, neither with the Yesterday nor with the Tomorrow, but with the Present as such, with the 'Now' in the sense of an absolute presence,"[113] since the mind as perceived by the thinking ego is "the Now as such," then philosophy has to reconcile the conflict between the thinking and the willing ego. It must unite the time speculations belonging to the perspective of the Will and its concentration on the future with Thinking and its perspective of an enduring present.

The attempt is far from being successful. As Koyré points out in the concluding sentences of his essay, the Hegelian notion of a "system" clashes with the primacy he accords to the future. The latter demands that time shall never be terminated so long as men exist on earth, whereas philosophy in the Hegelian sense—the owl of Minerva that starts its flight at dusk—demands an arrest in real time, not merely the suspension of time during the activity of the thinking ego. In other words, Hegel's philosophy could claim objective truth only on condition that history were factually at an end, that mankind had no more future, that nothing could still occur that would bring anything new. And Koyré adds: "It is possible that Hegel believed this . . . even that he believed . . . that this essential condition [for a philosophy of history] was *already* an actuality . . . and that this had been the reason why he himself was able—had been able—to complete it."[114] (That in fact is the conviction of Kojève, for whom the Hegelian system is *the* truth and therefore the definite end of philosophy as well as history.)

Hegel's ultimate failure to reconcile the two mental activities, thinking and willing, with their opposing time concepts, seems to me evident, but he himself would have disagreed: Speculative thought is precisely "the unity of thought and *time*";[115] it does not deal with Being but with *Becoming*, and the object of the thinking mind is not Being but an "intuited Becoming."[116] The only motion that can be intuited is a movement that swings in a circle forming "a cycle that returns into itself . . . that presupposes its beginning, and reaches its beginning only at the end." This cyclical time concept, as we saw, is in perfect accordance with Greek classical philosophy, while post-classical philosophy, following the discovery of the Will as the mental mainspring for action, demands a rectilinear time, without which Progress would be unthinkable. Hegel finds the solution to this problem, viz., how to transform the circles into a progressing line, by assuming that something exists behind all the individual members of the human species and that this something, named Mankind, is actually a kind of somebody that he called the "World Spirit," to him no mere thought-thing but a presence embodied (incarnated) in Mankind as the mind of man is incarnated in the body. This World Spirit embodied in Mankind, as distinguished from individual men and particular nations, pursues a rectilinear movement inherent in the succession of the generations. Each new generation forms a "new stage of existence, a new world" and thus has "to begin all over again," but "*it commences at a higher level*" because, being human and endowed with mind, namely Recollection, it "has conserved [the earlier] experience" (italics added).[117]

Such a movement, in which the cyclical and the rectilinear notions of time are reconciled or united by forming a *Spiral*, is grounded on the experiences of neither the thinking ego nor the willing ego; it is the non-experienced movement of the World Spirit that constitutes Hegel's *Geisterreich*, "the realm of spirits . . . assuming definite shape in existence, [by virtue of] a succession, where one detaches and sets loose the other and each takes over from the predecessor the empire of the spiritual world."[118] No doubt this is a most ingenious solution of the problem of the Will and its reconciliation with sheer thought, but it is won at the expense of both—the thinking ego's experience of an enduring present and the willing ego's insistence on the primacy of the future. In other words, it is no more than a hypothesis.

Moreover, the plausibility of the hypothesis depends entirely on the assumption of the existence of *one* World Mind ruling over the plurality of human wills and directing them toward a "meaningfulness" arising out of reason's need, that is, psychologically speaking, out of the very human wish to live in a world that *is* as it *ought* to be. We encounter a similar solution in Heidegger, whose insights into the nature of willing are incomparably more profound and whose lack of sympathy with that faculty is outspoken and constitutes the actual turning-about (*Kehre*) of the later Heidegger: not "the Human will is the origin of the will to will," but "man is willed by the Will to will without experiencing what this Will is about."[119]

A few technical remarks may be appropriate in view of the Hegel revival of the last decades in which some highly qualified thinkers have played a part. The ingenuity of the triadic dialectical movement—from Thesis to Antithesis to Synthesis—is especially impressive when applied to the modern notion of Progress. Although Hegel himself probably believed in an arrest in time, an end of History that would permit the Mind to intuit and conceptualize the whole cycle of Becoming, this dialectical movement seen in itself seems to guarantee an *infinite* progress, inasmuch as the first movement from Thesis to Antithesis results in a Synthesis, which immediately establishes itself as a new Thesis. Although the original movement is by no means progressive but swings back and returns upon itself, the motion from Thesis to Thesis establishes itself behind these cycles and constitutes a rectilinear line of progress. If we wish to visualize the kind of movement, the result would be the following figure:

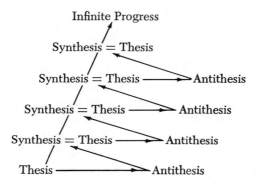

The advantage of the schema as a whole is that it assures progress and, without breaking up time's continuum, can still account for the undeniable historical fact of the rise and fall of civilizations. The advantage of the cyclical element in particular is that it permits us to look upon each end as a new beginning: Being and Nothingness "are the same thing, namely Becoming. . . . One direction is Passing Away: Being passes over into Nothing; but equally Nothing is its own opposite, a transition to Being, that is, Arising."[120] Moreover, the very infinity of the movement, though somehow in conflict with other Hegelian passages, is in perfect accord with the willing ego's time concept and the primacy it gives the future over the present and the past. The Will, untamed by Reason and its need to think, negates the present (and the past) even when the present confronts it with the actualization of its own project. Left to itself, man's Will "would rather will Nothingness than not will," as Nietzsche remarked,[121] and the notion of an infinite progress implicitly "denies every goal and admits ends only as means to outwit itself."[122] In other words, the famous power of negation inherent in the Will and conceived as the motor of History (not only in Marx but, by implication, already in Hegel) is an annihilating force that could just as well result in a process of permanent annihilation as of Infinite Progress.

The reason Hegel could construe the World-Historical movement in terms of an *ascending* line, traced by the "cunning of Reason" behind the backs of acting men, is to be found, in my opinion, in his never-questioned assumption that the dialectical process itself *starts* from Being, takes Being for granted (in contradistinction to a *Creatio ex nihilo*) in its march toward Not-Being and Becoming. The initial Being lends all further transitions their reality, their existential character, and prevents them from falling into the abyss of Not-Being. It is only because it follows on Being that "Not-Being contains [its] relation to Being; both Being and its negation are simultaneously asserted, and this assertion is Nothing as it exists in Becoming." Hegel justifies his starting-point by invoking Parmenides and the beginning of philosophy (that is, by "identifying logic and history"), thus tacitly rejecting

"Christian metaphysics," but one needs only to experiment with the thought of a dialectical movement starting from Not-Being in order to become aware that no Becoming could ever arise from it; the Not-Being at the beginning would annihilate everything generated. Hegel is quite aware of this; he knows that his apodictic proposition that "neither in heaven nor on earth is there anything not containing both Being and Nothing" rests on the solid assumption of the primacy of Being, which in turn simply corresponds to the *fact* that sheer nothingness, that is, a negation that does not negate something specific and particular, is unthinkable. All we can think is "a Nothing from which Something is to proceed; so that Being is already contained in the Beginning."[123]

Quaestio mihi factus sum

The Discovery of the Inner Man

II

7 The faculty of choice: proairesis, the forerunner of the Will

In my discussion of Thinking, I used the term "metaphysical fallacies," but without trying to refute them as though they were the simple result of logical or scientific error. Instead, I sought to demonstrate their authenticity by deriving them from the actual experiences of the thinking ego in its conflict with the world of appearances. As we saw, the thinking ego withdraws temporarily from that world without ever being able wholly to leave it, because of being incorporated in a bodily self, an appearance among appearances. The difficulties besetting any discussion of the Will have an obvious resemblance to what we found to be true of these fallacies, that is, they are likely to be caused by the nature of the faculty itself. However, while the discovery of reason and its peculiarities coincided with the discovery of the mind and the beginning of philosophy, the faculty of the Will became manifest much later. Our guiding question therefore will be: What experiences caused men to become aware of the fact that they were capable of forming volitions?

Tracing the history of a faculty can easily be mistaken for an effort to follow the history of an idea—as though here, for instance, we were concerned with the history of Freedom, or as though we mistook the Will for a mere "idea," which then indeed could turn out to be an "artificial concept" (Ryle) invented to solve artificial problems.[1] Ideas are thought-things, mental artifacts presupposing the identity of an artificer, and to assume that there is a history of the mind's faculties, as distinguished from the mind's products, seems like assuming that the human body, which is a toolmaker's and tool-user's body—the primordial tool being the human hand—is just as subject to change through the invention of new tools and implements as is the environment our hands continue to

55

reshape. We know this is not the case. Could it be different with our mental faculties? Could the mind acquire new faculties in the course of history?

The fallacy underlying these questions rests on an almost matter-of-course identification of the mind with the brain. It is the mind that decides the existence of both use-objects and thought-things, and as the mind of the maker of use-objects is a toolmaker's mind, that is, the mind of a body endowed with hands, so the mind that originates thoughts and reifies them into thought-things or ideas is the mind of a creature endowed with a human brain and brain power. The brain, the tool of the mind, is indeed no more subject to change through the development of new mental faculties than the human hand is changed by the invention of new implements or by the enormous tangible change they effect in our environment. But the mind of man, its concerns and its faculties, is affected both by changes in the world, whose meaningfulness it examines, and, perhaps even more decisively, by its own activities. All of these are of a reflexive nature—none more so, as we shall see, than the activities of the willing ego—and yet they could never function properly without the never-changing tool of brain power, the most precious gift with which the body has endowed the human animal.

The problem we are confronted with is well known in art history, where it is called "the riddle of style," namely, the simple fact "that different ages and different nations have represented the visible world in such different ways." It is surprising that this could come about in the absence of any physical differences and perhaps even more surprising that we do not have the slightest difficulty in recognizing the realities they point to even when the "conventions" of representation adopted by us are altogether different.[2] In other words, what changes throughout the centuries is the human mind, and although these changes are very pronounced, so much so that we can date the products according to style and national origin with great precision, they are also strictly limited by the unchanging nature of the instruments with which the human body is endowed.

In the line of these reflections, we shall begin by asking

ourselves how Greek philosophy dealt with phenomena and data of human experience that our post-classical "conventions" have been accustomed to ascribe to the Will as the mainspring of action. For the purpose, we turn to Aristotle, and that for two reasons. There is, first, the simple historical fact of the decisive influence that the Aristotelian analyses of the soul exerted on all philosophies of the Will—except in the case of Paul, who, as we shall see, was content with sheer descriptions and refused to "philosophize" about his experiences. There is, second, the no less indubitable fact that no other Greek philosopher came so close to recognizing the strange lacuna we have spoken of in Greek language and thought and therefore can serve as a prime example of how certain psychological problems could be solved before the Will was discovered as a separate faculty of the mind.

The starting-point of Aristotle's reflections on the subject is the anti-Platonic insight that reason by itself does not move anything.[3] Hence the question guiding his examinations is: "What is it in the soul that originates movement?"[4] Aristotle admits the Platonic notion that reason gives commands (*keleuei*) because it knows what one should pursue and what one should avoid, but he denies that these commands are necessarily obeyed. The incontinent man (his paradigmatic example throughout these inquiries) follows his desires regardless of the commands of reason. On the other hand, at the recommendation of reason, these desires can be resisted. Hence they, too, have no obligatory force inherent in them: by themselves they do not originate movement. Here Aristotle is dealing with a phenomenon that later, after the discovery of the Will, appears as the distinction between will and inclination. The distinction becomes the cornerstone of Kantian ethics, but it makes its first appearance in medieval philosophy—for instance, in Master Eckhart's distinction between "the inclination to sin and the will to sin, the inclination being no sin," which leaves the question of the evil deed itself altogether out of account: "If I never did evil but had only the will to evil . . . it is as great a sin as though I had killed all men even though I had done nothing."[5]

Still, in Aristotle desire retains a priority in originating movement, which comes about through a playing together of reason and desire. It is desire for an absent object that stimulates reason to step in and calculate the best ways and means to obtain it. This calculating reason he calls *"nous praktikos,"* practical reason, as distinguished from *nous theōrētikos,* speculative or pure reason, the former being concerned only with what depends exclusively on men (*eph' hēmin*), with matters in their power and therefore contingent (they can be or not-be), while pure reason is concerned only with matters that are beyond human power to change.

Practical reason is needed to come to the aid of desire under certain conditions. "Desire is influenced by what is just at hand," thus easily obtainable—a suggestion carried by the very word used for appetite or desire, *orexis,* whose primary meaning, from *oregō,* indicates the stretching out of one's hand to reach for something nearby. Only when the fulfillment of a desire lies in the future and has to take the time factor into account is practical reason needed and stimulated by it. In the case of incontinence, it is the force of desire for what is close at hand that leads to incontinence, and here practical reason will intervene out of concern for future consequences. But men do not only desire what is close at hand; they are able to imagine objects of desire to secure which they need to calculate the appropriate means. It is this future imagined object of desire that stimulates practical reason; as far as the resulting motion, the act itself, is concerned, the desired object is the beginning, while for the calculating process the same object is the end of the movement.

It appears that Aristotle himself found this outline of the relation between reason and desire unsatisfactory as an adequate explication of human action. It still relies, though with modifications, on Plato's dichotomy of reason and desire. In his early *Protreptikos,* Aristotle had interpreted it thus: "One part of the soul is Reason. This is the natural ruler and judge of things concerning us. The nature of the other part is to follow it and submit to its rule."[6] We shall see later that to issue commands is among the chief characteristics of the Will. In Plato reason could take this function on itself because of the assumption that reason is concerned with truth, and truth indeed is compelling. But reason itself, while it leads to truth, is persuasive, not imperative, in the soundless thinking dialogue between me and myself; only those who are not capable of thinking need to be compelled.

Within man's soul, reason becomes a "ruling" and commanding principle only because of the desires, which are blind and devoid of reason and therefore supposed to obey blindly. This obedience is necessary for the mind's tranquillity, the undisturbed harmony between the Two-in-One that is guaranteed by the axiom of non-contradiction—do not contradict yourself, remain a friend of yourself: "all friendly feelings toward others are an extension of the friendly feelings a person has for himself."[7] In the event that the desires do not submit to the commands of reason, the result in Aristotle is the "base man," who contradicts himself and is "at variance with himself" (*diapherein*). Wicked men either "run away from life and do away with themselves," unable to bear their own company, or "seek the company of others with whom to spend their days; but they avoid their own company. For when they are by themselves they remember many events that make them uneasy . . . but when they are with others they can forget. . . . Their relations with themselves are not friendly . . . their soul is divided against itself . . . one part pulls in one direction and the other in another as if to tear the individual to pieces. . . . Bad people are full of regrets."[8]

This description of internal conflict, a conflict between reason and the appetites, may be adequate to explain conduct— in this case the conduct, or, rather, misconduct, of the incontinent man. It does not explain action, the subject matter of Aristotelian ethics, for action is not mere execution of the commands of reason; it is itself a reasonable activity, though an activity not of "theoretical reason" but of what in the treatise *On the Soul* is called "*nous praktikos,*" practical reason. In the ethical treatises it is called *phronēsis,* a kind of insight and understanding of matters that are good or bad for men, a sort of sagacity—neither wisdom nor cleverness—needed for human affairs, which Sophocles, following common usage, ascribed to old age[9] and which Aristotle conceptualized. *Phronēsis* is required for any activity involving things within human power to achieve or not to achieve.

Such practical sense also guides production and the arts, but these have "an end other than themselves," whereas "action is itself an end."[10] (The distinction is the difference between the flute-player, for whom the playing is an end itself, and the flute-maker, whose activity is only a means and has come to an end when the flute is produced.) There is such a thing as *eupraxia*, action well done, and the doing of something well, regardless of its consequences, is then counted among the *aretai*, the Aristotelian excellences (or virtues). Actions of this sort are also moved not by reason but by desire, but the desire is not for an object, a "what" that I can grasp, seize, and use again as a means to another end; the desire is for a "how," a way of performing, excellence of appearance in the community—the proper realm of human affairs. Much later but quite in the Aristotelian spirit, Plotinus had this to say, as paraphrased by a recent interpreter: "What actually is in man's power in the sense that it depends entirely upon him . . . is the quality of his conduct, *to kalōs*"; man, if compelled to fight, is still free to fight bravely or in a cowardly way."[11]

Action in the sense of how men want to appear needs a deliberate planning ahead, for which Aristotle coins a new term, *proairesis*, choice in the sense of preference between alternatives—one rather than another. The *archai*, beginnings and principles, of this choice are desire *and* logos: logos provides us with the purpose for the sake of which we act; choice becomes the starting-point of the actions themselves.[12] Choice is a median faculty, inserted, as it were, into the earlier dichotomy of reason and desire, and its main function is to mediate between them.

The opposite of deliberate choice or preference is *pathos*, passion or emotion, as we would say, in the sense that we are motivated by something we suffer. (Thus a man may commit adultery out of passion and not because he has deliberately preferred adultery to chastity; he "may have stolen but not be a thief."[13]) The faculty of choice is necessary whenever men act for a purpose (*heneka tinos*), insofar as means have to be chosen, but the purpose itself, the ultimate end of the act for the sake of which it was embarked on in the first place, is not open to choice. The ultimate end of human acts is *eudaimonia,* happiness in the sense of "living well," which all men desire; all acts are but different means chosen to arrive at it. (The relationship between means and ends, whether in action or in fabrication, is that all means are equally justifiable by their ends; the specifically moral problem of the means-end relationship—whether all means can be justified by ends—is never even mentioned by Aristotle.) The element of reason in choice is called "deliberation," and we never deliberate about ends but about the means to attain them.[14] "No one chooses to be happy but to make money or run risks for the purpose of being happy."[15]

It is in the *Eudemian Ethics* that Aristotle explains in a more concrete way why he found it necessary to insert a new faculty into the old dichotomy and thus settle the old quarrel between reason and desire. He gives the example of incontinence: all men agree that incontinence is bad and not something to be desired; moderation or *sō-phrosynē*—that which saves (*sōzein*) practical reason (*phronēsis*)—is the naturally given criterion of all acts. If a man follows his desires, which are blind to future consequences, and thus indulges in incontinence, it is as though "the same man were to act at the same time both voluntarily [that is, intentionally] and involuntarily [that is, contrary to his intentions]," and this, Aristotle remarks, "is impossible."[16]

Proairesis is the way out of the contradiction. If reason and desire remained without mediation, in their crude natural antagonism, we would have to conclude that man, beset by the conflicting urges of both faculties, "forces himself away from his desire" when he remains continent and "forces himself away from his reason" when desire overwhelms him. But no such being-forced occurs in either case; both acts are done intentionally, and "when the principle is from within, there is no force."[17] What actually happens is that, reason and desire being in conflict, the decision between them is a matter of "preference," of deliberate choice. What intervenes is reason, not *nous,* which is concerned with things that are forever and cannot be otherwise than they are, but *dianoia* or *phronēsis,* which deal with things in our power, as distinguished from desires and imaginations that may stretch out to things we can never achieve, as when we wish to be gods or immortal.

Proairesis, the faculty of choice, one is tempted to conclude, is the precursor of the Will. It opens up a first, small restricted space for the human mind, which without it was delivered to two opposed compelling forces: the force of self-evident truth, with which we are not free to agree or disagree, on one side; on the other, the force of passions and appetites, in which it is as though nature overwhelms us unless reason "forces" us away. But the space left to freedom is very small. We deliberate only about *means* to an end that we take for granted, that we cannot choose. Nobody deliberates and chooses health or happiness as his aim, though we may think about them; ends are inherent in human nature and the same for all.[18] As to the means, "sometimes we have to find what [they] are, and sometimes how they are to be used or through whom they can be acquired."[19] Hence, the means, too, not just the ends, are given, and our free choice concerns only a "rational" selection between them; *proairesis* is the arbiter between several possibilities.

In Latin, Aristotle's faculty of choice is *liberum arbitrium.* Whenever we come upon it in medieval discussions of the Will, we are not dealing with a spontaneous power of beginning something new, nor with an autonomous faculty, determined by its own nature and obeying its own laws. The most grotesque example of it is Buridan's ass: the poor beast would have starved to death between two equidistant, equally nice-smelling bundles of hay, as no deliberation would give him a reason for preferring one to the other, and he only survived because he was smart enough to forgo free choice, trust his desire, and grasp what lay within reach.

The *liberum arbitrium* is neither spontaneous nor autonomous; we find the last vestiges of an arbiter between reason and desire still surviving in Kant, whose "good will" finds itself in a strange predicament: it is either "good without qualifications," in which case it enjoys complete autonomy but has no choice, or it receives its law—the categorical imperative—from "practical reason," which tells the will what to do and adds: Don't make an exception of yourself, obey the axiom of non-contradiction, which, since Socrates, has ruled the soundless dialogue of thought. The Will in Kant is in fact "practical reason"[20] much in the sense of Aristotle's *nous praktikos;* it borrows its obligatory power from the compulsion exerted on the mind by self-evident truth or logical reasoning. This is why Kant asserted time and again that every "Thou-shalt" that does not come from outside but rises up in the mind itself implies a "Thou-canst." What is at stake is clearly the conviction that whatever depends on us and concerns only ourselves is within our power, and this conviction is what Aristotle and Kant basically have in common, although their estimation of the importance of the realm of human affairs is greatly at variance. Freedom becomes a problem, and the Will as an independent autonomous faculty is discovered, only when men begin to doubt the coincidence of the Thou-shalt and the I-can, when the question arises: *Are things that concern only me within my power?*

8 *The Apostle Paul and the impotence of the Will*

The first and fundamental answer to the question I raised at the beginning of this chapter—what experiences caused men to become aware of their capability of forming volitions?—is that these experiences, Hebrew in origin, were not political and did not relate to the world, either to the world of appearances and man's position within it or to the realm of human affairs, whose existence depends upon deeds and actions, but were exclusively located within man himself. When we deal with experiences relevant to the Will, we are dealing with experiences that men have not only with themselves, but also *inside* themselves.

Such experiences were by no means unknown to Greek antiquity. In the previous volume, I spoke at some length of the Socratic discovery of the two-in-one, which we today would call "consciousness" and which originally had the function of what we today call "conscience." We saw how this two-in-one as a sheer fact of consciousness was actualized and articulated in the "soundless dialogue" that since Plato we have called "thinking." This thinking dialogue between me and myself takes place only in solitude, in a withdrawal from the world of appearances, where ordinarily we are together with others and appear as one to ourselves as well as to them. But the inwardness of the thinking dialogue that makes of philosophy Hegel's "solitary business" (although it is aware of itself—Descartes' *cogito me cogitare,* Kant's *Ich denke,* silently accompanying everything I do) is not thematically concerned with the Self but, on the contrary, with the experiences and questions that this Self, an appearance among appearances, feels are in need of examination. This meditating examination of everything given can be disturbed by the necessities of life, by the presence of others, by all kinds of urgent business. But none of the factors interfering with the mind's activity rises out of the mind itself, for the two-in-one are friends and partners, and to keep intact this "harmony" is the thinking ego's foremost concern.

The Apostle Paul's discovery, which he describes in great detail in the Letter to the Romans (written between A.D. 54 and 58), again concerns a two-in-one, but these two are not friends or partners; they are in constant struggle with each other. Precisely when he "wants to do right *(to kalon),*" he finds that "evil lies close at hand" (7:21), for "if the law had not said, 'You shall not covet,' " he "should not have known what it is to covet." Hence, it is the command of the law that occasioned "all kinds of covetousness. Apart from the law sin lies dead" (7:7, 8).

The function of the law is equivocal: it is "good, in order that sin might be shown to be sin" (7:13), but since it speaks in the voice of command, it "arouses the passions" and "revives sin." "The very commandment which promised life proved to be death to me" (7:9–10). The result is that "I do not understand my own actions. ["I have become a question to myself."] For I do not do what I want, but I do the very thing I hate" (7:15). And the point of the matter is that this inner conflict can never be settled in favor of either obedience to the law or submission to sin; this inner "wretchedness," according to Paul, can be healed only through grace, gratuitously. It was this insight that "flashed about" the man of Tarsus named Saul, who had been, as he said, an "extremely zealous" Pharisee (Galatians 1:14), belonging to the "strictest party of our religion" (Acts 26:4). What he wanted was "righteousness" (*dikaiosynē*), but righteousness, namely, to "abide by all things written in the book of the law, and do them" (Galatians 3:10), is impossible; this is the "curse of the law," and "if righteousness were through the law, then Christ died to no purpose" (Galatians 2:21).

That, however, is only one side of the matter. Paul became the founder of the Christian religion not only because, by his own declaration, he was "entrusted with the gospel to the uncircumcised" (Galatians 2:7), but also because wherever he went he preached the "resurrection of the dead" (Acts 24:21). The center of his concern, in sharp and obvious distinction from that of the gospels, is not Jesus of Nazareth, his preaching and his deeds, but Christ, crucified and resurrected. From this source he derived his new doctrine that became "a stumbling-block to Jews and folly to Gentiles" (I Corinthians 1:23).

It is the concern with eternal life, ubiquitous in the Roman Empire at the time, that separates the new era so sharply from antiquity and becomes the common bond that syncretistically united the many new Oriental cults. Not that Paul's concern with individual resurrection was Jewish in origin; to the Hebrews, immortality was felt to be necessary only for the people and granted only to them; the individual was content to survive in his progeny, content also to die old and "sated with years." And in the ancient world, Roman or Greek, the only immortality asked for or striven for was the non-oblivion of the great name and the great deed, and therefore of the institutions—the *polis* or *civitas*—which could guarantee a continuity of remembrance. (When Paul said that "the wages of sin is death" [Romans 6:23], he might have been recalling the words of Cicero, who had said that although men must die, communities [*civitates*] are meant to be eternal and perish only as a consequence of their sins.) Lying behind the many new beliefs is clearly the common experience of a declining, perhaps a dying, world; and the "good news" of Christianity in its eschatological aspects said clearly enough: You who have believed that men die but that the world is everlasting need only turn about, to a faith that the world comes to an end but that you yourself will have everlasting life. Then, of course, the question of "righteousness," namely, of being worthy of this eternal life, takes on an altogether new, personal importance.

Concern with personal, individual immortality appears in the gospels, too, all of them written during the last third of the first century. Jesus is commonly asked, "What shall I do to inherit eternal life?" (e.g., Luke 10:25), but Jesus seems not to have preached resurrection. Instead, he said that if people would do as he told them—"go and do likewise" or "follow me"—then "the kingdom of God is in the midst of you" (Luke 17:21) or "has come upon you" (Matthew 12:28). If people pressed him further, his answer was always the same: Fulfill the law as you know it *and* "sell all that you have and distribute it to the poor" (Luke 18:22). The thrust of Jesus' teaching is contained in this "and," which drove the well-known and accepted law to its inherent extreme. This is what he must have meant when he said, "I have come not to abolish [the law] but to fulfill [it]" (Matthew 5:17). Hence, not "Love your neighbors," but "Love your enemies"; "to him who strikes you on the cheek, offer the other also"; "from him who takes away your cloak do not withhold your coat as well." In short, not "What you don't want to be done to you, don't do to others," but "As you wish that men would do to you, do so to them" (Luke 6:27-31)—certainly the most radical possible version of "Love your neighbor *as yourself*."

Paul was certainly aware of the radical turn the old demand to fulfill the law had taken in the teaching of Jesus of Nazareth. And he may well have suddenly understood that in this lay the law's only true fulfillment, and then have found out

that such fulfillment was beyond human power: it led to an
I-will-but-can*not,* even though Jesus himself seems never to
have told any of his followers that they could not do what they
willed to do. Still, in Jesus, there is already a new stress on the
inner life. He would not have gone so far as Eckhart, more than
a thousand years later, and asserted that having the will to do
was enough to "earn eternal life," for "before God to will to do
according to my capacity and to have done are the same." Yet
Jesus' stress on the "Thou shall not covet," the only one of the
Ten Commandments that relates to an inner life, points in that
direction—"every one who looks at a woman lustfully has already committed adultery . . . in his heart" (Matthew 5:28).
Similarly, in Eckhart, a man who has the will to kill without
ever killing anybody has committed no less a sin than were
he to have murdered the whole human race.[21]

Of perhaps even greater relevance are Jesus' preachings
against hypocrisy as the sin of the Pharisees and his suspicion
of appearances: "Why do you see the speck that is in your
brother's eye but do not notice the log that is in your own eye?"
(Luke 6:41). And they "like to go about in long robes, and love
salutations in the market places" (Luke 20:46), which poses a
problem that must have been familiar to men of the Law. The
trouble is that whatever good you do, by the very fact of its
appearing either to others or to yourself becomes subject to
self-doubt.[22] Jesus knew about that: "Do not let your left hand
know what your right hand is doing" (Matthew 6:3), that is,
live in hiding, in hiding even from yourself, and do not bother
to *be* good—"No one is good but God alone" (Luke 18:19). Yet
this lovely carelessness could hardly be maintained when to do
good *and to be good* had become the requirement for overcoming death and being granted eternal life.

Hence, when we come to Paul, the accent shifts entirely
from doing to believing, from the outward man living in a
world of appearances (himself an appearance among appearances and therefore subject to semblance and illusion) to an
inwardness which by definition never unequivocally manifests
itself and can be scrutinized only by a God who also never
appears unequivocally. The ways of this God are inscrutable.
For the Gentiles, His chief property is His invisibility; for Paul

himself, what is the most inscrutable is that "Sin indeed was in the world before the law was given but sin is not counted where there is no law" (Romans 5:13), so that it is entirely possible "that Gentiles who did not pursue righteousness have attained it . . . but that Israel who pursued the righteousness which is based on the law did not succeed in fulfilling that law" (Romans 9:30–31). That the law cannot be fulfilled, that the will to fulfill the law activates another will, the will to sin, and that the one will is never without the other—that is the subject Paul deals with in the Letter to the Romans.

Paul, it is true, does not discuss it in terms of two wills but in terms of two laws—the law of the mind that lets him delight in the law of God "in his inmost self" and the law of his "members" that tells him to do what in his inmost self he hates. Law itself is understood as the voice of a master demanding obedience; the Thou-shalt of the law demands and expects a voluntary act of submission, an I-will of agreement. The Old Law said: thou shalt do; the New Law says: thou shalt *will*. It was the experience of an imperative demanding *voluntary* submission that led to the discovery of the Will, and inherent in this experience was the wondrous fact of a freedom that none of the ancient peoples—Greek, Roman, or Hebrew— had been aware of, namely, that there is a faculty in man by virtue of which, regardless of necessity and compulsion, he can say "Yes" or "No," agree or disagree with what is factually given, including his own self and his existence, and that this faculty may determine what he is going to do.

But this faculty is of a curiously paradoxical nature. It is actualized by an imperative that says not merely "Thou shalt" —as when the mind speaks to the body and, as Augustine put it later, the body immediately and, as it were, mindlessly obeys—but says "Thou *shalt will*," and this already implies that, whatever I may in fact eventually do, I can answer: I will, or I will not. The very commandment, the Thou-shalt, puts me before a choice between an I-will and an I-will-not, that is, theologically speaking, between obedience and disobedience. (Disobedience, it will be remembered, later becomes the mortal sin *par excellence*, and obedience, the very foundation of Christian ethics, the "virtue above all virtues" [Eckhart], and one, incidentally, that, unlike poverty and chastity, can hardly be derived from the teaching and preaching of Jesus of Nazareth.) If the will did not have the choice of saying "No," it would no longer be a will; and if there were not a *counter-will* within me that is aroused by the very commandment of the Thou-shalt, if, to speak in Paul's terms, "sin" did not dwell "within me" (Romans 7:20), I would not need a will at all.

I have spoken earlier of the reflexive nature of mental activities: the *cogito me cogitare*, the *volo me velle* (even judgment, the least reflexive of the three, recoils, acts back upon itself). Later we shall be seeing that this reflexivity is nowhere stronger than in the willing ego; the point is that every I-will arises out of a natural inclination toward freedom, that is, out of the natural revulsion of free men toward being at someone's bidding. The will always addresses itself to itself; when the command says, Thou shalt, the will replies, Thou shalt *will* as the command says—and not mindlessly execute orders. That is the moment when the internal contest begins, for the aroused counter-will has a like power of command. Hence, the reason "all who rely on works of the law are under a curse" (Galatians 3:10) is not only the I-will-and-can*not* but also the fact that the I-will inevitably is countered by an I-nill, so that even if the law is obeyed and fulfilled, there remains this inner resistance.

In the fight between the I-will and the I-nill, the outcome can depend only on an act—if works no longer count, the Will is helpless. And since the conflict is between *velle* and *nolle*, persuasion nowhere enters, as it did in the old conflict between reason and the appetites. For the phenomenon itself, that "I do not do the good I want, but the evil I do not want is what I do" (Romans 7:19), is of course not new. We find almost the same words in Ovid: "I see what is better and approve of it; I follow what is worse,"[23] and this is probably a translation of the famous passage in Euripides' *Medea* (lines 1078–80): "I know indeed what evil I intend to do; but stronger than my deliberations [*bouleumata*] is my *thymos* [what makes me move], which is the cause of the greatest evils among mortals." Euripides and Ovid might have deplored the weakness of reason when confronted with the passionate drive of the desires, and Aristotle might have gone a step farther and detected a self-contradiction in the choosing of the worse, an act that provided him with his definition of the "base man," but none of them would have ascribed the phenomenon to a free choice of the Will.

The Will, split and automatically producing its own counter-will, is in need of being healed, of becoming one again. Like thinking, willing has split the one into a two-in-one, but for the thinking ego a "healing" of the split would be the worst thing that could happen; it would put an end to thinking altogether. Well, it would be very tempting to conclude that divine mercy, Paul's solution for the wretchedness of the Will, actually abolishes the Will by miraculously depriving it of its counter-will. But this is no longer a matter of volitions, since mercy cannot be striven for; salvation "depends not upon man's will or exertion, but upon God's mercy," and He "has mercy upon whomever he wills, and he hardens the heart of whomever he wills" (Romans 9:16, 18). Moreover, just as "the law came in" not merely to make sin identifiable but to "increase the trespass," so grace "abounded" where "sin increased"—*felix culpa* indeed, for how could men know the glory if they were unacquainted with wretchedness; how would we know what day was if there were no night?

In brief, the will is impotent not because of something outside that prevents willing from succeeding, but because the will hinders itself. And wherever, as in Jesus, it does not hinder itself, it does not yet exist. For Paul, the explanation is relatively simple: the conflict is between flesh and spirit, and the trouble is that men are both, carnal and spiritual. The flesh will die, and therefore to live according to the flesh means certain death. The chief task of the spirit is not just to rule over the appetites and make the flesh obey but to bring about its mortification—to crucify it "with its passions and desires" (Galatians 5:24), which in fact is beyond human power. We saw that from the perspective of the thinking ego a certain suspicion of the body was only natural. Man's carnality, though not necessarily the source of sin, interrupts the mind's thinking activity and offers a resistance to the soundless, swift dialogue of the mind's exchange with itself, an exchange whose very "sweetness" consists in a spirituality in which no material factor intervenes. This is a far cry from the aggressive hostility to the body that we find in Paul, a hostility, moreover, that, quite apart from prejudices against the flesh, arises out of the very essence of the Will. Its mental origin notwithstanding, the will grows aware of itself only by overcoming resistance, and "flesh" in Paul's reasoning (as in the later disguise of "inclination") becomes the metaphor for an internal resistance. Thus, even in this simplistic scheme, the discovery of the Will has already opened a veritable Pandora's box of unanswerable questions, of which Paul himself was by no means unaware and which from then on were to plague with absurdities any strictly Christian philosophy.

Paul knew how easy it would be to infer from his presentation that we are "to continue in sin that grace may abound" (Romans 6:1) ("why not do evil that good may come?—as some people slanderously charge us with saying" [Romans 3:8]) although he hardly foresaw how much discipline and rigidity of dogma would be required to protect the Church against the *pecca fortiter*. He was also quite aware of the greatest stumbling-block for a Christian *philosophy:* the obvious contradiction between an all-knowing, all-powerful God and what Augustine later called the "monstrosity" of the Will. How can God permit this human wretchedness? Above all, how can He "still find fault," since no one "can resist his will" (Romans 9:19)? Paul was a Roman citizen, spoke and wrote koine Greek, and was obviously well informed about Roman law and Greek thought. Yet the founder of the Christian religion (if not of the Church) remained a Jew, and there could perhaps be no more forceful proof of it than his answer to the unanswerable questions his new faith and the new discoveries of his own inwardness had raised.

It is almost word for word the answer Job gave when he was led to question the inscrutable ways of the Hebrew God. Like Job's, Paul's reply is very simple and entirely unphilosophical: "But, who are you, a man, to answer back to God? Will what is molded say to its molder, 'Why have you made me thus?" Has the potter no right over the clay, to make out of the same lump one vessel for beauty and another for menial use? What if God, desiring . . . to make known his power, has endured . . . the vessels of wrath made for destruction, in order to make known the riches of his glory for the vessels of mercy, which he has prepared beforehand for glory . . . ?" (Romans 9:20–23; Job 10). In the same vein, God, cutting off all interrogation, had spoken to Job, who had dared to question *Him:* "I will question you and you shall declare to me. Where were you when I laid the foundations of the earth? . . . Shall a fault-finder contend with the Almighty?" And to this there exists indeed only Job's answer: "I have uttered what I did not understand, things too wonderful for me, which I did not know" (Job 42:3).

Unlike his doctrine of the resurrection of the dead, Paul's *argumentum ad hominem,* as it were, cutting short all questions with a Who-are-you-to-ask? failed to survive the early stages of the Christian faith. Historically speaking, that is, since of course we cannot know how many Christians in the long centuries of an *imitatio Christi* remained untouched by the ever-repeated attempts to reconcile absolute Hebrew faith in the Creator-God with Greek philosophy. The Jewish communities, at any rate, were warned against any kind of speculation; the Talmud, provoked by Gnosticism, told them: "It were better for the man never to be born who thinks about four matters: what is above and what is below, what was before and what will be afterward."[24]

Like a faint echo of this faithful awe before the mystery of all Being, centuries later we hear Augustine repeating what must have been a well-known joke at the time: "I answer the man who says: What did God do before He made heaven and earth? . . . : He was preparing Hell for those who pry into such deep matters." But Augustine did not let the matter rest at that. Several chapters further on (in the *Confessions*), after denouncing unjokingly those who ask such questions as men attacked "by a criminal disease that makes them thirst for more than they can hold," gives the logically correct and existentially unsatisfactory answer that, since the Creator-God is eternal, He must have created time when He created Heaven and Earth, so that there could be no "before" prior to the Creation. "Let them see that there could be no time without a created being."[25]

9   *Epictetus and the omnipotence of the Will*

In the Letter to the Romans, Paul describes an inner experience, the experience of the I-will-and-I-can*not*. This experience, followed by the experience of God's mercy, is overwhelming. He explains what happened to him and tells us how and why the two occurrences are interconnected. In the course of the explanation he develops the first comprehensive theory of history, of what history is all about, and he lays the foundations of Christian doctrine. But he does so in terms of facts; he does not *argue*, and this is what distinguishes him most sharply from Epictetus, with whom otherwise he had much in common.

They were just about contemporaries, came from roughly the same region in the Near East, lived in the Hellenized Roman Empire, and spoke the same language (the Koine), though one was a Roman citizen and the other a freedman, a former slave, one was a Jew and the other a Stoic. They also have in common a certain moral rigidity which sets them apart from their surroundings. They both declare that to covet your neighbor's wife means to have committed adultery. They denounce in almost the same words the intellectual establishment of their time—the Pharisees in Paul's case, the philosophers (Stoics and Academicians) in Epictetus'—as hypocrites who do not conduct themselves in accordance with their teaching. "Show me a Stoic if you can!" exclaims Epictetus. "Show me one who is sick and yet happy, in peril and yet happy, dying and yet happy, in exile and happy, in disgrace and happy. . . . By the gods I would fain see a Stoic."[26] This scorn is more outspoken and plays an even greater role in Epictetus than in Paul. Finally, they share an almost instinctive contempt for the body—this "bag," in Epictetus' words, which day by day

I stuff, and then empty: "what could be more tiresome?"[27]— and insist on the distinction between an "inmost self" (Paul) and "outward things."[28]

In each, the actual content of inwardness is described exclusively in terms of the promptings of the Will, which Paul believed to be impotent and Epictetus declared to be almighty: "Where lies the good? In the will. Where lies evil? In the will. Where lies neither? In what is not within the will's control."[29] At first glance, this is old Stoic doctrine but without any of the old Stoa's philosophical underpinnings; from Epictetus, we do not hear about the intrinsic goodness of nature according to which (*kata physin*) men ought to live and think—think away, that is, all apparent evil as a necessary component of an all-comprehensive good. In our context the interest of Epictetus lies precisely in the absence of such metaphysical doctrines from his teaching.

He was primarily a teacher and, since he taught and did not write,[30] he apparently thought of himself as a follower of Socrates, forgetting, like most of Socrates' so-called followers, that Socrates had nothing to teach. Anyhow, Epictetus considered himself a philosopher and he defined philosophy's subject matter as "the art of living one's life."[31] This art consisted mainly in having an argument ready for every emergency, for every situation of acute misery. His starting-point was the ancient *omnes homines beati esse volunt,* all men wish to be happy, and the only question for philosophy was to find out how to arrive at this matter-of-course goal. Except that Epictetus, in agreement with the mood of the time and in contrast to the pre-Christian era, was convinced that life, as it is given on earth, with the inevitable ending in death, and hence beset by fear and trembling, was incapable of giving real happiness without a special effort of man's will. Thus "happiness" changed its meaning; it was no longer understood as *eudaimonia,* the *activity* of *eu zēn,* living well, but as *euroia biou,* a Stoic metaphor indicating a free-flowing life, undisturbed by storms, tempests, or obstacles. Its characteristics were serenity, *galēnē,* the stillness after the storm, and tranquillity, *eudia,* fair weather[32]—metaphors unknown to classical antiquity. They all relate to a mood of the soul that is best described in negative terms (like *ataraxia*) and indeed consists in something wholly negative: to be "happy" now meant primarily "not to be miserable." Philosophy could teach "the processes of reason," the arguments, "like weapons bright and ready for use,"[33] to be directed against the wretchedness of real life.

Reason discovers that what makes you miserable is not death threatening from the outside but the fear of death within you, not pain but the fear of pain—"it is not death or pain which is a fearful thing, but the fear of pain or death."[34] Hence the only thing to be rightly afraid of is fear itself, and while men cannot escape death or pain, they can argue themselves out of the fear within themselves by eliminating the impressions fearful things have imprinted on their minds: "if we kept our fear not for death or exile, but for fear itself, then we should practice to avoid what we think evil."[35] (We need only recall the many instances that testify to the role played in the household of the soul by an overwhelming fear of being afraid, or imagine how reckless human courage would be if experienced pain left no memory behind—Epictetus' "impression"—in order to realize the down-to-earth psychological value of these apparently far-fetched theories.)

Once reason has discovered this inward region where man is confronted only by the "impressions" outward things make on his mind rather than by their factual existence, its task has been accomplished. The philosopher is no longer the thinker examining whatever may come his way but the man who has trained himself never to "turn to outward things," no matter where he happens to be. Epictetus gives an illuminating example of the attitude. He lets his philosopher go to the games like everybody else; but unlike the "vulgar" crowd of other spectators, he is "concerned" there only with himself and his own "happiness"; hence, he forces himself to "wish only that to happen which does happen, and only him to win who does win."[36] This turning away from reality while still in the midst of it, in contrast to the withdrawal of the thinking ego into the solitude of the soundless dialogue between me and myself, where every thought is an after-thought by definition, has the most far-reaching consequences. It means, for instance, that when one is going somewhere one pays *no* attention to one's goal but is interested only in one's "own activity" of walking, "or when deliberating is interested [only] in the act of deliberation, and not in getting that for which he is planning."[37] In terms of the game parable, it is as though these spectators, looking with blinded eyes, were mere ghostlike apparitions in the world of appearances.

It may be helpful to compare this attitude with that of the philosopher in the old Pythagorean parable about the Olympic Games; the best were those who did not participate in the struggle for fame or gain but were mere spectators, interested in the games for their own sake. Not a trace of such disinterested interest is left here. Only the self is of interest, and the self's unchallengeable ruler is argumentative reason, not the old *nous,* the inner organ for truth, the invisible eye of the mind directed toward the invisible in the visible world, but a *dynamis logikē,* whose greatest distinction is that it takes "cognizance of itself and of all things else" and "has the power to approve or disapprove its own action."[38] At first glance this may look like the Socratic two-in-one actualized in the thinking process but in reality it is much closer to what we today would call consciousness.

Epictetus' discovery was that the mind, because it could retain outward "impressions" (*phantasiai*), was able to deal with all "outside things" as mere "data of consciousness," as we would say. The *dynamis logikē* examines both itself and the "impressions" imprinted on the mind. Philosophy teaches us how to "deal with impressions aright"; it tests them and "distinguishes them and makes use of none which is untested." Looking at a table does not enable us to decide whether the table is good or bad; vision does not tell us, nor do any of our other senses. Only the mind, which deals not with real tables but with impressions of tables, can tell us. ("What tells us that gold is a goodly thing? For the gold does not tell us. Clearly it is the faculty that deals with impressions."[39]) The point is that you don't have to go outside yourself if your concern is wholly for that self. Only insofar as the mind can draw things into itself are they of any value.

Once the mind has withdrawn from outside things into the

inwardness of its own impressions, it discovers that in one respect it is entirely independent of all outside influences: "Can anyone prevent you from agreeing to what is true? No one. Can anyone compel you to accept the false? No one. Do you see that in this sphere your faculty is free from let and hindrance and constraint and compulsion?"[40] That it is in the nature of truth to "necessitate" the mind is an old insight: "*hōsper hyp' autēs tēs alētheias anagkasthentes,*" "necessitated as it were by truth itself," as Aristotle says when talking of self-evident theories standing in need of no special reasoning.[41] But in Epictetus this truth and its *dynamis logikē* have nothing at all to do with knowledge or cognition, for which "the processes of logic are unfruitful"[42]—literally good for nothing (*akarpa*). Knowledge and cognition concern "outside things," independent of man and beyond his power; hence, they are not, or should not be, of concern to him.

The beginning of philosophy is "an awareness [*synaisthē-sis*] of one's own weakness in regard to necessary things." We have no "innate conception" of things we ought to know, such as "a right-angled triangle," but we can be taught by people who know, and those who do not yet know *know* that they don't know. It is quite different with things which actually concern us and on which the kind of life we lead depends. In this sphere everybody is born with an it-seems-to-me, *dokei moi*, an opinion, and there our difficulty begins: "in the discovery of conflict in men's minds with one another" and the "attempt to discover a standard, just as we discover the balance to deal with weights and the rule to deal with things straight and crooked. This is the beginning of philosophy."[43]

Philosophy, then, sets the standards and norms and teaches man how to *use* his sensory faculties, how "to deal with impressions aright," and how "to test them and calculate the value of each." The criterion of every philosophy is therefore its usefulness in the business of leading a life free from pain. More specifically, it teaches certain lines of thought that can defeat the innate impotence of men. In this general philosophical framework it ought to be reason, argumentative reasoning, that is given primacy over all the mental faculties; but this is not the case. In his violent denunciation of men who were "philosophers only with their lips," Epictetus points to the appalling gap between a man's teachings and his actual conduct, and by implication hints at the old insight that reason by itself neither moves nor achieves anything. The great achiever is not reason but the Will. "Consider who you are" is an exhortation addressed to reason, it seems, but what is then discovered is that "man . . . has nothing more sovereign [*kyriōteros*] than will [*proairesis*] . . . all else [is] subject to this, and will itself is free from slavery and subjection." Reason (*logos*), it is true, distinguishes man from the animals, which therefore are "marked for service," while man is "fitted for command";[44] yet the organ capable of command is not reason but Will. If philosophy deals with the "art of living your own life" and if its supreme criterion is usefulness in these terms, then "philosophy means very little else but this— to search how it is practicable to exercise the will to get and the will to avoid without hindrance."[45]

The first thing reason can teach the will is the distinction between things that depend on man, those that are in his power (the Aristotelian *eph' hēmin*), and those that are not. The power of the will rests on its sovereign decision to concern itself only with things within man's power, and these reside exclusively in human inwardness.[46] Hence, the will's first decision is not-to-will what it cannot get and to cease nilling what it cannot avoid—in short, not to concern itself with anything over which it has no power. ("What matters it whether the world is composed of atoms or of infinite parts or of fire and earth? Is it not enough to know . . . the limits of the will to get and the will to avoid . . . and to dismiss those things that are beyond us?"[47]) And since "it is impossible that what happens should be other than it is,"[48] since man, in other words, is entirely powerless in the real world, he has been given the miraculous faculties of reason and will that permit him to reproduce the outside—complete but deprived of its reality—inside his mind, where he is undisputed lord and master. There he rules over himself and over the objects of his concern, for the will can be hindered only by itself. Everything that seems to be real, the world of appearances, actually needs my consent in order to be real *for me*. And this consent cannot be forced on me: if I withhold it, then the reality of the world disappears as though it were a mere apparition.

This faculty of turning away from the outside toward an invincible inside obviously needs "training" (*gymnazein*) and constant arguing, for not only does man live his ordinary life in the world as it is; but his inside itself, so long as he is alive, is located within some outside, a body that is not in his power but belongs to the "outside things." The constant question is whether your will is strong enough not merely to distract your attention from external, threatening things but to fasten your imagination on different "impressions" in the actual presence of pain and misfortune. To withhold consent, or bracket out reality, is by no means an exercise in sheer thinking; it has to prove itself in actual fact. "I must die. I must be imprisoned. I must suffer exile. But: must I die groaning? Must I whine as well? Can anyone hinder me from going into exile with a smile?" The master threatens to chain me: "What say you? Chain me? My leg you will chain—yes, but not my will—no, not even Zeus can conquer that."[49]

Epictetus gives many examples, which we do not need to enumerate here; they make tedious reading, like exercises in a schoolbook. The upshot is always the same. What bothers men is not what actually happens to them but their own "judgment" (*dogma*, in the sense of belief or opinion): "You will be harmed only when you think you are harmed. No one can harm you without your consent."[50] "For instance, what does it mean to be slandered? Stand by a stone and slander it: what effect will you produce?"[51] Be stonelike and you will be invulnerable. *Ataraxia*, invulnerability, is all you need in order to *feel* free once you have discovered that reality itself depends on your consent to recognize it as such.

Like almost all Stoics, Epictetus recognized that the body's vulnerability puts certain limits on this inner freedom. Unable to deny that it is not mere wishes or desires that make us unfree, but the "fetters attached to us in the shape of the body,"[52] they therefore had to prove that these fetters are not unbreakable. An answer to the question What restrains us from suicide? becomes a necessary topic of these writings. Epictetus, at any rate, seems to have quite clearly realized that this kind of unlimited inner freedom actually presupposes that "one must remember and hold fast to this, that *the door is open*."[53] For a philosophy of total world-alienation, there is much truth in the remarkable sentence with which Camus began his first book: "*Il n'y a qu'un problème philosophique vraiment sérieux: c'est le suicide.*"[54]

At first glance, this doctrine of invulnerability and apathy (*apatheia*)—how to shield yourself against reality, how to lose your ability to be affected by it, for better or worse, in joy or in sorrow—seems so obviously open to refutation that the enormous argumentative as well as emotional influence of Stoicism on some of the best minds of Western mankind seems well-nigh incomprehensible. In Augustine, we find such a refutation in its shortest and most plausible form. The Stoics, he says, have found the trick of how to pretend to be happy: "Since a man cannot get what he wants, he wants what he can get" ("*Ideo igitur id vult quod potest, quoniam quod vult non potest*").[55] Moreover, he goes on, the Stoics assume that "all men by nature wish to be happy" but they do not believe in immortality, at least not in bodily resurrection, that is, not in a future deathless *life,* and this is a contradiction in terms. For "if all men really will to be happy they must necessarily also will to be immortal. . . . In order to *live* happily you must first be alive" ("*Cum ergo beati esse omnes homines velint, si vere volunt, profecto et esse immortales volunt. . . . Ut enim homo beate vivat, oportet ut vivat*").[56] In other words, mortal men cannot be happy, and the Stoics' insistence on the fear of death as the main source of unhappiness testifies to this; the most they can achieve is to become "apathetic," to be unaffected by either life or death.

This refutation, however, so plausible on this level of argument, misses a number of rather important points. There is first the question of why a will should be necessary in order *not* to will, why it should not be possible simply to lose the faculty under the sway of the superior insights of right reasoning. After all, don't we all know how relatively easy it has always been to lose at least the habit, if not the faculty, of thinking? Nothing more is needed than to live in constant distraction and never leave the company of others. It may be argued that it is harder to break men of the habit of wanting what is beyond their power than of the habit of thinking, but for a sufficiently "trained" man, it ought not to be necessary to repeat the not-willing over and over—since the *mē thele*, the "do not will" where you cannot prevent, is at least as important to this schooling as the mere appeal to will power.

Closely connected with the foregoing, and even more puzzling, is the fact that Epictetus is by no means content with the will's power *not*-to-will. He does not just preach indifference to everything that is not within our power; he insistently demands that man will what happens anyhow. I have already cited the game parable in which the man whose sole concern is with the feeling-well of the self is admonished to wish "only that to happen which does happen, and only him to win who does win." In a different context Epictetus goes much farther and praises (unnamed) "philosophers" who said "that 'if the good man knew coming events beforehand he would help on nature, even if it meant working with disease, and death and maiming.' "[57] To be sure, in his argument he falls back on the old Stoic notion of *heimarmenē*, the doctrine of fate which holds that everything happens in harmony with the nature of the universe and that every particular thing, man or animal, plant or stone, has its task allotted to it by the whole and is justified by it. But not only is Epictetus very explicitly uninterested in any question relating to nature or the universe; but also nothing in the old doctrine indicates that man's will, totally ineffectual by definition, would be of avail in the "ordering of the universe." Epictetus is interested in what happens to him: "I will a thing and it does not happen; what is there more wretched than I? I will it not and it happens; what is more wretched than I?"[58] In short, in order "to live well" it is not enough to "ask *not* that events should happen as you will"; you must "let your will be that events should happen as they do."[59]

It is only when will power has reached this climactic point, where it can will what *is* and thus never be "at odds with outward things," that it can be said to be omnipotent. Underlying all the arguments for such omnipotence is the matter-of-course assumption that reality *for me* gets its realness from my consent; and underlying that assumption, guaranteeing its practical effectiveness, is the simple fact that I can commit suicide when I truly find life unbearable—"the door is always open." And here this solution does not imply, as it does, for instance, in Camus, a kind of cosmic rebellion against the human condition; to Epictetus, such a rebellion would be entirely pointless, since "it is impossible that what happens should be other than it is."[60] It is unthinkable because even an absolute negation depends on the sheer inexplicable thereness of all that is, including myself, and Epictetus nowhere demands an explanation or justification of the inexplicable. Hence, as Augustine will later argue,[61] those who believe they choose non-being when they commit suicide are in error; they choose a form of being that will come about one day anyhow and they choose peace, which of course is only a form of being.

The sole force that can hinder this basic, active consent given by the will is the will itself. Hence the criterion for right conduct is: "Will to be pleased, you with yourself" (*"theleson aresai autos seauto"*). And Epictetus adds: "Will to appear noble to the god" (*"theleson kalos phanenai to theo"*),[62] but the addendum is actually redundant, for Epictetus does not believe in a transcendent God but holds that the soul is godlike and that the god is "within you, you are a fragment of him."[63] The willing ego, it turns out, is no less split in two than the Socratic two-in-one of Plato's dialogue of thought. But, as we saw with Paul, the two in the willing ego are far from enjoying a friendly, harmonious intercourse with each other, although in Epictetus their frankly antagonistic relationship does not subject the self to the extremes of despair that we hear so much of in Paul's lamentation. Epictetus characterizes their relation as an ongoing "struggle" (*agon*), an Olympic contest demanding an ever-attentive suspicion of myself by myself: "In one word, [the philosopher, who always looks to himself for benefit and harm] keeps watch and guard on himself *as his own* enemy [*hos echthron heautou*], lying in wait for him."[64] We need only remind ourselves of Aristotle's insight ("all friendly feelings toward others are an extension of the friendly feelings a person has for himself") to gauge the distance the human mind has traveled since antiquity.

The philosopher's self, ruled by the willing ego that tells him that nothing can hinder or constrain it but the will itself, is engaged in a never-ending fight with the counter-will, engendered, precisely, by his own will. The price paid for the Will's omnipotence is very high; the worst that, from the viewpoint of the thinking ego, could happen to the two-in-one, namely, to be "at variance with yourself," has become part and parcel of the human condition. And the fact that this fate is no longer assigned to Aristotle's "base man" but, on the contrary, to the good and wise man who has learned the art of conducting his own life in no matter what external circumstances may well cause one to wonder whether this "cure" of human misery was not worse than the disease.

Still, in this lamentable business there is one decisive discovery that no argument can eliminate and that at least explains why the feeling of omnipotence as well as of human freedom could come out of the experiences of the willing ego. A point we touched on marginally in our discussion of Paul, namely, that all obedience presumes the power to disobey, is at the very center of Epictetus' considerations. There the heart of the matter is the Will's power to assent or dissent, say Yes or No insofar, at any rate, as I myself am concerned. This is why things that in their pure existence—i.e., "impressions" of outside things—depend only on me are also in my power; not only can I will to change the world (though the proposition is of doubtful interest to an individual subject totally alienated from the world in which it finds itself), I can also deny reality to anything and everything by virtue of an I-will-not. This power must have had something awful, truly overpowering, for the human mind, for there has never been a philosopher or theologian who, after having paid due attention to the implied No in every Yes, did not squarely turn around and demand an emphatic consent, advising man, as Seneca did in a sentence quoted with great approbation by Master Eckhart, "to accept all occurrences as though he himself had desired them and asked for them." To be sure, if in this universal agreement one sees no more than the willing ego's last and deepest resentment of its existential impotence in the world as it factually is, he will also see only another argument here for the illusionary character of the faculty, an ultimate confirmation of its being an "artificial concept." Man in that case would have been given a truly "monstrous" faculty (Augustine), compelled by its nature to demand a power it is able to exercise only in the illusion-ridden region of sheer phantasy—the inwardness of a mind that has successfully separated itself from all outward appearance in its relentless quest for absolute tranquillity. And as the last and ironic reward for so much effort, it will have obtained an uncomfortably intimate acquaintance with the "painful storehouse and treasure of evils," in the words of Democritus, or with the "abyss" which, according to Augustine, lies hidden "in the good heart and in the evil heart."[65]

10 *Augustine, the first philosopher of the Will*

> If it is due to Scripture that there is
> a philosophy which is Christian,
> it is due to the Greek tradition that
> Christianity possesses a philosophy.
> Etienne Gilson

Augustine, the first Christian philosopher and, one is tempted to add, the only philosopher the Romans ever had,[66] was also the first man of thought who turned to religion because of philosophical perplexities. Like many educated people of the time, he had been brought up as a Christian; yet what he himself eventually described as a conversion—the subject matter of his *Confessions*—was utterly different from the experience that changed the extremely zealous Pharisee Saul into Paul, the Christian Apostle and follower of Jesus of Nazareth.

In the *Confessions,* Augustine tells how his heart had first been set "on fire" by Cicero's *Hortensius,* a book (now lost) that contained an exhortation to philosophy. Augustine kept quoting from it till the end of his life. He became the first Christian philosopher because throughout his life he held fast to philosophy. His treatise *On the Trinity,* a defense of the crucial dogma of the Christian Church, is at the same time the most profound and the most articulated development of his own very original philosophical position. But its starting-point remained the Roman and Stoic quest for happiness—"Certain it is, said Cicero, that we all want to be happy."[67] In his youth he had turned to philosophy out of inner wretchedness and as a man he turned to religion because philosophy had failed him. This pragmatic attitude, the demand that philosophy be "life's leader" (Cicero),[68] is typically Roman; it had a more lasting influence on the formation of Augustine's thought than did Plotinus and the Neoplatonists, to whom he owed whatever he knew of Greek philosophy. Not that the general human wish to be happy had escaped the attention of the Greeks —the Roman proverb seems to have been a translation from the Greek—but this desire was not what made them do philosophy. Only the Romans were convinced that "there is no reason for man to philosophize unless in order to be happy."[69]

We find this pragmatic concern for private happiness throughout the Middle Ages; it underlies the hope for eternal salvation and the fear of eternal damnation and clarifies many otherwise rather abstruse speculations whose Roman origins are difficult to detect. That the Roman Catholic Church, despite the decisive influx of Greek philosophy, remained so profoundly Roman was due in no small measure to the strange coincidence that her first and most influential philosopher should also have been the first man of thought to draw his deepest inspiration from Latin sources and experiences. In Augustine, the striving for eternal life as the *summum bonum* and the interpretation of eternal death as the *summum malum* reached the highest level of articulation because he combined them with the new era's discovery of an *inward* life. He understood that the exclusive interest in this inner self meant that "I have become a question for myself" ("*quaestio mihi factus sum*")—a question that philosophy as it was then taught and learned neither raised nor answered.[70] The famous analyses of the concept of Time in the eleventh book of the *Confessions* are a paradigmatic illustration of the challenge of the new and problematic: time is something utterly familiar and ordinary so long as no one asks What is Time?—at which moment it turns into an "intricate riddle" whose challenge is that it is both entirely ordinary and entirely "hidden."[71]

There is no doubt that Augustine belongs among the great and original thinkers, but he was not a "systematic thinker," and it is true that the main body of his work is "littered with lines of thought that are not worked through to their conclusion and with abandoned literary enterprises"[72]—besides being shot through with repetitions. What is remarkable under the cirmcumstances is the continuity of the chief topics that finally, at the end of his life, he subjected to a searching examination titled *Retractationes*, or "Recantations," as though the Bishop and Prince of the Church were his own Inquisitor. Perhaps the most crucial of these ever-recurring topics was the "Free Choice of the Will" (the *Liberum arbitrium voluntatis*), as a faculty distinct from desire and reason, although he devoted but one whole treatise to it under that title. This was an early work, whose first part is still entirely in the vein of his other early philosophical writings despite its having been written after the dramatic event of his conversion and baptism.

It rather speaks, I think, for the quality of the man and the thinker that it took him ten years to write down in minute detail what to him was the most momentous event of his life— and this not just for remembrance's or piety's sake but for the sake of its mental implications. As his most recent biographer, Peter Brown, puts it a bit simplistically, "he was very definitely not a *type croyant*, such as had been common among educated men in the Latin world before his time";[73] for Augustine, it was not a matter of abandoning the uncertainties of philosophy in favor of revealed Truth but of finding the philosophical implications of his new faith. In that tremendous effort he relied first of all on the Letters of the Apostle Paul, and the measure of his success can perhaps best be gauged by the fact that his authority throughout the subsequent centuries of Christian philosophy became equal to that of Aristotle—for the Middle Ages "the philosopher."

Let us start with Augustine's early interest in the faculty of the Will as expounded in the first part of the early treatise (the two concluding parts were written almost ten years later, roughly at the same time as the *Confessions*). Its leading question is an inquiry into the cause of evil: "for evil could not have come into being without a cause" and God cannot be the cause of evil because "God is good." The question, current even then, had "disturbed [him] exceedingly since his youth . . . and indeed driven [him] into heresy," namely, into adhering to the teachings of Mani.[74] What follows is strictly argumentative reasoning (though in dialogue form) as we found it in Epictetus, and the telling points at this late time sound like a summing up for educational purposes until we reach the conclusion, where the disciple is made to say: "I question whether free will . . . ought to have been given to us by Him who made us. For it seems that we would not have been able to sin, if we did not have free will. And it is to be feared that in this way God may appear to be the cause of our evil deeds." At this point Augustine reassures the questioner and postpones the discussion.[75] Thirty years later, in a different way, in the *City of God*, he takes up the question of the "purpose of the Will" as the "purpose of Man."

The question whose answer he postponed for so many years is the starting-point for Augustine's own philosophy of the Will. But a close interpretation of Paul's Letter to the Romans was the original occasion of his framing it. In the *Confessions*, as well as in the last two sections of *On Free Choice of the Will*, he draws the philosophical inferences and articulates the consequences of the strange phenomenon (that it is possible to will and, in the absence of any outside hindrance, still be unable to perform) which Paul had described in terms of antagonistic laws. But Augustine does not speak of two laws but of "*two wills*, one new and the other old, one carnal and the other spiritual," and describes in detail, like Paul, how these wills struggled "within" him and how their "discord undid [his] soul."[76] In other words, he is careful to avoid his own earlier Manichaean heresy, which taught that two antagonistic principles rule the world, one good and one evil, one carnal and one spiritual. For him now, there is only one law, and the first insight therefore is the most obvious but also the most startling one: "*Non hoc est velle quod posse*," "to will and to be able are not the same."[77]

It is startling because the two faculties, willing and performing, are so closely connected: "Will must be present for
power to be operative"; and power, needless to say, must be
present for the will to draw on. "If you act . . . it can never
be without willing" even if "you do a thing unwillingly, under
compulsion." "When you do not act" it may be that "will is
lacking" or that "the power is lacking."[78] This is all the more
surprising as Augustine agrees with the Stoics' main argument
for the predominance of the Will, namely, that "nothing is so
much in our power as the will itself, for there is no interval,
the moment we will—there it is,"[79] except that he does not
believe that the Will is enough. "The law would not command
if there were no will, nor would grace help if will were
enough." The point here is that the Law does not address
itself to the mind, in which case it would simply reveal and not
command; it addresses itself to the Will because "the mind is
not moved until it wills to be moved." And this is why only the
Will, and neither reason nor the appetites and desires, is "in our
power; it is free."[80]

This proof of the freedom of the Will draws exclusively on
an inner power of affirmation or negation that has nothing to
do with any actual *posse* or *potestas*—the faculty needed to
perform the Will's commands. The proof obtains its plausibility from a comparison of willing with reason, on the one hand,
and with the desires, on the other, neither of which can be said
to be free. (We saw that Aristotle introduced his *proairesis* to
avoid the dilemma of saying either that the "good man" *forces*
himself away from his appetites or that the "base man" *forces*
himself away from his reason.) Whatever reason tells me is
compelling as far as reason is concerned. I may be able to say
"No" to a truth disclosed to me, but I cannot possibly do this
on rational grounds. The appetites rise in my body automatically, and my desires are aroused by objects outside myself; I
may say "No" to them on the advice given by reason or the law
of God, but reason itself does not move me to resistance.
(Duns Scotus, very much influenced by Augustine, later
elaborates on the argument. To be sure, carnal man, in the
sense Paul understood him, cannot be free; but spiritual man is
not free either. Whatever power the intellect may have over

the mind is a necessitating power; what the intellect can never prove to the mind is that it should not merely subject itself to it but also will to do so.[81])

The faculty of Choice, so decisive for the *liberum arbitrium*, here applies not to the deliberative selection of means toward an end but primarily—and, in Augustine, exclusively— to the choice between *velle* and *nolle*, between willing and nilling. This *nolle* has nothing to do with the will-not-to-will, and it cannot be translated as I-will-not because this suggests an absence of will. *Nolle* is no less actively transitive than *velle*, no less a faculty of will: if I will what I do not desire, I nill my desires; and in the same way I can nill what reason tells me is right. In every act of the will, there is an I-will *and I-nill* involved. These are the two wills whose "discord" Augustine said "undid [his] soul." To be sure, "he who wills, wills something," and this something is presented to him "either from without through the body's senses or comes into the mind in hidden ways," but the point is that none of these objects determine the will.[82]

What is it then that causes the will to will? What sets the will in motion? The question is inevitable, but the answer turns out to lead into an infinite regress. For if the question were to be answered, "will you not inquire again for the cause of that cause if you find it?" Will you not wish to know "the cause of the will prior to the will"? Could it not be inherent in the Will to have no cause in this sense? "For either the will is its own cause or it is not a will."[83] The Will is a fact which in its sheer contingent factuality cannot be explained in terms of causality. Or—to anticipate a late suggestion of Heidegger's— since the will experiences itself as *causing* things to happen which otherwise would not have happened, could it not be that it is neither the intellect nor our thirst for knowledge (which could be stilled by straightforward information), but precisely the will that lurks behind our quest for causes—as though behind every Why there existed a latent wish not just to learn and to know but to learn the know-how?

Finally, still tracing the difficulties that are described but not explained in the Letter to the Romans, Augustine comes to interpret the scandalous side of Paul's doctrine of grace: "Law came in to increase the trespass; but where sin increased, grace abounded all the more." From that it is indeed difficult not to conclude: "Let us do evil that good may come." Or, to put it more mildly, that it is worthwhile to have been incapable of doing good because of the overwhelming joy of grace—as Augustine himself once said.[84] His answer in the *Confessions* points to the strange ways of the soul even in default of any specifically religious experiences. The soul is "more delighted at finding or recovering the things it loves, than if it had always had them. . . . The victorious commander triumphs . . . and the greater the peril in battle, the greater joy in triumph. . . . A friend is sick . . . he is restored, and though he walks not with his former strength, there is such joy, as there had not been when he was able to walk strongly and soundly." And so it is with all things; human life is "full of witnesses" to it. "The greatest joy is ushered in by the greatest painfulness"—this is the "allotted mode of being" of all living things, from "the angel to the worm." Even God, since He is a living god, "doth joy more over one sinner that repenteth than over ninety and nine persons that need no repentance."[85] This mode of being (*modus*) is equally valid for base and for noble things, for mortal things and things divine.

This is certainly the quintessence of what Paul had to say, but expressed in a non-descriptive, conceptual way: without appealing to any purely theological interpretation, it effaces the edge of Paul's lamentations and latent accusations, from which only the *argumentum ad hominem*, the Job-like question "Who are *you* to ask such questions and to raise such objections?" could save him.

In Augustine's refutation of Stoicism, we can see a similar transformation and solidification brought about by means of conceptual thought. What was actually scandalous in that doctrine was not that man could will to say "No" to reality but that this No was not enough; in order to find tranquillity, man was told, he had to train his will to say "Yes" and to "let your will be that events should happen as they do." Augustine understands that this willed submissiveness presupposes a severe limitation of the willing capacity itself. Although in his view every *velle* is accompanied by a *nolle*, the freedom of the faculty is limited because no created being can will against creation, for this would be—even in the case of suicide—a will directed not only against a counter-will but against the very existence of the willing or nilling subject. The will, the faculty of a living being, cannot say "I'd rather not *be*," or "I would prefer nothingness as such." Anybody who says "I'd rather not exist than be unhappy" cannot be trusted, since while he is saying it he is still alive.

Yet this may be so only because being alive always implies a wish to go on being; therefore most people prefer "to be unhappy than to be nothing at all." But what about those who say "If I had been consulted before I existed, I'd have preferred not to exist rather than be unhappy"? They have not considered that even this proposition is stated on the firm ground of Being; if they would consider the matter properly, they would find that their very unhappiness makes them, as it were, exist less than they wish; it takes some existence from them. "The degree of their unhappiness is commensurate with the distance from that which *is* in the highest degree [*quod summe est*]" and therefore outside the temporal order, which is shot through with non-existence—"for temporal things have no existence before they exist; while they exist, they are passing away; once they have passed away, they will never exist again." All men fear death, and this feeling is "truer" than any opinion that may lead you "to think that you ought to will not to exist," for the fact is that "beginning to exist is the same as proceeding toward non-existence." In short, "all things by the very fact that they *are* are good," evil and sin included; and this not only because of their divine origin and because of a belief in a Creator-God, but also because your own existence prevents you from either thinking or willing absolute non-existence. In this context it should be noted that Augustine (although most of what I have been quoting is drawn from the last part of his *De libero arbitrio voluntatis*) nowhere demands, as Eckhart later does, that "A good man ought to conform his will to the divine will, so that he will what God wills: hence, if God has willed me to sin, I should not will not to have committed my sin; this is my true repentance."[86]

What Augustine infers from this theory of Being is not Will but Praise: "Give thanks that you are"; "praise all things for the very fact that they are." Avoid saying not only " 'It would be better if [sinners] had not existed,' but also 'They ought to have been made differently.' " And the same is true for everything, since "all things have been created in their proper order," and if you "dare to find fault with a desert," do so only because you can compare it "with what is better." It is "as if a man who grasped by his reason perfect roundness became disgusted" because he could not find it in nature. He should be grateful for having the idea of roundness.[87]

In the previous volume, I spoke of the ancient Greek notion that all appearances, inasmuch as they *appear,* not only imply the presence of sentient creatures capable of perceiving them but also demand recognition and *praise.* This notion was a kind of philosophical justification of poetry and the arts; world-alienation, which preceded the rise of Stoic and Christian thought, succeeded in obliterating it from our tradition of philosophy—though never entirely from the reflections of poets. (You can still find it, very emphatically expressed, in W. H. Auden—who speaks of "That singular command / I do not understand, / *Bless what there is for being,* / Which has to be obeyed, for / What else am I made for, / Agreeing or disagreeing?"[88]—in the Russian poet Osip Mandelstam, and, of course, in the poetry of Rainer Maria Rilke.) Where we find it in a strictly Christian context, it already has an uncomfortably argumentative flavor, as though it were simply a necessary inference from the unquestioned faith in a Creator-God, as though Christians were duty-bound to repeat God's words after the Creation—"And God saw everything . . . and . . . it was very good." In any event, Augustine's observations on the impossibility of nilling absolutely because you cannot nill your own existence while you are nilling—hence cannot nill absolutely even by committing suicide—are an effective refutation of the mental tricks Stoic philosophers had recommended to enable men to withdraw from the world while still living in it.

. . . . . .

We return to the question of the Will in the *Confessions,* which are almost entirely non-argumentative and rich in what we today would call "phenomenological" descriptions. For although Augustine starts by conceptualizing Paul's position, he goes far beyond that, also far beyond his own first conceptual conclusions—that "to will and to be able to perform are not the same," that "the law would not command if there were no will, nor would grace help if will were enough," that it is our mind's allotted mode of being to perceive only through the succession of opposites, of day becoming night and night becoming day, and we learn about justice only by experiencing injustice, about courage only through cowardice, and so on. Reflecting on what had actually happened during the "hot contention wherein he had engaged with himself" before his conversion, he discovered that Paul's interpretation of a struggle between flesh and spirit was wrong. For "more easily did my body obey the weakest willing of my soul, in moving its limbs at its nod, than my soul had obeyed itself in carrying out this great will that could be done in the will alone."[89] Hence the trouble was not the dual nature of man, half carnal and half spiritual; it was to be found in the faculty of the Will itself.

"Whence is this monstrosity? and why is it? . . . The mind commands the body, and is obeyed instantly; the mind commands itself and is resisted?" ("*Unde hoc monstrum, et quare istud? Imperat animus corpori, et paretur statim; imperat animus sibi et resistitur?*") The body has no will of its own and is obedient to the mind although that is different from the body. But the moment "the mind commands the mind to will, and the mind is not something different, yet it does not [will]. Whence is this monstrosity and why? I say it commands that itself would will a thing, and would not give that command unless it willed, and it does not that which is commanded." Perhaps, he continues, this can be explained by a weakness in the will, a lack of commitment: The mind perhaps "willeth not entirely, and therefore does not command entirely . . . and therefore what it commands *is* not." But who does the commanding here, the mind or the will? Does the mind (*animus*) command the will, and does it hesitate, so that the will does not receive an unequivocal command? The answer is no, for it is "the will [that] commandeth that there be a will, not another will [as would be the case if the *mind* were divided between conflicting wills], but the same will itself."[90]

The split occurs in the will itself; the conflict arises neither out of a split between mind and will nor out of a split between flesh and mind. This is attested by the very fact that the Will always speaks in imperatives: "Thou shalt will," says the Will to itself. Only the Will itself has the power to issue such commands, and "if the will were 'entire,' it would not command itself to be." It is in the Will's nature to double itself, and in this sense, wherever there is a will, there are always "two wills neither of which is entire [*tota*], and what is present to one of them is absent from the other." For this reason you always need two antagonistic wills to will at all; it is "not monstrous therefore partly to will and partly to nill" ("*Et ideo sunt duae voluntates, quia una earum tota non est. . . . Non igitur monstrum partim velle, partim nolle*"). The trouble is that it is the same willing ego that simultaneously wills and nills: "It was I who willed, I who nilled, I, I myself; I neither willed totally nor nilled entirely"—and this does not mean that I was of "two minds, one good, the other evil," but that the uproar of two wills in one and the same mind "rent me asunder."[91]

The Manicheans explained the conflict by the assumption of two contrary natures, one good and the other evil. But "if there were as many contrary natures as there are wills that resist themselves, there would not be two natures only but many." For we find the same conflict of wills where no choice between good and evil is at stake, where both wills must be called evil or both good. Whenever a man tries to come to a decision in such matters, "you find one soul fluctuating between various wills." Suppose somebody tries to make up his mind between "going to the circus or the theatre, if both be open the same day; or, thirdly, to rob another's house . . . or, fourthly, to commit adultery . . . all these meeting together in the same junction of time, and all being equally desired, which cannot at one time be acted." Here we have four wills, all bad and all conflicting with each other and "rending" the willing ego. And the same is true for "wills that are good."[92]

Augustine does not say here how these conflicts are resolved except that he admits that at a certain moment a goal is chosen "whither the one entire will may be borne which before was divided into many." But the healing of the will, and this is decisive, does not come about through divine grace. At the end of the *Confessions* he returns once more to the problem and relying on certain very different considerations that are explicitly argued in the treatise *On the Trinity* (which he was to spend fifteen years writing, from 400 to 416), he diagnoses the ultimate unifying will that eventually decides a man's conduct as *Love*.

Love is the "weight of the soul," its law of g.avitation, that which brings the soul's movement to its rest. Somewhat influenced by Aristotelian physics, he holds that the end of all movement is rest, and now he understands the emotions—the motions of the soul—in analogy to the movements of the physical world. For "nothing else do bodies desire by their weight than what souls desire by their love." Hence, in the *Confessions:* "My weight is my love; by it I am borne whithersoever I am borne."[93] The soul's gravity, the essence of who somebody is, and which as such is inscrutable to human eyes, becomes manifest in this love.

Let us retain the following. First: The split within the Will is a conflict, and not a dialogue, and it is independent of the content that is willed. A bad will is no less split than a good one and vice versa. Second: The will as the commander of the body is no more than an executive organ of the mind and as such quite unproblematic. The body obeys the mind because it is possessed of no organ that would make disobedience possible. The will, addressing itself to itself, arouses the counter-will because the exchange is entirely mental; a contest is possible only between equals. A will that would be "entire," without a counter-will, could no longer be a will properly speaking. Third: Since it is in the nature of the will to command and demand obedience, it is also in the nature of the will to be resisted. Finally: Within the framework of the *Confessions,* no solution to the riddle of this "monstrous" faculty is given; how the will, divided against itself, finally reaches the moment when it becomes "entire" remains a mystery. If this is the way the will functions, how does it ever arrive at moving me to act—to prefer, for instance, robbery to adultery? For Augustine's "fluctuations of the soul" between many equally desirable ends are quite unlike Aristotle's deliberations, which concern not ends but means to an end that is given by human nature. No such ultimate arbiter appears in Augustine's main analyses except at the very end of the *Confessions,* when he suddenly begins to speak of the Will as a kind of Love, "the weight of our soul," but without giving any account of this strange equation.

Some such solution is evidently required, since we know that these conflicts of the willing ego are finally resolved. Actually, as I shall show later, what looks like a *deus ex machina* in the *Confessions* is derived from a different theory of the Will. But before we turn to *On the Trinity,* it may be useful to stop to see how the same problem is treated in terms of consciousness by a modern thinker.

John Stuart Mill, examining the question of free will, suggests that "the confusion of ideas" current in this philosophical area "must . . . be very natural to the human mind," and he describes—less vividly and also less precisely but in words strangely similar to those we have just been hearing—the conflicts the willing ego is subject to. It is wrong, he insists, to describe them as "taking place between me and some foreign power, which I conquer or by which I am overcome. [For] it is obvious that 'I' am both parties in the contest; the conflict is between me and myself. . . . What causes Me, or, if you please, my Will, to be identified with one side rather than with the other, is that one of the Me's represents a more *permanent* state of my feelings than the other does."

Mill needed this "permanence" because he "disputed altogether that we are conscious of being able to act in opposition to the strongest desire or aversion"; he therefore had to explain the phenomenon of regret. What he then discovered was that "after the temptation has been yielded to [that is, the strongest desire at the moment], the desiring 'I' will come to an end, but the conscience-stricken 'I' may *endure* to the end of life." Though this enduring, conscience-stricken "I" plays no role in Mill's later considerations, here it suggests the intervention of something, called "conscience" or "character," that survives all single, temporally limited, volitions or desires. According to Mill, the "enduring I," which manifests itself only after volition has come to its end, should be similar to whatever prevented Buridan's ass from starving between two equally nice-smelling hay bundles: "From mere lassitude . . . combined with the sensation of hunger" the animal "would cease thinking of the rival objects at all." But this Mill could hardly admit, as the "enduring I" is of course one of the "parties in the contest," and when he says "the object of moral education is to educate the will," he is assuming that it is possible to teach one of the parties to win. Education enters here as a *deus ex machina:* Mill's proposition rests on an unexamined assumption—such as moral philosophers often adopt with great confidence and which actually can be neither proved nor disproved.[94]

That strange confidence cannot be expected from Augustine; it arose much later in order to neutralize, at least in the sphere of ethics and, as it were, by fiat the universal doubt that characterizes the modern age—which Nietzsche, rightly, I think, called the "era of suspicion." When men could no longer *praise,* they turned their greatest conceptual efforts to *justifying* God and His Creation in theodicies. But of course Augustine, too, needed some means of redemption for the Will. Divine grace would not help once he had discovered that the brokenness of the Will was the same for the evil and for the good will; it is rather difficult to imagine God's gratuitous grace deciding whether I should go to the theater or commit adultery. Augustine finds his solution in an entirely new approach to the problem. He now undertakes to investigate the Will not in isolation from other mental faculties but in its interconnectedness with them; the leading question now is: What function has the will in the life of the mind as a whole? Yet the phenomenal datum that suggested the answer even before it was found and duly outlined is curiously like Mill's "enduring I." In Augustine's words, it is "that there is One within me who is more myself than my self."[95]

The dominant insight of the treatise *On the Trinity* is derived from the mystery of the Christian trinity. Father, Son, and Holy Ghost, three substances when each is related to itself, can at the same time form a One, thus insuring that the dogma does not signify a break with monotheism. The unity comes about because all three substances are "mutually predicated relatively" to each other without thereby losing their existence "in their own substance." (This is not the case, for instance, when color and the colored object are "mutually predicated" in their relation to each other, for color has "not any proper substance in itself, since colored body is a substance but color is *in* a substance."[96])

The paradigm for a mutually predicated relationship of independent "substances" is *friendship:* two men who are friends can be said to be "independent substances" insofar as they are related to themselves; they are friends only relatively to each other. A pair of friends forms a unity, a One, insofar and as long as they are friends; the moment the friendship ceases they are again two "substances," independent of each other. This demonstrates that somebody or something can be a One when related only to itself and still be so related to another, so intimately *bound* together with it, that the two can appear as a One without changing their "substance," losing their substantial independence and identity. This is the way of the Holy Trinity: God remains One while related only to Himself but He is three in the unity with Son and Holy Ghost.

The point here is that such a mutually predicated relationship can occur only among "equals"; hence one cannot apply it to the relationship of body and soul, of carnal man and spiritual man, even though they always appear together, because here the soul is obviously the ruling principle. However, for Augustine the mysterious three-in-one must be found somewhere in human nature since God created man in His own image; and since it is precisely man's mind that distinguishes him from all other creatures, the three-in-one is likely to be found in the structure of the mind.

We find the first inklings of this new line of investigation at the end of the *Confessions,* the work that most closely precedes *On the Trinity.* There for the first time it occurs to him to use the theological dogma of the three-in-one as a general philosophical principle. He asks the reader to "consider these three things that are in themselves . . . [and] are far other than the Trinity . . . the three things I speak of are, to Be, to Know, and to Will. [The three are interconnected.] For I Am, and I Know, and I Will; I Am Knowing and Willing; and I know myself to Be and to Will; and I Will to Be and to Know. In these three let him discern who can, how inseparable is one life, one mind, one essence; finally, how inseparable a distinction there is, and yet there is a distinction."[97] The analogy of course does not mean that Being is an analogy of the Father, Knowing an analogy of the Son, and Willing of the Holy Ghost. What interests Augustine is merely that the mental "I" contains three altogether different things that are inseparable and yet distinct.

This triad of Being, Willing, and Knowing occurs only in the rather tentative formula of the *Confessions:* obviously Being does not belong here, since it is not a faculty of the mind. In *On the Trinity,* the most important mental triad is Memory, Intellect, and Will. These three faculties are "not three minds but one mind. . . . They are mutually referred to each other . . . and each one is comprehended by" the other two and relates back to itself: "I remember that I have memory, understanding, and will; and I understand that I understand, will, and remember; and I will that I will, remember, and understand."[98] These three faculties are equal in rank, but their Oneness is due to the Will.

The Will tells the memory what to retain and what to forget; it tells the intellect what to choose for its understanding. Memory and Intellect are both contemplative and, as such, passive; it is the Will that makes them function and eventually "binds them together." And only when by virtue of one of them, namely, the Will, the three are "forced into one do we speak of *thought*"—*cogitatio*, which Augustine, playing with etymology, derives from *cogere* (*coactum*), to force together, to unite forcefully. ("*Atque ita fit illa trinitas ex memoria, et interna visione, et quae utrumque copulat voluntate. Quia tria* [*in unum*] *coguntur, ab ipso coactu cogitatio dicitur.*"[99])

The Will's binding force functions not only in purely mental activity; it is manifest also in sense perception. This element of the mind is what makes sensation meaningful: In every act of vision, says Augustine, we must "distinguish the following three things . . . the object which we see . . . and this can naturally exist before it is seen; secondly, the vision which was not there before we perceived the object . . . and thirdly the power that fixes the sense of sight on the object . . . namely, the attention of the mind." Without the latter, a function of the Will, we have only sensory "impressions" without any actual perceiving of them; an object is *seen* only when we concentrate our mind on the perception. We can see without perceiving, and hear without listening, as frequently happens when we are absent-minded. The "attention of the mind" is needed to transform sensation into perception; the Will that "fixes the sense on that thing which we see and binds both together" is essentially different from the seeing eye and the visible object; it is mind and not body.[100]

Moreover, by fixing our mind on what we see or hear, we tell our memory what to remember and our intellect what to understand, what objects to go after in search of knowledge. Memory and intellect have withdrawn from outside appearances and deal not with these themselves (the real tree) but with images (the seen tree), and these images clearly are inside us. In other words, the Will, by virtue of *attention,* first unites our sense organs with the real world in a meaningful way, and then drags, as it were, this outside world into ourselves and prepares it for further mental operations: to be remembered, to be understood, to be asserted or denied. For the inner images are by no means mere illusions. "Concentrating exclusively on the inner phantasies and turning the mind's eye completely away from the bodies which surround our senses," we come "upon so striking a likeness of the bodily species expressed from memory" that it is hard to tell whether we are seeing or merely imagining. "So great is the power of the mind over its body" that sheer imagination "can arouse the genital organs."[101] And this *power* of the mind is due not to the Intellect and not to Memory but only to the Will that unites the mind's inwardness with the outward world. Man's privileged position within the Creation, in the outward world, is due to the mind which "imagines within, yet imagines things that are from without. For no one could use these things [of the outward world] . . . unless the images of sensible things were retained in the memory, and unless . . . the same will [were] adapted both to bodies without and to their images within."[102]

This Will as the unifying force binding man's sensory apparatus to the outside world and then joining together man's different mental faculties has two characteristics that were entirely absent from the various descriptions we have had of the Will up to now. This Will could indeed be understood as "the spring of action"; by directing the senses' attention, presiding over the images impressed on memory, and providing the intellect with material for understanding, the Will prepares the ground on which action can take place. This Will, one is tempted to say, is so busy preparing action that it hardly has time to get caught in the controversy with its own counter-will. "And just as in man and woman there is one flesh of two, so the one nature of the mind [the Will] embraces our intellect and action, or our council and execution . . . so as it was said of those: 'They shall be two in one flesh,' so it can be said of these [the inward and the outward man]: 'Two in one mind.' "[103]

Here is a first intimation of certain consequences that Duns Scotus much later will draw from Augustinian voluntarism: the Will's redemption cannot be mental and does not come by divine intervention either; redemption comes from the act which—often like a *"coup d'état,"* in Bergson's felicitous phrase—interrupts the conflict between *velle* and *nolle*. And the price of the redemption is, as we shall see, *freedom.* As Duns Scotus expressed it (in the summary of a modern commentator), "It is possible for me to be writing at this moment, just as it is possible for me not to be writing." I am still entirely free, and I pay for this freedom by the curious fact that the Will always wills and nills at the same time: the mental activity in its case does not exclude its opposite. "Yet my *act* of writing excludes its opposite. By one act of the will I can determine myself to write, and by another I can decide not to write, but I cannot be simultaneously in act in regard to both things together."[104] In other words, the Will is redeemed by ceasing to will and starting to act, and the cessation cannot originate in an act of the will-not-to-will because this would be but another volition.

In Augustine, as well as later in Duns Scotus, the solution of the Will's inner conflict comes about through a transformation of the Will itself, its transformation into *Love*. The Will—seen in its functional operative aspect as a coupling, binding agent—can also be defined as Love (*voluntas: amor seu dilectio*[105]), for Love is obviously the most successful coupling agent. In Love, there are again "three things: he that loves, and that which is loved, and Love. . . . [Love] is a certain life which couples . . . together two things, namely, him that loves and that which is loved."[106] In the same way, Will qua attention was needed to effect perception by coupling together the one with eyes to see and that which is visible; it is only that the uniting force of love is stronger. For what love unites is "marvelously glued together" so that there is a cohesion between lover and the beloved—"*cohaerunt enim mirabiliter glutino amoris.*"[107] The great advantage of the transformation is not only Love's greater force in uniting what remains separate—when the Will uniting "the form of the body that is seen and its image which arises in the sense, that is, the vision . . . is so violent that [it keeps the sense *fixed* on the vision once it has been formed], it can be called love, or desire, or passion"[108]—but also that love, as distinguished from will and desire, is not extinguished when it reaches its goal but enables the mind "to remain *steadfast* in order to *enjoy*" it.

What the will is not able to accomplish is this steadfast enjoyment; will is given as a mental faculty because the mind "is not sufficient to itself" and "through its need and want, it becomes excessively intent upon its own actions."[109] The will decides how to *use* memory and intellect, that is, it "refers them to something else," but it does not know how "to use with the joy, not of hope, but of the actual thing."[110] That is the reason the will is never satisfied, for "satisfaction means that the will is at rest,"[111] and nothing—certainly not hope— can still the will's restlessness "save endurance," the quiet and lasting enjoyment of something present; only "the force of love is so great that the mind draws in with itself those things upon which it has long reflected with love."[112] The whole mind "is in those things upon which it thinks with love," and these are the things "without which it cannot think of itself."[113]

The emphasis here is on the mind *thinking* of itself, and the love that stills the will's turmoil and restlessness is not a love of tangible things but of the "footprints" "sensible things" have left on the inwardness of the mind. (Throughout the treatise, Augustine is careful to distinguish between thinking and knowing, or between wisdom and knowledge. "It is one thing not to know oneself, and another thing not to think of oneself."[114]) In the case of Love, the lasting "footprint" that the mind has transformed into an intelligible thing would be neither the one who loves nor his beloved but the third element, namely, Love itself, the love with which the lovers love each other.

The difficulty with such "intelligible things" is that although they are as "present to the gaze of the mind as . . . tangible things are present . . . to the senses of the body," a man "who arrives [at them] does not abide in them . . . and thus a transitory thought is formed of a thing that is not transitory. And this transitory thought is committed to the memory . . . so that there may be a place to which the thought may again return." (The example he gives of lastingness in the midst of human transience is drawn from music. It is as if "one were to grasp [a melody] passing through intervals of time while it stands apart from time in a kind of secret and sublime silence"; without memory to record the sequence of sounds, one could never even "conceive of the melody as long as that singing could be heard."[115]) What Love brings about is last-ingness, a perdurance of which the mind otherwise seems incapable. Augustine has conceptualized Paul's words in the Letter to the Corinthians: "Love never ends"; of the three that "abide"—Faith, Hope, Love—"the greatest [the most durable, as it were] is love" (I Corinthians 13:8).

To summarize: this Will of Augustine's, which is not understood as a separate faculty but in its function within the mind as a whole, where all single faculties—memory, intellect, and will—are "mutually referred to each other,"[116] finds its redemption in being transformed into Love. Love as a kind of enduring and conflictless Will has an obvious resemblance to Mill's "enduring I," which finally prevails in the will's decisions. Augustine's Love exerts its influence through the "weight"—"the will resembles a weight"[117]—it adds to the soul, thus arresting its fluctuations. Men do not become just by knowing what is just but by loving justice. Love is the soul's gravity, or the other way round: "the specific gravity of bodies is, as it were, their love."[118] What is saved, moreover, in this transformation of his earlier conception is the Will's power of assertion and denial; there is no greater assertion of something or somebody than to love it, that is, to say: I will that you be—*Amo: Volo ut sis.*

Thus far, we have left to one side all strictly theological questions and with them the chief problem free will presents to all strictly Christian philosophy. In the first centuries after Christ, the existence of the universe could be explained as emanation, the outflow of divine and anti-divine forces, requiring no personal God behind it. Or, following the Hebrew tradition, it could be explained as creation having a divine person for its author. The divine author created the world of His own free will and out of nothingness. And He created man after His image, that is, endowed, too, with a free will. From then on, the theories of emanation corresponded to the fatalist or determinist theories of necessity; the creation theories had to deal theologically with the Free Will of God, Who decided to create the world, and to reconcile this Freedom with the freedom of the creature, man. Insofar as God is omnipotent (He can overrule man's will), and has foreknowledge, human freedom seems to be doubly canceled out. The standard argument, then, is: God only foreknows; He does not compel. You find the argument in Augustine, too, but at his best he proposes a very different line of thought.

Earlier, we took up the basic arguments put forward for determinism and fatalism because of their great importance to the mentality of the ancient world, especially Roman antiquity. And we saw, following Cicero, how this reasoning always ended in contradictions and paradoxes. You remember the so-called idle argument—When you were sick, whether you would recover or not recover was predestined, hence why have called a doctor; but whether you called a doctor or did not call him was also predetermined, and so on. In other words, all your faculties become *idle* once you think along these lines without cheating. The reasoning relies on antecedent causes; that is, it relies on the past. But what you actually are interested in is of course the future. You want the future to be predictable—"it was to be"—but the moment you start arguing along these lines, you are up against another paradox: "If I can foresee that I am going to be killed tomorrow in an airplane crash, then I will not get out of bed tomorrow. But then I will not be so killed. But then I will not have correctly foreseen the future."[119] The flaw in the two arguments, the one relating to the past, the other to the future, is the same: the first extrapolates the present into the past, the second extrapolates it into the future, and both assume that the extrapolator stands outside the sphere in which the real event takes place and that he, the outside observer, has no power at all to act—he himself is not a cause. In other words, since man is himself part and parcel of the temporal process, a being with a past and a special faculty for the past, called "memory," since he lives in the present and looks forward to the future, he cannot jump out of the temporal order.

I pointed out earlier that the argument of determinism receives its actual poignancy only if a Foreknower is introduced who stands outside the temporal order and looks on what is happening from the perspective of eternity. By introducing such a Foreknower, Augustine was able to arrive at the most dubious and also most terrible of his teachings, the doctrine of predestination. We are not interested here in this doctrine, a perverse radicalization of Paul's teaching that salvation lies not in works but in faith and is given by God's grace—so that not even faith is within man's power. You find it in one of the last treatises, *On Grace and Free Will*, written against the Pelagians, who, referring precisely to Augustine's earlier doctrines of the Will, had emphasized "the merits of the antecedent good will" for the reception of grace, which was given wholly gratuitously only in the forgiveness of sins.[120]

The philosophical arguments, not for predestination but for the possible co-existence of God's omniscience and man's free will, occur in a discussion of Plato's *Timaeus*. Human knowledge is of "various kinds"; men know

in different ways things which as yet are not, things which are, and things which have been. [But] not in our fashion does He look forward to what is future, nor does He look at what is present nor look back at what is past, but in a manner far and profoundly different from the way of our thoughts. For He does not pass from this to that [following in thought what has changed from past to present to future], but He sees altogether unchangeably; so that all things which [for us] emerge temporally—the future which is not yet as well as the present that already is and the past which is no more— are comprehended by Him in a stable and sempiternal presence: nor does He see differently with the eyes of the body and differently with the mind, for He is not composed of mind and body: nor [does He see] in different fashion the now, the before, the later; for His knowledge, unlike ours, is not a knowledge of three different times, present, past, and future through whose variations our knowledge is affected. . . . Nor is there any intention that passes from thought to thought in Whose bodyless intuition all things which He knows are present together at once. For He knows all times with no temporal notions, just as He moves all temporal things with no temporal movements.[121]

In this context, one can no longer speak of God's *Fore*knowledge; for Him, past and future do not exist. Eternity, understood in human terms, is an everlasting present. "If the present were always present . . . it would no longer be time but eternity."[122]

I have quoted this argument at some length because if one can assume that there is a *person* for whom the temporal order does not exist, the co-existence of God's omniscience and man's free will ceases to be an insoluble problem. At the very least it can be approached as part of the problem of man's temporality, that is, in a consideration of all our faculties as related to time. This new view, explicated in the *City of God,* is prepared for in the famous eleventh book of the *Confessions,* to which we now briefly turn.

Regarded in temporal categories, "the present of things past is in memory, the present of things present is in a mental intuition [*contuitus*—a gaze that gathers things together and "pays attention" to them], and the present of things future is in expectation."[123] But these threefold presents of the mind do not in themselves constitute time; they constitute time only because they pass into each other "from the future through the present by which it passes to the past"; and the present is the least lasting of them, since it has no "space" of its own. Hence time passes "from that which does not yet exist, by that which has no space, into that which no longer exists."[124] Time, therefore, cannot possibly be constituted by "the movements of the heavenly bodies"; the movements of bodies are "in time" only insofar as they have a beginning and an end; and time that can be measured is in the mind itself, namely, "from the time I began to see until I cease to see." For "we measure in fact the interval from some beginning up to some kind of end," and this is possible only because the mind retains in its own present the expectation of that which is not yet, which it then "pays attention to and remembers when it passes through."

The mind performs this temporalizing action in each everyday act: "I am about to recite a psalm. . . . The life of this action of mine is distended into memory in respect to the part I have already recited and into expectation in respect to the part I am about to recite. Attention is present, through which what was future is conveyed over [*traiiciatur*], that it may become past." Attention, as we have seen, is one of the major functions of the Will, the great unifier, which here, in what Augustine calls the "distention of the mind," binds together the tenses of time into the mind's present. "Attention abides and through it what will be present proceeds to become something absent," namely, the past. And "the same holds for the whole of man's life," which without the mind's distention would never be a whole; "the same [also] for the whole era of the children of men, of which all the lives of men are parts," namely, insofar as this era can be recounted as a coherent continuous story.[125]

From the perspective, then, of the temporality of the human faculties, Augustine in the last of the great treatises, the *City of God,* returns once more to the problem of the Will.[126] He states the main difficulty: God, "though Himself eternal, and *without beginning,* caused time to have a beginning; and man, whom He had not made previously, He made in time."[127] The creation of the world and of time coincide— "the world was made *not* in time, but simultaneously with time"—not only because creation itself implies a beginning but also because living creatures were made before the making of man. "Where there is no creature whose changing movement admits of succession, there cannot be time at all . . . time being impossible without the creature."[128] But what, then, was God's purpose in creating man, asks Augustine; why did He "will to make him in time," him "whom He had never made before"? He calls this question "a depth indeed" and speaks of "the unsearchable depth of this purpose" of creating *"temporal man [hominem temporalem]* who has never before been," that is, a creature that does not just live "in time" but is essentially temporal, is, as it were, time's essence.[129]

To answer "this very difficult question of the eternal God creating new things," Augustine first finds it necessary to refute the philosophers' cyclical time concepts, inasmuch as novelty could not occur in cycles. He then gives a very surprising answer to the question of why it was necessary to create Man, apart from and above all other living things. In order, he says, that there may be novelty, a *beginning* must exist; "and this beginning never before existed," that is, not before Man's creation. Hence, that such a beginning "might be, man was created before whom nobody was" (*"quod initium eo modo antea nunquam fuit. Hoc ergo ut esset, creatus est homo, ante quem nullus fuit"*).[130] And Augustine distinguishes this from the beginning of the creation by using the word *"initium"* for the creation of Man but *"principium"* for the creation of the heaven and the earth.[131] As for the living creatures, made before Man, they were created "in numbers," as species beings, unlike Man, who was created in the singular and continued to be "propagated from individuals."[132]

It is Man's character of individuality that explains Augustine's saying that there was "nobody" before him, namely, nobody whom one could call a "person"; this individuality manifests itself in the Will. Augustine proposes the case of identical twins, both "of a like temperament of body and soul." How can we tell them apart? The only endowment by which they are distinguished from each other is their will—"if both are tempted equally and one yields and consents to the temptation while the other remains unmoved . . . what causes this but their own wills in cases . . . where the temperament is identical?"[133]

In other words, and somehow elaborating on these speculations: Man is put into a world of change and movement as a new beginning because he knows that he has a beginning and will have an end; he even knows that his beginning is the beginning of his end—"our whole life is nothing but a race toward death."[134] In this sense, no animal, no species being, has a beginning or an end. With man, created in God's own image, a being came into the world that, because it was a beginning running toward an end, could be endowed with the capacity of willing and nilling.

In this respect, he was the image of a Creator-God; but since he was temporal and not eternal, the capacity was entirely directed toward the future. (Wherever Augustine speaks of the three tenses, he stresses the primacy of the future—like Hegel, as we saw; the primacy of the Will among the mental faculties necessitates the primacy of the future in time speculations.) Every man, being created in the singular, is a new beginning by virtue of his birth; if Augustine had drawn the consequences of these speculations, he would have defined men, not, like the Greeks, as mortals, but as "natals," and he would have defined the freedom of the Will not as the *liberum arbitrium*, the free choice between willing and nilling, but as the freedom of which Kant speaks in the *Critique of Pure Reason*.

His "faculty of spontaneously beginning a series in time," which "occurring in the world can have only a relatively first beginning" and still is "an absolutely first beginning not in time but in causality" must once again be invoked here. "If, for instance, I at this moment arise from my chair in complete freedom . . . a new series, with all its natural consequences *in infinitum,* has its absolute beginning in this event."[135] The distinction between an "absolute" and a "relative" beginning points to the same phenomenon we find in Augustine's distinction between the *principium* of the Heaven and the Earth and the *initium* of Man. And had Kant known of Augustine's philosophy of natality he might have agreed that the freedom of a *relatively* absolute spontaneity is no more embarrassing to human reason than the fact that men are *born*—newcomers again and again in a world that preceded them in time. The freedom of spontaneity is part and parcel of the human condition. Its mental organ is the Will.

Will and Intellect III

11 Thomas Aquinas and the primacy
of Intellect

More than forty years ago, Etienne Gilson, the great re-
viver of Christian philosophy, speaking at Aberdeen as the
Gifford Lecturer, addressed himself to the magnificent revival
of Greek thought in the thirteenth century; the result was a
classical and, I think, lasting statement—*The Spirit of Medieval
Philosophy*—on "the basic principle of all medieval speculation." He was referring to the *fides quaerens intellectum*, Anselm's "faith asking the intellect for help" and thereby making
philosophy *ancilla theologiae*, the handmaid of faith. There
was always the danger that the handmaid might become the
"mistress," as Pope Gregory IX warned the University of Paris,
anticipating Luther's fulminant attacks on this *stultitia*, this
folly, by more than two hundred years. I mention Gilson's
name, certainly not to invite comparisons—which would be
fatal to myself—but, rather, out of a feeling of gratitude and
also in order to explain why, in what follows, I shall avoid discussing matters that were dealt with long ago in such a mas-
terly way and whose result is available—even in paperback.

Eight hundred years separate Thomas from Augustine,
time enough not just to make a saint and Father of the Church
out of the Bishop of Hippo but to confer on him an authority
equal to that of Aristotle and almost equal to that of the
Apostle Paul. In the Middle Ages such authority was of the
utmost importance; nothing could be more damaging to a new
doctrine than a frank avowal that it was new; never was what
Gilson called "ipsedixitism" more dominant. Even when
Thomas expressly disagrees with an opinion, he needs an
authoritative quote to establish the doctrine against which he
will then argue. To be sure, this had something to do with the
absolute authority of God's word, recorded in books, the Old
and the New Testament, but the point here is that almost

every author that was known—Christian, Jewish, Moslem—was quoted as an "authority," either for the truth or for some important untruth.

In other words, when we study these medieval works we must remember that their authors lived in monasteries—without which such a thing as a "history of ideas" in the Western world would not exist—and that means that these writings came out of a world of books. But Augustine's reflections, by contrast, had been intimately connected with his experiences; it was important to him to describe them in detail, and even when he treated such speculative matters as the origin of evil (in the early dialogue *On Free Choice of the Will*), it scarcely occurred to him to quote the opinions of a host of erudite and worthy men on the subject.

The Scholastic authors use experience only to give an example supporting their argument; experience itself does not inspire the argument. What actually arises from the examples is a curious kind of casuistry, a technique of bringing general principles to bear on particular cases. The last author still to write clearly of the perplexities of his mind or soul, entirely undisturbed by bookish concerns, was Anselm of Canterbury, and that was two hundred years before Thomas. This, of course, is not to say that the Scholastic authors were unconcerned with the actual issues and merely inspired by arguments, but to say that we are now entering an "age of commentators" (Gilson), whose thoughts were always guided by some written authority, and it would be a grave error to believe that this authority was necessarily or even primarily ecclesiastical or scriptural. Yet Gilson, whose mentality was so admirably attuned to the requirements of his great subject, and who recognized that "it is due to scripture that there is a philosophy which is Christian, [as] it is due to the Greek tradition that Christianity possesses a philosophy," could seriously suggest that the reason Plato and Aristotle failed to penetrate to the ultimate truth was to be found in the unfortunate fact that they had not "the advantage of reading the first lines of Genesis . . . had they done so the whole history of philosophy might have been different."[1]

Thomas' great unfinished masterwork, the *Summa Theo-*

logica, was originally intended for pedagogical purposes, as a textbook for the new universities. It enumerates in a strictly systematic manner all possible questions, all possible arguments, and presumes to give final answers to each of them. No later system I know of can rival this codification of presumably established truths, the *sum* of coherent knowledge. Every philosophical system aims at offering the restless mind a kind of mental habitat, a secure home, but none has ever succeeded so well, and none, I think, was so free of contradictions. Anyone willing to make the considerable mental effort to enter that home was rewarded by the assurance that in its many mansions he would never find himself perplexed or estranged.

To read Thomas is to learn how such domiciles are built. First, the Questions are raised in the most abstract but nonspeculative manner; then, the points of inquiry for each question are sorted out, followed by the Objections that can be made to every possible answer; whereupon an "On the contrary" introduces the opposite position; only when this whole ground has been laid does Thomas' own answer follow, complete with specific replies to the Objections. This schematic order never alters, and the reader patient enough to follow the sequence of question upon question, answer upon answer, taking account of each objection and each contrary position, will find himself spellbound by the immensity of an intellect that seems to know it all. In every instance, an appeal is made to some authority, and this is particularly striking when arguments that are being refuted have first been brought forward backed by an authoritative quotation.

Not that the citation of authority is the only or even the dominant way of argumentation. It is always accompanied by a kind of sheer rational demonstration, usually iron-clad. No rhetoric, no kind of persuasion is ever used; the reader is compelled as only truth can compel. The trust in compelling truth, so general in medieval philosophy, is boundless in Thomas. He distinguishes three kinds of necessity: absolute necessity, which is rational—for instance, that three angles of a triangle are equal to two right angles; relative necessity, which is that of utility—for instance, food is necessary for life or a horse is necessary for a journey; and coercion imposed by an outside agent. And of these only the last is "repugnant to the will."[2] Truth compels; it does not command as the will commands, and it does not coerce. It is what Scotus later called the *dictamen rationis,* the "dictate of reason," that is, a power which prescribes in the form of speech (*dicere*) and whose force has its limits in the limitations of rational intercourse.

With unsurpassed clarity, Thomas distinguishes between two "apprehensive" faculties, intellect and reason; these have their corresponding intellectually appetitive faculties, will and *liberum arbitrium* or free choice. Intellect and reason deal with truth. Intellect, also called "universal reason," deals with mathematical or self-evident truth, first principles needing no demonstration to be assented to, whereas reason, or particular reason, is the faculty by which we draw particular conclusions from universal propositions as in syllogisms. Universal reason is by nature contemplative, while the task of particular reason is "to come from one thing to the knowledge of another, and so . . . we reason about conclusions, that are known from the principles."[3] This discursive reasoning process dominates all his writings. (The Age of Enlightenment has been called the Age of Reason—which may or may not be an apt description; these centuries of the Middle Ages are certainly best called the Age of Reasoning.) The distinction would be that truth, perceived by the intellect only, is revealed to and compels the mind without any activity on the mind's part, whereas in the discursive reasoning process the mind compels itself.

The argumentative reasoning process is set in motion by the faith of a rational creature whose intellect naturally turns to its Creator for help in seeking out "such knowledge of the true being" that He is "as may lie within the power of my natural reason."[4] What was revealed to faith in Scripture was not subject to doubt, any more than the self-evidence of first principles was doubted by Greek philosophy. Truth is compelling. What distinguishes this power of compulsion in Thomas from the necessitation of Greek *alētheia* is not that the decisive revelation comes from without but that "to the truth promulgated from without by revelation, responded the light of reason from within. Faith, *ex auditu* [for instance, Moses listening to the divine voice], at once awoke an answering chord."[5]

If one comes to Thomas and Duns Scotus from Augustine, the most striking change is that neither is interested in the problematic structure of the Will, seen as an isolated faculty; what is at stake for them is the relation between Will and Reason or Intellect, and the dominant question is which of these mental faculties is "nobler" and therefore entitled to primacy over the other. It may be of even greater significance, especially in view of Augustine's enormous influence on both thinkers, that, of Augustine's three mental faculties—Memory, Intellect, and Will—one has been lost, namely, Memory, the most specifically Roman one, binding men back to the past. And this loss turned out to be final; nowhere in our philosophical tradition does Memory again attain the same rank as Intellect and Will. Quite apart from the consequences of this loss for all strictly political philosophy,[6] it is obvious that what went out with memory—*sedes animi est in memoria*—was a sense of the thoroughly temporal character of human nature and human existence, manifest in Augustine's *homo temporalis*.[7]

The Intellect, which in Augustine related to whatever was present in the mind, in Thomas relates back to *first principles,* that is, to what comes logically before anything else; it is from them that the reasoning process that deals with particulars takes off.[8] The proper object of the Will is the end, yet this end is no more the future than the "first principle" is the past; principle and end are logical, not temporal, categories. So far as the Will is concerned, Thomas, closely following the *Nicomachean Ethics,* insists chiefly on the means-end category, and as in Aristotle, the end, though the Will's object, is given to the Will by the apprehensive faculties, that is, by the Intellect. Hence, the proper "order of action" is this: "First there is the apprehension of the end . . . then counsel [deliberation] about the means; and finally desire for the means."[9] At each step, the apprehensive power precedes, and has primacy over, the appetitive movement.

The conceptual foundation of all these distinctions is that

"goodness and Being" differ only in thought; they are "the same *realiter*," and this to the point where they can be said to be "convertible": "As much as [a man] has of Being, so much has he of goodness, while so far as something is lacking in the fullness of [his] Being, so far does this fall short of goodness and is said to be evil."[10] No being, insofar as it *is*, can be said to be evil, "but only insofar as it lacks Being." All this of course is no more than an elaboration of Augustine's position, but the position is enlarged and conceptually sharpened. From the perspective of the apprehensive faculties, Being appears under the aspect of truth; from the perspective of the Will, where the end is the good, it appears "under the aspect of desirableness, which Being does not express." Evil is not a principle, because it is sheer *absence*, and absence can be stated "in a privative and in a negative sense. Absence of good, taken negatively, is not evil . . . for instance, if a man lacks the swiftness of the horse; evil is an absence where something is *deprived* of a good that belongs to it essentially—for instance, the blind man, who is deprived of sight."[11] Because of its privative character, absolute or radical evil cannot exist. No evil exists in which one can detect "the total absence of good." For *"if the wholly evil could be, it would destroy itself."*[12]

Thomas was not the first to regard evil as nothing but "privation," a kind of optical illusion that comes about if the whole, of which evil is only a part, is not taken into account. Already Aristotle had had the notion of a universe "wherein every part has its own perfectly ordered place" so that the inherent goodness of fire "causes evil to water" by accident.[13] And it remains the most resilient, and ever-repeated traditional argument against the real existence of evil; even Kant, who coined the concept of "radical evil," by no means believed that one who "cannot prove a lover" may on that account be "determined to prove a villain," that, to use Augustine's language, *velle* and *nolle* are interconnected and that the true choice of the Will is between willing and nilling. Still, it is true that this old *topos* of philosophy makes more sense in Thomas than in most other systems because the center of Thomas' system, its "first principle," is Being. In the context of his philosophy, "to say that God created not only the world but the evil in it, would be to say that God created nothingness," as Gilson pointed out.[14]

All created things, whose main distinction is that they *are*, aspire "to Being [each] after its own manner," but only the Intellect has "knowledge" of Being as a whole; the senses "do not know Being except under the conditions of *here* and *now*."[15] The Intellect "apprehends Being absolutely, and for all time," and man, insofar as he is endowed with this faculty, cannot but desire "always to exist." This is the "natural inclination" of the Will, whose ultimate goal is as "necessary" to it as truth is compelling to the Intellect. The Will is free, properly speaking, only with respect to "particular goods," by which it is not "necessarily moved," although the appetites may be moved by them. The ultimate goal, the Intellect's desire to exist forever, keeps the appetites under control so that the concrete distinction between men and animals manifests itself in the fact that man "is not moved at once [by his appetites, which he shares with all other living things] . . . but *awaits* the command of the Will, which is the superior appetite . . . and so the lower appetite is not sufficient to cause movement unless the higher appetite consents."[16]

It is obvious that Being, Thomas' first principle, is simply a conceptualization of Life and the life instinct—the fact that every living thing instinctively preserves life and shuns death. This, too, is an elaboration of thoughts we found expressed in more tentative formulae by Augustine, but its inherent consequence, an equation of the Will with the life instinct—without any relation to a possible eternal life—is commonly drawn only in the nineteenth century. In Schopenhauer it is explicitly stated; and in Nietzsche's will to power, truth itself is understood as a function of the life process: what we call truth is those propositions without which we could not go on living. Not reason but our will to live makes truth compelling.

We now turn to the question of which of the two mental powers, if compared with one another, is "absolutely higher and nobler." At first sight the question seems not to make much sense, since the ultimate object is the same; it is Being that appears good and desirable to the Will and true to the Intellect. And Thomas agrees: these two powers "include one another in their acts, because the Intellect understands that the Will wills, and the Will wills the Intellect to understand."[17] Even if we distinguish between the "good" and the "true" as corresponding to different faculties of the mind, it turns out that they are very similar because both are *universal* in scope. As the Intellect is "apprehensive of universal being and truth," so the Will is "appetitive of universal good," and, just as the Intellect has reasoning as its subordinate power for dealing with the particulars, so the Will has the faculty of free choice (*liberum arbitrium*) as its subservient helper in sorting out the appropriate particular means to a universal end. Moreover, since both faculties have Being as their ultimate objective—in the guise of the True or of the Good—they seem to be equals, each of them attended by its proper servant to handle mere particulars.

Hence, the really distinctive line separating higher and lower faculties seems to be the line dividing "superior" and "subservient" faculties, and that distinction is never questioned. For Thomas—as for nearly all his successors in philosophy, of whom there are more than avowed Thomists—it was a matter of course, actually the very touchstone of philosophy as a separate discipline, that the universal is "nobler and higher in rank" than the particular, and the only proof this needed was and remained the old Aristotelian statement that the whole is always greater than the sum of its parts.

The great and rather lonely distinction of John Duns Scotus is to have questioned and challenged that assumption: Being in its universality is but a thought, what it lacks is *reality;* only particular things (*res*), which are characterized by "thisness" (*haecceity*) can be said to be real for man. Hence Scotus sharply contrasted "intuitive cognition, whose proper object is the existing singular perceived as existing, and abstractive cognition, whose proper object is the *quiddity* or essence of the known thing."[18] Therefore—and this is decisive—the mental image (the seen tree), because it has lost its actual existence, is of less ontological stature than the actual tree, although no knowledge of what a thing is would be possible without mental images. The consequence of this reversal is that *this* particular man, for instance, in his living existence is higher in rank than, and precedes, the species or the mere thought of mankind. (Kierkegaard later raised a very similar argument against Hegel.)

The reversal seems a rather obvious consequence for a philosophy that drew its main inspiration from the Bible, that is, from a Creator-God, who certainly was a person, who created men in His own image, that is, necessarily as persons. And Thomas is enough of a Christian to hold that *"persona significat id quod est perfectissimum in tota natura"* ("the person signifies what is most perfect in the whole of nature").[19] The Biblical basis, as Augustine showed, is in Genesis, where all natural species were created in the plural—*"plura simul iussit exsistere"* ("He commanded them to be many at once"). Only man was created as a singular, so that the human species (taken as an animal species) multiplied out of a One: *"ex uno . . . multiplicavit genus humanum."*[20] In Augustine and in Scotus, but not in Aquinas, the Will is the mental organ that actualizes this singularity; it is the *principium individuationis*.

To return to Thomas, he insists: "If Intellect and Will be compared with one another according to the universality of their respective objects then . . . the Intellect is absolutely higher and nobler than the Will." And this proposition is all the more significant because it does not follow from his general philosophy of Being. This is admitted in a way by Thomas himself. For him the primacy of the Intellect over the Will does not lie so much in the primacy of their respective objects—Truth over the Good—as in the way the two faculties "concur" within the human mind: "Every movement of the will [is] . . . preceded by apprehension"—no one can will what he does not know—"whereas . . . apprehension is not preceded by an act of the will."[21] (Here, of course, he parts company with Augustine, who maintained the primacy of the Will qua attention even for acts of sense perception.) This precedence shows itself in every volition. In "free choice," for instance, in which the means to an end are "elected," the two powers concur in the election: "cognitive power . . . by which we judge one thing to be preferred to another . . . and appetitive power [whereby] it is required that the appetite should accept the judgment of counsel."[22]

If we look upon the Augustinian and the Thomistic positions in purely psychological terms, as their authors frequently used to argue them, we have to admit that their opposition is somewhat spurious because they are equally plausible. Who would deny that no one can will what he does not somehow know or, on the contrary, that some volition precedes, and decides upon, the direction we want our knowledge or our search for knowledge to go? Thomas' true reason for maintaining the primacy of the Intellect—like Augustine's final reason for electing the primacy of the Will—lies in the undemonstrable answer to the ultimate question of all medieval thinkers: In what does "man's last end and happiness consist?"[23] We know that Augustine's answer was love; he intended to spend his after-life in an undesiring, never-to-be-sundered union of the creature with its creator. Whereas Thomas, obviously replying (though without mentioning them) to Augustine and the Augustinians, answers: Although someone might think that man's last end and happiness consists "not in knowing God, but in loving Him, or in some other act of will toward Him," he, Thomas, maintains that "it is one thing to possess the good which is our end, and another to love it; for love was imperfect before we possessed the end, and perfect after we obtained possession." For him, a love without desire is unthinkable and therefore the answer is categorical: "Man's ultimate happiness is essentially to know God by the Intellect; it is not an act of the Will." Here Thomas is following his teacher, Albertus Magnus, who had declared that "the supreme bliss comes to pass when the Intellect finds itself in the state of contemplation."[24] It is noteworthy to see Dante in full agreement:

> Hence may be seen how the celestial bliss
> Is founded on the act that seeth God,
> Not that which loves, which comes after this.[25]

At the start of these considerations I tried to stress the distinction between Will and desire, and by implication distinguish the concept of Love in Augustine's philosophy of the

Will from the Platonic *eros* in the *Symposium,* where it indicates a deficiency in the lover and a longing for the possession of whatever he may be lacking. What I have just quoted from Thomas shows, I think, to what an extent his concept of the appetitive faculties is still indebted to the notion of a desire to *possess* in a hereafter whatever may be lacking in earthly life. For the Will, basically understood as desire, stops when the desired object is brought into its possession, and the notion that "the Will is blessed when it is in possession of what it wills"[26] is simply not true—this is precisely the moment when the Will ceases to will. The Intellect, which, according to Thomas, is "a passive power,"[27] is assured of its primacy over the Will not only because it "presents an object to the appetite," and hence is prior to it, but also because it survives the Will, which is extinguished, as it were, when the object has been attained. The transformation of Will into Love—in Augustine as well as in Duns Scotus—was at least partly inspired by a more radical separation of the Will from appetites and desires as well as by a different notion of "man's last end and happiness." Even in the hereafter man still remains man, and his "ultimate happiness" cannot be sheer "passivity." Love could be invoked to redeem the Will because it is still active, though without restlessness, neither pursuing an end nor afraid of losing it.

That there could be an *activity* that has its end in itself and therefore can be understood outside the means-end category never enters Thomas' considerations. For him, "every agent acts for an end . . . the principle of this motion lies in the end. Hence it is that the art, which is concerned with the end, by its command moves the art which is concerned with the means; just as the *art of sailing commands the art of shipbuilding.*"[28] To be sure, this comes right out of the *Nicomachean Ethics,* except that in Aristotle it is true of only one kind of activity, namely, *poiēsis,* the productive arts, as distinguished from the performing arts, where the end lies in the activity itself—flute-playing, compared with flute-making, or just going for a walk, compared with walking in order to reach a predetermined destination. In Aristotle it is quite clear that *praxis* must be understood in analogy to the performing arts and cannot be understood in terms of the means-end category; and it is quite striking that Thomas, who depended so heavily on the Philosopher's teachings and especially on the *Nicomachean Ethics,* should have neglected the distinction between *poiēsis* and *praxis.*

Whatever the advantages of this distinction may be—and I think they are crucial for any theory of action—they are of little relevance to Thomas' notion of ultimate happiness. He opposes Contemplation to any kind of doing, and here he is quite in agreement with Aristotle, for whom the *energeia tou theou* is contemplative, since action as well as production would be "petty and unworthy of the gods." ("If we take away action from a living being, to say nothing of production, what is left but contemplation?") Hence, humanly speaking, contemplation is "not-doing-anything," being blessed by sheer intuition, blissfully at rest. Happiness, says Aristotle, "depends on leisure, for our purpose in being busy [either acting or making] is to have leisure, and we wage war in order to have peace."[29] For Thomas, only this last end—the bliss of contemplation—"moves the will" necessarily; "the will cannot not-will it." Hence "the Will moves the Intellect to be active in the way an agent is said to move; but the Intellect moves the Will in the way the end moves"[30]—that is, in the way Aristotle's "unmoved mover" was supposed to move, and how could that move except by virtue of "being loved," as the lover is moved by the beloved?[31]

What in Aristotle was the "most continuous of all pleasures" is now hoped for as eternal bliss, not the pleasure that may attend volitions but a delight that puts the will to rest, so that the ultimate end of the Will, seen in reference to itself, is to cease willing—in short, to attain its own non-being. And in the context of Thomas' thought, this implies that every activity, since its end is never reached while it is still active, ultimately aims at its own self-destruction; the means disappear when the end is reached. (It is as though, while writing a book, one were constantly driven by the desire to have it finished and be rid of writing.) To what extremes Thomas, in his single-minded predilection for contemplation as sheer seeing and not-doing, was prepared to go becomes manifest in a rather casual side remark he lets drop when interpreting a Pauline text dealing with human love between two persons. Could the "enjoyment" of loving somebody, he asks, signify that the Will's ultimate "end" has been placed in man? The answer is "No," for, according to Thomas, what Paul said in effect was that "he enjoyed his brother as a *means* toward the enjoyment of God"[32]—and God, as we have seen, cannot be reached by Man's Will or Love but only by his Intellect.

This is of course a far cry from Augustine's Love, which loves the love of the beloved, and it is also rather offensive to the ears of those who, schooled by Kant, are pretty well convinced that we ought to "treat humanity, whether in [our] own person or in that of any other . . . as an end withal, never as means only."[33]

12 *Duns Scotus and the primacy of the Will*

When we now come to Duns Scotus, no leap over the centuries, with the inevitable discontinuities and discords that make the historian suspicious, will be involved. He was not more than a generation younger than Thomas Aquinas, almost his contemporary. We are still in the midst of Scholasticism. In the texts you will find the same curious mixture of ancient quotations—treated as authorities—and argumentative reason. Although Scotus did not write a *Summa*, he proceeds in the same way as Aquinas: first, the Question states what is being inquired about (for instance, monotheism: "I ask whether there is but one God"); then the Pros and Contras, based on authoritative quotations, are discussed; next the arguments of other thinkers are given; finally, under *Respondeo*, Scotus states his own opinions, the *viae*, "Ways," as he calls them, for thought-trains, along with correct arguments, to travel.[34] No doubt at first glance it looks as though the only point of difference with Thomistic scholasticism were the question of the primacy of the Will, which is "proved" by Scotus with no less argumentative plausibility than Thomas had deployed in proving the primacy of the Intellect, and with scarcely fewer quotations from Aristotle. To put the opposing arguments in a nut-shell: If Thomas had argued that the Will is an executive organ, necessary to execute the insights of the Intellect, a merely "subservient" faculty, Duns Scotus holds that "*Intellectus . . . est causa subserviens voluntatis.*" The Intellect serves the Will by providing it with its objects as well as with the necessary knowledge; i.e., the Intellect in its turn becomes a merely subservient faculty. It needs the Will to direct its attention and can function properly only when its object is "confirmed" by the Will. Without this confirmation the Intellect ceases to function.[35]

It would be somewhat pointless here to enter the old controversy as to whether Scotus was an "Aristotelian" or an "Augustinian"—scholars have gone so far as to maintain that "Duns Scotus is as much a disciple of Aristotle as St. Thomas is"[36]—because Scotus actually was neither. But to the extent that the debate makes sense, that is, so to speak, biographically, it seems that Bettoni, the Italian Scotus scholar, is right: "Duns Scotus remains an Augustinian who profited to the utmost degree from the Aristotelian method in the exposition of the thoughts and doctrines that form his metaphysical vision of reality."[37]

These and similar evaluations are surface reactions, but unhappily they have succeeded in obliterating to a large degree the originality of the man and the significance of his thought, as though the *Doctor subtilis'* chief claim to our attention *were* subtlety, the unique complexity and intricacy of his presentation. Scotus was a Franciscan, and Franciscan literature was always greatly affected by the fact that Thomas, a Dominican, despite early difficulties, was recognized as a saint by the Church and his *Summa Theologica,* first used, and finally prescribed, as *the* textbook for the study of philosophy and theology in all Catholic schools. In other words, Franciscan literature is apologetic, usually cautiously defensive, even though Scotus' own polemics are directed at Henry of Ghent rather than turned on Thomas.[38]

A closer reading of the texts will soon disabuse one of those first impressions; the difference and distinction of the man show most clearly when he seems to be in complete conformity with the rules of Scholasticism. Thus, in a lengthy interpretive rendering of Aristotle, he suddenly proposes to "reinforce the Philosopher's reasoning" and, in discussing Anselm of Canterbury's "proof" of the existence of God, he will almost casually yield to the inclination to "touch it up" a bit, indeed quite considerably. The point is that he insisted on "establishing by reason" arguments derived from authority.[39]

Standing at the turning-point—the early fourteenth century—when the Middle Ages were changing into the Renaissance, he could indeed have said what Pico della Mirandola said at the end of the fifteenth century, in the middle of the Renaissance: "Pledged to the doctrine of no man, I have ranged through all the masters of philosophy, investigated all books, and come to know all schools."[40] Except that Scotus would not have shared the naïve trust of later philosophers in reason's persuasive power. At the heart of his reflection, as well as at the heart of his piety, is the firm conviction that, touching the questions that "pertain to our end and to our sempiternal perpetuity, the most learned and most ingenious men could know almost nothing by natural reason."[41] For "to those who have no faith, right reason, as it seems to itself, shows that the condition of its nature is to be mortal both in body and soul."[42]

It is his close attention to opinions to which he remained uncommitted, but whose examination and interpretation make up the body of his work, that is likely to lead the reader astray. Scotus certainly was not a skeptic—ancient or modern—but he had a critical turn of mind, something that is, and always has been, very rare. From this perspective, large portions of his writings read like a relentless attempt to *prove* by sheer argumentation what he suspected could not be proved; how could he be sure of being right against almost everybody else unless he followed all the arguments and subjected them to what Petrus Johannis Olivi had called an "*experimentum suitatis,*" an experiment of the mind with itself? That was why he found it necessary to "reinforce" the old arguments or "touch them up" a bit. He knew very well what he was doing. As he said: "I wish to give the most reasonable interpretation to [other thinkers'] words that I possibly can."[43] Only in this essentially non-polemical way could the inherent weakness of the argumentation be demonstrated.

In Scotus' own mature thought, this manifest weakness of natural reason can never be used as an argument for the superiority of irrational faculties; he was no mystic, and the notion that "man is irrational" was to him "unthinkable" ("*incogitabile*").[44] What we are dealing with, according to him, is the natural limitation of an essentially *limited* creature whose finitude is absolute, "prior to any reference it may have to another essence." "For, just as a body is first limited in itself by its own proper boundaries before it is limited in respect to anything else . . . so the finite form is first limited in itself before it is limited with respect to matter."[45] This finitude of the human intellect—very much like that of Augustine's *homo temporalis*—is due to the simple fact that man qua man has not created himself, though he is able to multiply like other animal species. Hence for Scotus the question is never how to derive (draw down, deduce) finitude from divine infinity or how to ascend from human finitude to divine infinity, but how to explain that an absolutely finite being can conceive of something infinite and call it "God." "Why is it that the intellect . . . does not find the notion of something infinite repugnant?"[46]

To put it differently: What is it in the human mind that makes it capable of transcending its own limitations, its absolute finitude? And the answer to this question in Scotus, as distinguished from Thomas, is the Will. To be sure, no philosophy can ever be a substitute for divine revelation, which the Christian accepts on the strength of testimony in which he has faith. Creation and resurrection are articles of faith; they cannot be proved or refuted by natural reason. As such they are *contingent,* factual truths whose opposite is not inconceivable; they relate to events that might not have happened. For those brought up in the Christian faith they have the same validity as other events of which we know only because we trust the testimony of witnesses—for instance, the fact that the world existed before we were born or that there are places on the earth where we have never been, or even that certain persons are our parents.[47]

A radical doubt that rejects the testimony of witnesses and relies on reason alone is impossible for men; it is a mere rhetorical device of solipsism, constantly refuted by the doubter's own existence. All men live together on the solid foundation of a *fides acquisita,* an acquired faith they have in common. The test for the countless facts whose trustworthiness we constantly take for granted is that they must make sense for men as they are constituted. And in this respect, the dogma of resurrection makes much more sense than the philosophers' notion of the soul's immortality: a creature endowed with body and soul can find sense only in an after-life in which he is resurrected from death as he is and knows himself to be. The philosophers' "proofs" of the soul's immortality, even if they were logically correct, would be irrelevant. To be existentially relevant for the *"viator,"* the wayfarer or pilgrim on earth, the after-life must be a "second life," not an entirely different mode of being as a disembodied entity.

Yet while it seems obvious to Scotus that the philosophers' natural reason never attained the "truths" proclaimed by divine revelation, it remains undeniable that the notion of divinity antedated any Christian revelation, and that means that there must be a mental capacity in man by which he can transcend whatever is given to him, transcend, that is, the very factuality of Being. He seems to be able to transcend himself. For man, according to Scotus, was created together with Being, as part and parcel of it—just as man, according to Augustine, was created not in time but together with time. His intellect is attuned to this Being as his sense organs are fitted for the perception of appearances; his intellect is "natural," *"cadit sub natura"*;[48] whatever the intellect proposes to him, man is *forced* to accept, compelled by the evidence of the object: *"Non habet in potestate sua intelligere et non intelligere."*[49]

It is different with the Will. The Will may find it difficult not to accept what reason dictates, *but the thing is not impossible,* just as it is not impossible for the Will to resist strong natural appetites: *"Difficile est, voluntatem non inclinari ad id, quod est dictatum a ratione practica ultimatim, non tamen est impossibile, sicut voluntas naturaliter inclinatur, sibi dismissa, ad condelectandum appetitui sensitivo, non tamen impossibile, ut frequenter resistat, ut patet in virtuosis et sanctis.*"[50] It is the possibility of resistance to the needs of desire, on the one hand, and the dictates of intellect and reason, on the other, that constitutes human freedom.

The Will's autonomy, its complete independence of things as they are, which the schoolmen call "indifference"—by which they mean that the will is "undetermined" (*indeterminata*) by any object presented to it—has only one limitation: it cannot deny Being altogether. Man's limitation is nowhere more manifest than in the fact that his mind, the willing faculty included, can hold as an article of faith that God created Being *ex nihilo*, out of nothingness, and yet be unable to conceive "nothingness." Hence the Will's indifference relates to contradictories—*voluntas autem sola habet indifferentiam ad contradictoria;* only the willing ego knows that "a decision actually taken need not have been taken and a choice other than the one actually made might have been made."[51]

This is the test by which freedom is demonstrated, and neither desire nor the intellect can measure up to it: an object presented to desire can only attract or repel, and an issue presented to the intellect can only be affirmed or negated. But it is the basic quality of our will that we may will or nill the object presented by reason or desire: *"in potestate voluntatis nostrae est habere nolle et velle, quae sunt contraria, respectu unius obiecti"* ("It is in the power of our will to will and to nill, which are contraries, with respect to the same object").[52] In saying this, Scotus, of course, does not deny that two successive volitions are necessary to will and nill the same object; but he does maintain that the willing ego in performing one of them is aware of being free to perform its contrary also: "The essential characteristic of our volitional acts is . . . the power to choose between opposite things *and to revoke the choice once it has been made"* (italics added).[53] Precisely this freedom, which is manifest only as a mental activity—the power to revoke disappears once the volition has been executed—is what we spoke of earlier in terms of a brokenness of the will.

Besides being open to contraries, the Will can *suspend* itself, and while such suspension can only be the result of another volition—in contradistinction to the Nietzschean and

Heideggerian Will-not-to-will, which we shall discuss later—this second volition, in which "indifference" is directly chosen, is an important testimony to human freedom, to the mind's ability to avoid all coercive determination from the outside. It is because of their freedom that men, though part and parcel of created Being, can praise God's creation, for if such praise derived from their reason it would be no more than a natural reaction caused by our given harmony with all the other parts of the universe. But by the same token they can also abstain from such praise and even "hate God and find satisfaction in such hatred" or at least refuse to love Him.

This refusal, which Scotus does not mention in his discussion of the possible hatred of God, is posited in analogy to his objection to the old "all men will to be happy." He admits that of course all men by nature wish to be happy (although no agreement about happiness exists), but the Will—and here is the crucial point—can transcend nature, in this case suspend it: there is a difference between man's natural inclination to happiness and happiness as the deliberately chosen goal of one's life; it is by no means impossible for man to discount happiness altogether in making his willed projects. As far as natural inclination is concerned, and the limitation nature sets on the power of the Will, all that can be affirmed is that no man can "will to be miserable."[54] Scotus avoids giving a clear answer to the question of whether hatred of God is possible or not, because of the close relation of that question to the question of evil. In line with all his predecessors and successors, he, too, denies that man can will evil as evil, "but not without raising some doubts as to the possibility of the opposite view."[55]

The Will's autonomy—"nothing else but the will is the total cause of volition" ("*nihil aliud a voluntate est causa totalis volitionis in voluntate*")[56]—decisively limits the power of reason, whose dictate is not absolute, but it does not limit the power of nature, be it the nature of the inner man, called "inclinations," or that of exterior circumstances. The will is by no means omnipotent in its actual effectiveness: its force consists solely in that it cannot be coerced to will. To illustrate this mental freedom, Scotus gives the example of a man "who hurls himself from a high place."[57] Does not this act terminate his freedom since he now necessarily falls? According to Scotus, it does not. While the man is necessarily falling, compelled by the law of gravity, he remains free to continue "to will to fall," and can also of course change his mind, in which case he would be unable to undo what he started voluntarily and would find himself in the hands of necessity. We remember Spinoza's example of the rolling stone which, if endowed with consciousness, would necessarily be prey to the illusion that it had hurled itself and was now rolling of its own free will. Such comparisons are useful in order to realize to what an extent such propositions and their illustrations, disguised in the form of plausible arguments, depend on preliminary assumptions about necessity or freedom as self-evident facts. To stay with the present illustration—no law of gravity can have power over the freedom guaranteed in interior experience; no interior experience has any direct validity in the world as it really and necessarily is according to outer experience and the correct reasoning of the intellect.

Duns Scotus distinguishes between two kinds of will: "natural will" (*ut natura*), which follows the natural inclinations, and may be inspired by reason as well as by desire, and "free will" (*ut libera*) properly speaking.[58] He agrees with nearly every other philosopher that it is in human nature to incline toward the good and explains the evil will as human weakness, the blemish of a creature that has come from nothingness ("*creatio ex nihilo*") and has therefore a certain inclination to sink back into nothingness ("*omnis creatura potest tendere in nihil et in non esse, eo quod de nihilo est*").[59] Natural will works like "gravity in bodies," and he calls it "*affectio commodi*," our being affected by what is proper and expedient. If man had only his natural will, he would at best be a *bonum animal*, a kind of enlightened brute, whose very rationality would help him to choose appropriate means to ends given by human nature. Free will—as distinguished from the *liberum arbitrium*, which is only free to select the means to a pre-designed end—freely designs ends that are pursued *for their own sake*, and of this pursuance only the Will is capable: "[*voluntas*] *enim est productiva actum,*" "for the Will produces its own act."[60] The trouble is that Scotus does not seem to say anywhere what this freely designed end actually is, although he seems to have understood the activity of free designing as the Will's actual perfection.[61]

It is with great regret that I admit that this cannot be the place (and that I would not be qualified if it were the place) to do justice to Duns Scotus' originality of thought, especially to the "passion for constructive thinking that pervades all of [his] genuine work,"[62] which he had neither the time—he died too young, too young for a philosopher—nor perhaps the inclination to present systematically. It is hard to think of any great philosopher, any one of the great thinkers—of whom there are not many—who still "needs [so much] to be discovered and helped by our attention and understanding."[63]

Such help will be all the more welcome and all the more difficult to provide, for the very good reason that finding a comfortable niche for him between predecessors and successors in the history of ideas will not be possible. Avoiding the textbook cliché of the "systematic opponent of St. Thomas" will not be enough, and in his insistence on the Will as the nobler faculty compared with the Intellect he had many predecessors among the schoolmen—the most important was Petrus Johannis Olivi.[64] Nor will it be enough to clarify and bring out in detail his undoubtedly great influence on Leibniz and Descartes, even though it is still true, as Windelband said more than seventy years ago, that their links with "the greatest of the scholastics . . . have unfortunately not found the consideration or treatment that they deserve."[65] Certainly the intimate presence of the Augustinian inheritance in his work is too patent to escape notice—there is no one who read Augustine with greater sympathy and deeper understanding—and his indebtedness to Aristotle was perhaps even greater than that of Aquinas. Still the simple truth is that for his quintessential thought—contingency, the price gladly paid for freedom—he had neither predecessors nor successors. Nor for his method: a careful elaboration of Olivi's *experimentum suitatis* in thought-experiments, which were framed as the ultimate test of the mind's critical examination in the course of its transactions with and within itself (*experimur in nobis, experientia interna*[66]).

In the following I shall try to summarize those strikingly original and highly relevant thought-trains—or thought-experiments—which clearly go against the grain of our philosophical and theological traditions but are easily overlooked because they are presented in the manner of the schoolmen and easily lost in the intricacies of Scotian argumentations. I have already mentioned some of the striking insights: first, his objection to the old cliché that "all men will to be happy" (of which nothing more was left than "no man can will to be miserable"); second, his no less surprising proof of the existence of contingency ("let all those who deny contingency be tortured until they admit that it would be possible *not* to be tortured"[67]). Stumbling on such down-to-earth remarks in their erudite surroundings, one is tempted to read them as mere witticisms. Their validity, according to Scotus, depends on the *experientia interna*, an experience of the mind whose evidence can be denied only by those who lack the experience, as a blind man would deny the experience of color. The dry, tindery quality of such remarks could suggest flashes of insight rather than thought-trains, but these abrupt flashes usually occur only in the thought-thing, a single pithy sentence that is the result of long previous critical examinations. It is characteristic of Scotus that, despite his "passion for constructive thinking," he was no system builder; his most surprising insights often appear casually and, as it were, out of context; he must have known of the disadvantages of this, for he warns us explicitly against entering into disputes with "contentious" opponents who, lacking "internal experience," are likely to win an argument and lose the issue at stake.[68]

Let us start with Contingency as the price to be paid for freedom. Scotus is the only thinker for whom the word "contingent" has no derogatory association: "I say that contingency is not merely a privation or defect of Being like the deformity . . . which is sin. Rather, contingency is a positive mode of

Being, just as necessity is another mode."[69] This position seems to him unavoidable, a matter of intellectual integrity, if one wishes to save freedom. The primacy of the Intellect over the Will must be rejected "because it cannot save freedom in any way"—*"quia hoc nullo modo salvat libertatem."*[70] For him the main distinction between Christians and pagans lies in the Biblical notion of the origin of the universe: the universe of Genesis did not come into being through the emanation of predetermined necessary forces, so that its existence would also be necessary, but was created *ex nihilo* by the decision of a Creator-God Who, we must suppose, was entirely free to create a different world in which neither our mathematical truths nor our moral precepts would be valid. From this it follows that everything that is might possibly not have been—save God Himself. His existence is necessary from the perspective of a non-necessary world which He freely "designed," but not necessary in the sense that there had ever been a necessity that coerced or inspired Him in His creation; such a necessity working through Him would be in clear contradiction to God's omnipotence as well as to His supremacy.

Men are part and parcel of this Creation, and all their natural capabilities, including their intellect, naturally follow the laws laid down by divine Fiat. Yet Man, in contradistinction to all other parts of Creation, was not freely designed; he was created in God's own image—as though God needed not only angels in some supranatural world, but some creatures after His likeness in the midst of worldly nature to keep Him company. The hallmark of this creature, obviously closer to God than any other, is by no means creativity; in that case the creature would indeed have been something like a "mortal god" (and to my mind this is very likely the reason that Scotus did not follow up his notion of a "freely designed goal of the Will" even though he seems to have thought of such a "contentless ability to design freely" as "true perfection"[71]). Rather, God's creature is distinguished by the mental capacity to affirm or negate freely, uncoerced by either desire or reasoning. It is as though Being, having come into existence, needed God's final judgment for its fulfillment—"And God saw everything that He had made, and behold, it was very good"—and this judgment was elicited also from the mortal that had been created in His likeness.

At any rate the price of the Will's freedom is to be free vis-à-vis every object; man can "hate God and find satisfaction in such hatred," because some pleasure (*delectatio*) attends every volition.[72] The Will's freedom does not consist in the selection of means for a predetermined end—*eudaimonia* or *beatitudo* or *blessedness*—precisely because this end is already *given* by human nature; it consists in freely affirming or negating or hating whatever confronts it. It is this freedom of the will mentally to *take a position* that sets man apart from the rest of creation; without it he would be an enlightened animal (*bonum animal*) at best, or, as Olivi had said earlier, a *bestia intellectualis*, an intellectual beast.[73] The miracle of the human mind is that by virtue of the Will it can transcend everything ("*voluntas transcendit omne creatum*," as Olivi said[74]), and this is the sign of man's being created in God's image. The Biblical notion that God showed him His preference by giving him dominion over all the works of His hands (Psalm 8) would only make him the highest of all created things; it would not set him absolutely apart from them. The willing ego, when it says in its highest manifestation, "*Amo: Volo ut sis*," "I love you; I want you to be"—and not "I want to have you" or "I want to rule you"—shows itself capable of the same love with which supposedly God loves men, whom He created only because He willed them to exist and whom He *loves without desiring them.*

That is how the matter presented itself to the Christian; it is why "Christians . . . say that God acts contingently . . . freely and contingently."[75] But it is also possible, according to Scotus, to arrive at the same evaluation of contingency by way of philosophy. After all, it was the Philosopher who had defined the contingent and the accidental (*to symbēbekos*) as that which "could as well not be" (*endechomenon mē einai*),[76] and what was the willing ego more aware of in every volition than that it could also not will (*experitur enim qui vult se posse non velle*[77])? How would man ever have been capable of distinguishing a free act of will from an overwhelming desire without that infallible internal test?

What apparently spoke against the Will's freedom to will or to nill was the law of causality, which Scotus also knew in the Aristotelian version: a chain of causation that would make movement intelligible and ultimately lead to an unmoved source of all motion, "the unmoved mover," a cause that itself is not caused. The strength of the argument, or, rather, its explicatory force, lies in the assumption that no more than one cause is sufficient to explain why something should be rather than not-be, that is, to explain motion and change. Scotus challenges the whole notion of a chain of causality leading in an unbroken line through a succession of sufficient and necessary causes and having to arrive finally at a First uncaused Cause in order to avoid an infinite regress.

He starts the discussion by asking "whether the act of the will is caused in the will by the object moving it or by the will moving itself" and rejects the answer that the will is moved by an object outside itself, since in no way can that save freedom (*"quia hoc nullo modo salvat libertatem"*). The opposite answer, that the Will is omnipotent, he rejects because it cannot account for all the consequences that follow a volition (*"quia tunc non possunt salvari omnes conditiones quae consequuntur actum volendi"*). Thus he arrives at his "median position," actually the only position that saves both phenomena— freedom and necessity. Presented in this form, it sounds like one of the usual Scholastic logical exercises, a rather empty play with abstract concepts. Scotus, however, at once pursues the inquiry further and arrives at a theory of "partial causes . . . [which] may concur on an equal basis and independently of one another."

Taking as his prime example procreation, where two independent substances, male and female, must come together to bring forth the child, he reaches the theory that all change occurs because a plurality of causes happens to coincide, and the coincidence engenders the texture of reality in human affairs.[78] Therefore the crux of the matter is not simply to insist on God's original freedom in creating the world, and hence on the possibility that He might have created a totally different one, but to show that change and motion as such, the phenomena that originally, in Aristotle, had led to the Law of Causality, the *aitiai* as well as the *archai,* are ruled by Contingency.

"By 'contingent,' " said Scotus, "I do not mean something that is not necessary or which was not always in existence, but something whose opposite could have occurred at the time that this actually did. That is why I do not say that something is contingent, but that something is *caused contingently.*"[79] In other words, it is precisely the causative element in human affairs that condemns them to contingency and unpredictability. Nothing indeed could be in greater contradiction to every philosophical tradition than this insistence on the contingent character of processes. (We need only think of the libraries that have been produced to explain the necessity of the outbreaks of the last two wars, each theory picking out a different single cause—when in truth nothing seems more plausible than that it was a coincidence of causes, perhaps finally set in motion by one more additional one, that "contingently caused" the two conflagrations.)

Although this notion of contingency corresponds to the experience of the willing ego, which in the act of volition knows itself to be free, uncoerced by its aims to act or not to act in their pursuit, at the same time it is in apparently unsolvable opposition to another, equally valid experience of the mind and of common sense telling us that actually we live in a factual world of *necessity.* A thing may have happened quite at random, but, once it has come into existence and assumed reality, it loses its aspect of contingency and presents itself to us in the guise of necessity. And even if the event is of our own making, or at least we are one of its contributing causes —as in contracting marriage or committing a crime—the simple existential fact that it now is as it has become (for whatever reasons) is likely to withstand all reflections on its original randomness. Once the contingent has happened, we can no longer unravel the strands that entangled it until it became an *event*—as though it could still be or not be.[80]

The reason for this strange switch of perspective, which is

at the root of many of the paradoxes connected with the problem of freedom, is that there is no substitute, real or imagined,
for existence as such. To be sure, the flux of time and change
may dissolve facts and events; but each of these dissolutions,
even the most radical change, already presupposes the reality
that preceded it. In Scotus' words, "*everything that is past is
absolutely necessary.*"[81] It has *become* the necessary condition
for my own existence, and I cannot, mentally or otherwise,
conceive of my own non-existence since, being part and parcel
of Being, I am unable to conceive of nothingness, just as I
conceive of God as the Creator of Being but not of a God prior
to the *creatio ex nihilo.*

In other words, the Aristotelian understanding of actuality
as necessarily growing out of a preceding potentiality would
be verifiable only if it were possible to revolve the process
back from actuality into potentiality, at least mentally; but this
cannot be done. All we can say about the actual is that it
obviously was *not* impossible; we can never prove that it was
necessary just because it now turns out to be impossible for us
to imagine a state of affairs in which it had not happened.

This is what made John Stuart Mill say that "our internal
consciousness tells us that we have a power [i.e., freedom],
which the whole outward experience of the human race tells
us that we never use"; for what does this "outward experience
of the human race" consist of but the record of historians,
whose backward-directed glance looks toward what *has been*
—*factum est*—and has therefore already become necessary?
At this moment "outward experience" displaces the certainties
of "internal consciousness" without, however, destroying them,
and the result is that for a mind wanting to co-ordinate and
keep in balance both "internal consciousness" and "outward
experience," it looks as though the ground of necessity itself
depends on a contingency.

If, on the other hand, the mind, in its uneasiness about the
apparent contradiction it faces, decides to take its bearings
exclusively from its own inwardness and enters into a state of
reflection on the past, it will find that here, too, factually, as
the result of Becoming, has already re-arranged and eliminated the randomness of the processes into a pattern of neces-

sity. That is the necessary condition of the existential presence of the thinking ego pondering on the meaning of what has become and now *is*. Without an a priori assumption of some unilinear sequence of events having been caused necessarily and not contingently, no explanation of any coherence would be possible. The obvious, even the only possible, way to prepare and tell a story is to eliminate from the real happening the "accidental" elements, a faithful enumeration of which may be impossible anyhow, even for a computerized brain.

Scotus is reported to have cheerfully admitted that "there is no real answer to the question as to the way in which freedom and necessity can be reconciled."[82] He was still unacquainted with Hegelian dialectics in which the process of necessity can produce freedom. But to his way of thinking, no such reconciliation was needed, for freedom and necessity were two altogether different dimensions of the mind; if there was a conflict at all, it would amount to an intramural conflict between the willing and the thinking ego, a conflict in which the will directs the intellect and makes man ask the question: Why? The reason for this is simple: the will, as Nietzsche was later to discover, is incapable of "willing backwards"; hence, let the intellect try to find out what went wrong. The question Why?—what is the *cause?*—is suggested by the will because the will experiences itself as a causative agent.

It is this aspect of the Will we stress when we say that "the Will is the spring of action"; or, in the language of the schoolmen, that "our will . . . is productive of acts, and is that by which its possessor operates in formally willing."[83] Speaking in terms of causality, the will first causes volitions, and these volitions then cause certain effects which no will can undo. The intellect, trying to provide the will with an explicatory cause to quiet its resentment at its own helplessness, will fabricate a story to make the data fall into place. Without an assumption of necessity, the story would lack all coherence.

In other words, the past, precisely because it is the "absolutely necessary," is beyond the reach of the Will. For Scotus himself, the matter presented itself more simply: the decisive opposites are not freedom and necessity, but freedom and nature—Will *ut natura* and Will *ut libera*.[84] Like the Intellect, the Will is *naturally* inclined to necessity, except that the Will, unlike the Intellect, can successfully resist the inclination.

Closely connected with this doctrine of contingency is Scotus' surprisingly simple solution to the age-old problem of freedom insofar as the problem arises out of the willing faculty itself. We discussed at some length the curious brokenness of the will, the fact that the two-in-one division, characteristic of all processes of the mind and first discovered—by Socrates and Plato—in the thinking process, turns into a deadly struggle between an I-will and I-nill (between *velle* and *nolle*) which must both be present in order to guarantee freedom: *"Experitur enim qui vult se posse non velle,"* "One who experiences a volition also has the experience of being able not to will."[85] The schoolmen, following the Apostle Paul and Augustine's philosophy of the Will, were in accord that divine grace was necessary to heal the Will's misery. Scotus, perhaps the most pious among them, disagreed. No divine intervention is necessary to redeem the willing ego.

It knows very well how to heal itself of the consequences of the priceless and yet highly questionable gift of human freedom, questionable because the fact that the will is free, undetermined and unlimited by either an exterior or an internally given object, does not signify that man qua man enjoys unlimited freedom. Man's normal way of escaping from his freedom is simply to *act* on the propositions of the will: "For example, it is possible for me to be writing at this moment, just as it is possible for me not to be writing; yet, my act of writing excludes its opposite. By one act of the will I can determine myself to write, and by another act I can decide not to write, but I cannot be simultaneously in act in regard to both things together."[86] In other words, the human will is indetermined, open to contraries, and hence broken only so long as its sole activity consists in forming volitions; the moment it stops willing and starts to act on one of the will's propositions, it loses its freedom—and man, the possessor of the willing ego, is as happy over the loss as Buridan's ass was happy to resolve the problem of choosing between two bundles of hay by following his instinct: stop choosing and start eating.

Underlying this solution, which seems simplistic at first

glance, there is a distinction Scotus made—probably under Aristotle's influence—between *activum* and *factivum*. It is between sheer activity, the Aristotelian *energeia*, which has its end and *ergon* within itself, and fabrication, *facere*, which consists in "producing or fashioning some external object," and this implies "that the operation is transient, that is, has a term outside the agent. Man's artifacts are produced by a transient activity."[87] Mental activities, such as thinking or willing, are activities of the first kind, and these, Scotus considered, though they are resultless in the real world, are of higher "perfection" because essentially they are not transient. They cease, not because they have reached their own end but only because man as a limited and conditioned creature is unable to continue them indefinitely.

Scotus likens these mental activities to the "activity" of light, which "is permanently renewed from its source and thus conserves its inner constancy and simply abides."[88] Because the gift of free will was bestowed upon an *ens creatum*, this being in order to save itself is forced to switch from the *activum* to the *factivum*, from sheer activity to the fashioning of something that finds its term naturally with the emergence of the product. The switch is possible because there is an I-can inherent in every I-will, and this I-can sets limitations on the I-will that are not outside the willing activity itself. "*Voluntas est potentia quia ipsa aliquid potest*," "the Will is a power because it *can* achieve something," and this potency, inherent in the Will, is indeed the "opposite of the *potentia passiva* of the Aristotelians. It is an active . . . powerful I-can . . . which the ego experiences."[89]

With this experience of the Will as a mental potency whose power does not consist, as in Epictetus, in shielding the mind against reality but on the contrary, inspires it and endows it with self-confidence, it is as though we have reached the end of a history whose beginning was the Apostle Paul's discovery that *velle* and *posse* do not coincide—a coincidence taken for granted in pre-Christian antiquity. Scotus' last word about the Will as a mental faculty relates to the same phenomenon that was elucidated more fully many centuries later in Nietzsche's and Heidegger's equation of Will and Power—except that

Scotus was still unaware of the annihilating (nihilistic) aspect of the phenomenon, that is, of the power generated by negation. He does not yet look upon the future as an anticipated negation of the present—or only perhaps in the general sense of perceiving the inherent futility of all merely worldly events (as Augustine said: *"quod futurum est, transiturum expectatur,"* "what is in the future is expected as something that will have been"[90]).

Man is capable of transcending the world of Being together with which he was created and which remains his habitat until death; yet even his mental activities are never unrelated to the world given to the senses. Thus the intellect is "bound up with the senses," and "its innate function is to understand sensory data"; in a similar way, the Will is "bound up with the sensory appetite" and its innate function is "to enjoy itself." *"Voluntas conjuncta appetitui sensitivo nata est condelectari sibi, sicut intellectus conjunctus sensui natus est intelligere sensibilia."*[91] The decisive words here are the *condelectari sibi,* a delight inherent in the willing activity itself as distinct from the delight of desire in having the desired object, which is transient—possession extinguishes the desire and the delight. The *condelectatio sibi* borrows its delight from its closeness to desire, and Scotus said explicitly that no mental delight can compete with the delight arising from the fulfillment of sensual desire, except that this delight is almost as transient as the desire itself.[92] Hence, he distinguishes sharply between will and desire because only the will is not transient. An inherent delight of the will in itself is as natural to the will as understanding and knowing are to the intellect, and can be detected even in hatred; but its innate perfection, the final peace between the two-in-one, can come about only when the will is transformed into *love*. If the will were mere desire to possess, it would cease to be once the object is possessed: I do not desire what I have.

To the extent that Scotus speculates about an after-life—that is, an "ideal" existence for man qua man—this hoped-for transformation of the will into love with its inherent *delectatio* is decisive. The transformation of willing into loving does not signify that loving ceases to be an activity whose end is within itself; hence future blessedness, the beatitude enjoyed in an after-life, cannot possibly consist in rest and contemplation. Contemplation of the *summum bonum*, of the highest "thing," ergo, God, would be the ideal of the intellect, which is always grounded in intuition, the grasping of a thing in its "thisness," *haecceitas*, which in this life is imperfect not only because here the highest remains unknown but also because intuition of thisness is imperfect: "the intellect . . . has recourse to universal concepts, precisely because it is incapable of grasping the haecceity."[93] The notion of "eternal peace," or of Rest, arises out of the experience of restlessness, of the desires and appetites of a needy being that can transcend them in mental activities without ever being capable of escaping them altogether. What the will in a state of blessedness, that is, in an after-life, no longer needs or is no longer capable of, is *rejection* and hatred, but this does not mean that man in a state of blessedness has lost the faculty of saying "Yes."

That unconditional acceptance is called "Love" by Scotus: "*Amo: volo ut sis.*" "Beatitude is therefore the act by which the will comes in contact with the object presented to it by the intellect and loves it, thus fully satisfying its natural desire for it."[94] Here again love is understood as an activity but no longer a mental one, as its object is no longer absent from the senses and no longer imperfectly known to the intellect. For "beatitude . . . consists in the full and perfect attainment of the object as it is in itself, and not merely as it is in the mind."[95] The mind, transcending the existential conditions of the "wayfarer," or pilgrim on earth, has an intimation of such future blessedness in its experience of sheer activity, that is, in a transformation of willing into *loving*. Falling back on the Augustinian distinction of *uti* and *frui*, using something for the sake of something else and enjoying it for its own sake, Scotus says that the essence of beatitude consists in "*fruitio*," the "perfect love of God for God's sake . . . thus distinct from the love of God for one's own sake." Even if the latter is love for the sake of one's soul's salvation, it is still *amor concupiscentiae*, desirous love.[96] Already in Augustine we find the transformation of willing into loving, and it is more than likely that the reflections of both thinkers were guided by Paul's words about the "love that never ends," not even when "that which is perfect comes" and all else has "passed away" (I Corinthians 13:8–13). In Augustine the transformation comes about because of the binding force of the will; there is no stronger binding force than the love with which the lovers love each other ("marvelously glued together").[97] But for Scotus the experiential ground of love's everlastingness is that he conceives of a love that is not only, as it were, emptied, purified of desires and needs, but in which the very *faculty* of the Will is transformed into sheer activity.

If in this life it is the miracle of the human mind that man at least mentally and provisionally can transcend his earthly conditions and enjoy the sheer actuality of an exercise that has its end in itself, then it is the hoped-for miracle of an after-life that man in his whole existence will be spiritualized. Scotus speaks of a "Glorified body,"[98] no longer dependent on "faculties" whose activities are interrupted either by the *factivum*, the making and fashioning of objects, or by the desires of a needy creature—both of which render transient every activity in this life, the mental ones not excluded. Transformed into love, the restlessness of the will is stilled but not extinguished; love's abiding power is felt not as the arrest of motion—as the end of the fury of war is felt as the quiet of peace—but as the serenity of a self-contained, self-fulfilling, everlasting movement. Here are not the quiet and delight that follow upon a perfect operation, but the stillness of an act resting in its end. In this life we know of such acts in our *experientia interna*, and, according to Scotus, we should be able to understand them as intimations of an uncertain future when they would last forever. Then "the operating faculty will find itself calmed in its object through the perfect act [love] by which it attains it."[99]

The idea that there could be an activity that finds its rest within itself is as surprisingly original—without precedent or sequel in the history of Western thought—as Scotus' ontological preference of the contingent over the necessary and of the existent particular over the universal. I have tried to show that in Scotus we meet not simple conceptual reversals but genuine new insights, all of which could probably be explicated as the speculative conditions for a philosophy of freedom. As far as I can see, in the history of philosophy only Kant can equal Duns Scotus in his unconditional commitment to freedom. And yet certainly Kant had no knowledge of him. I shall therefore end with an odd passage from the *Critique of Pure Reason* that at least deals with the same problem though without any mention of Freedom or the Will:

There is something very strange in the fact, that once we assume something to exist we cannot avoid inferring that something exists necessarily. . . . On the other hand, if I take the concept of anything, no matter what, I find that the existence of this thing can never be represented by me as absolutely necessary, and that, whatever it may be that exists, nothing prevents me from thinking its non-existence. Thus while I may indeed be obliged to assume something necessary as a condition of the existent in general, I cannot think any particular thing as in itself necessary. In other words, I can never *complete* the regress to the conditions of existence save by assuming a necessary being, and yet am never in a position to *begin* with such a being. [And concluding this deliberation a few pages later] . . . there is nothing which absolutely binds reason to accept such an existence; on the contrary it can always annihilate it in thought, without contradiction; absolute necessity is a necessity that is to be found in thought alone.[100]

To which, taught by Scotus, one may add that absolute nothingness cannot be found in thought. We shall have occasion later to come back to this idea when we discuss the uncertain destinies of the willing faculty at the close of the modern age.

Conclusions IV

13 *German Idealism and the*
"rainbow-bridge of concepts"

Before we come to the final part of these considerations I shall try to justify the last and largest leap over the centuries in this sketchy and fragmentary presentation that I had the presumption to announce as a history of the Will. I have already mentioned my doubts as to whether there can legitimately be a "history of ideas," a *Geistesgeschichte* that rests on the assumption that ideas follow and generate one another in a temporal succession. The assumption makes sense only in the system of Hegel's dialectics. But, apart from any theories, a record does exist of the thoughts of great thinkers whose place in factual history is unchallengeable and whose testimony affirming or negating the Will we have touched on here only in passing—Descartes and Leibniz on one side of the argument, Hobbes and Spinoza on the other.

The only great thinker in these centuries who would be truly irrelevant to our context is Kant. His Will is not a *special* mental capability distinct from thinking, but practical reason, a *Vernunftwille* not unlike Aristotle's *nous praktikos;* the statement that "pure reason can be practical is the chief thesis of the Kantian moral philosophy"[1] is perfectly right. Kant's Will is neither freedom of choice (*liberum arbitrium*) nor its own cause; for Kant, sheer spontaneity, which he often called "absolute spontaneity," exists only in thinking. Kant's Will is delegated by reason to be its executive organ in all matters of conduct.

Much more embarrassing, and thus in need of justification, is the omission from our considerations of the development of German idealism after Kant, the leap we have made over Fichte, Schelling, and Hegel, who in their speculative way summed up the centuries of the modern age. For the rise and decline of the modern age is not a figment of the "history of

149

ideas" but a factual event that can be dated: the discovery of the whole earth and of part of the universe, the rise of modern science and its technology, followed by the decline of the Church's authority, by secularization and enlightenment.

This momentous factual break occurring in our past has been characterized and interpreted from many different and legitimate viewpoints; in our context, the most decisive development that took place during these centuries was the subjectivization of cognitive as well as metaphysical thought. Only during these centuries did man become the center of concern to science as well as to philosophy. It had not happened in earlier times, even though, as we saw, the discovery of the Will coincided with the discovery of the "interior man" at a moment when man had become a "question for himself." Only when science had proved not merely that human senses were subject to error—which could be corrected in the light of new evidence in order to reveal "truth"—but that his sensory apparatus was forever incapable of self-evident certainties, did man's mind, now entirely thrown back upon itself, begin, with Descartes, to look for a "certainty" that would be a pure datum of consciousness. When Nietzsche called the modern age the "school of suspicion," he meant that, starting at least with Descartes, man was no longer sure of anything, not even of being real; he needed proof, not only of God's existence but also of his own. The certainty of the I-am is what Descartes found in his *cogito me cogitare;* that is, in a mental experience for which none of the senses, which give us the reality of ourselves and of an exterior world, is necessary.

To be sure, this certainty is very questionable. Already Pascal, himself influenced by Descartes, objected that this consciousness would hardly be sufficient to distinguish between dream and reality: a poor artisan dreaming for twelve hours every night that he was king would have the same life (and enjoy the same amount of "happiness") as a king who dreamed every night that he was nothing but a poor artisan. Moreover, since "one frequently dreams that he is dreaming," nothing can guarantee that what we call our life is not wholly a dream from which we shall awaken in death. To doubt everything (*"de omnibus dubitandum est"*) and find certainty

in the very activity of doubting demanded by the "new Philosophy [that] calls all in doubt" (Donne) does not help, for is
the doubter not obliged to doubt that he doubts? True, no one
went that far, but that only means that "no one was ever a perfect skeptic [*pyrrhonien*, in Pascal]," though not because reason fortified him; he was restrained by "nature, [which] helped
impotent reason"; and so Cartesianism was "something like the
story of Don Quixote."[2]

Centuries later, Nietzsche, still thinking in the same vein,
suspected that it was our Cartesian "belief in the [thinking]
'ego' . . . as the sole reality [that made us] . . . ascribe reality
to things in general."[3] Indeed, nothing became more characteristic of the last stages of metaphysics than this kind of turning-
of-the-tables, of which Nietzsche, with his mercilessly honest
thought-experiments, was the greatest master. But that
game—still a thought-game rather than a language-game—did
not become possible until, with the rise of German idealism,
all bridges had been broken "except the rainbow-bridges of
concepts,"[4] or, to put it less poetically, until it dawned on the
philosophers that "the novelty of our contemporary position in
philosophy lies in the conviction, which no era had before us,
that we do not possess the truth. All previous generations
'possessed the truth,' even the skeptics."[5]

Nietzsche and Heidegger are wrong, I think, in their dating
of that modern conviction; actually it had accompanied the
rise of modern science and then was attenuated by the Cartesian "certainty" as a substitute for truth; this in its turn was
destroyed by Kant along with the remnants of Scholasticism,
which in the form of logical exercises and the dogmatism of
the "schools" had led a rather brittle existence of sheer erudition. But only at the end of the nineteenth century (here
Heidegger is right) did the conviction of not possessing the
truth become the common opinion of the educated classes and
establish itself as something like the Spirit of the Age, of which
Nietzsche was probably the most fearless representative.

However, the mighty factor that delayed this reaction for
centuries itself sprang up with the rise of the sciences as the
natural response of every thinking man to the enormous and
enormously rapid advance in human knowledge, an advance

that was bound to make the previous centuries since antiquity appear as sheer stagnation by comparison. The concept of *Progress* as a vast co-operative drive in the interest of knowledge for its own sake, "in which all scientists of the past, the present and the future have a part . . . appeared for the first time fully developed in the works of Francis Bacon."[6] With it there came about, at first almost automatically, an important shift in the understanding of Time, the emergence of the Future to the rank formerly occupied by the Present or the Past. The notion that each subsequent generation would necessarily know more than its predecessor and that this progressing would never be completed—a conviction that only in our time has found challengers—was important enough; but for our context, even more important is the simple, matter-of-fact perception that "scientific knowledge" has been and can be attained only "step by step through contributions of *generations* of explorers building upon and gradually amending the findings of their predecessors."

The rise of science had begun with the new discoveries of the astronomers, scientists who not only had "used most systematically" the findings of their predecessors, but who, without the records of past generations, and reliable records at that, would have been unable to make any "progress" at all, since the life-span of one man, or one generation of men, is evidently too short to verify findings and validate scientific hypotheses. But "the astronomers composed star catalogues to be used by future scientists," i.e., they had laid a basis for scientific advances. (Astronomy, of course, was not wholly alone in initiating progress. Thomas Aquinas was conscious of an "increase in scientific knowledge"—"*augmentum factum est*" —which he explained by "the defects of knowledge of those who first invented the sciences." Craftsmen, too, used to the method of trial and error, were keenly aware of certain improvements in their crafts. Yet the guilds themselves "stressed the continuity rather than the progress of craftsmanship," and "the only passage in the extant literature which clearly expresses the idea of the gradual progress of knowledge, or better, technological skill, occurs in a treatise on artillery."[7]) Still, the decisive breakthrough that gave modern science its impetus occurred in astronomy, and the idea of Progress, which from then on dominated every other science till it finally became the dominant notion of the equally modern concept of History, was originally based on the pooling of data, the exchange of knowledge, and the slow accumulation of records that were the requisites of astronomical advance. It was only after the world-shaking discoveries of the sixteenth and seventeenth centuries that what had been going on in that field came to the attention of those who were concerned with the general human condition.

Thus, while the "new philosophy" proving the inadequacy of our senses had "called all in doubt" and given rise to suspicion and despair, the equally manifest forward movement of knowledge gave rise to an immense optimism as to what man can know and learn. Except that this optimism did not apply to men in the singular, not even to the relatively small community of scientists; it applied only to the succession of generations, that is, to Mankind as a whole. In the words of Pascal, who was the first to detect that the idea of Progress was a necessary complement to the idea of Mankind, it was the "particularly [human] prerogative [distinguishing man from animal] that not only each human being can daily advance in knowledge, but that all men together progress continually while the universe grows older . . . so that the whole succession of men throughout the centuries should be *considered as one and the same man who lives forever* and continually learns" (italics added).[8]

What is decisive in this formulation is that the notion of "all men together," which is of course a thought, not a reality, was immediately construed on the model of "man," of a "subject" that could serve as a noun for all kinds of activities expressed in verbs. This concept was not a metaphor, properly speaking; it was a full-fledged *personification* such as we find in the allegories of Renaissance narratives. In other words, *Progress became the project of Mankind,* acting behind the backs of real men—a personified force that we find somewhat later in Adam Smith's "invisible hand," in Kant's "ruse of nature," Hegel's "cunning of Reason," and Marx's "dialectical materialism." To be sure, the historian of ideas will see in these notions nothing more than the secularization of divine Providence, an interpretation that is all the more questionable since we find the personification of Mankind in Pascal, who would certainly have been the last to desire a secular replacement for God as the true ruler of the world.

However that may be, the interconnected ideas of Mankind and Progress came to the foreground of philosophical speculations only after the French Revolution had demonstrated to the minds of its most thoughtful spectators the possible actualization of such invisibles as *liberté, fraternité, égalité,* and thus seemed to constitute a tangible refutation of the oldest conviction of thinking men, to wit, that the ups and downs of history and the ever-changing affairs of men are not worth serious consideration. (To contemporary ears Plato's famous dictum in the *Laws* that a serious man keeps his seriousness for serious things and "does not waste it on trifles"[9] such as human affairs may sound extreme; in fact, it was never challenged before Vico, and Vico had no influence or echo till the nineteenth century.) The event of the French Revolution, the climax in many respects of the modern age, changed "the pale cast of thought" for almost a century; philosophers, a notoriously melancholy tribe of men, became cheerful and optimistic. They now believed in the Future and left the age-old lamentations over the course of the world to the historians. What centuries of scientific advances, fully grasped only by the participants in the great enterprise yet by no means beyond the general comprehension of the philosopher, had been unable to achieve was now brought about in a matter of a few decades: philosophers were converted to a faith in the progress not only of knowledge but also of human affairs generally.

And while they began to reflect, with a commitment never before witnessed, on the course of *History,* they could not help becoming aware almost immediately of the greatest riddle presented to them by their new subject matter. That was the simple fact that no action ever attains its intended goal and that Progress—or any other fixed meaningfulness in the historical process—arises out of a senseless "mixture of error and violence" (Goethe), out of a "melancholy haphazardness" in

the "meaningless course of human affairs" (Kant). What sense
there is can be detected only by the wisdom of hindsight,
when men no longer act but begin to tell the story of what has
happened; then it seems as though men, while pursuing their
aims at cross-purposes, without rhyme and reason, had been
led by an "intention of nature," by the "guiding thread of reason."[10] I have quoted Kant and Goethe, both of whom,
as it were, stopped at the threshold of the new generation,
that of the German Idealists for whom the events of the
French Revolution were the decisive experiences of their lives.
But that "the facts of known history" taken by themselves
"possess neither a common basis nor continuity nor coherence"
was already known to Vico, and Hegel, long after, was still
insisting that "passions, private aims, and the satisfaction of
selfish desires, are . . . the most effective springs of action."
Hence, not the record of past events but only the story makes
sense, and what is so striking in Kant's remarks at the end of
his life is that he immediately understood that the subject of
History's action would have to be Mankind, rather than man
or any verifiable human community. Striking, too, is the fact
that he was able to realize the great flaw in History's project:
"It will always remain bewildering that the earlier generations
seem to carry on their burdensome business only for the sake
of the later . . . and that only the last should have the good
fortune to dwell in the [completed] building."[11]

   Probably it was sheer coincidence that the generation that
grew to maturity under the impact of the eighteenth-century
revolutions was also mentally formed by Kant's liberation of
thought, by his resolution of the old dilemma between dogmatism and skepticism through the introduction of a self-
critique of Reason. And as the revolution encouraged them to
transfer the notion of Progress from scientific advancement to
the realm of human affairs and understand it as the progress
of History, it was only natural that their attention should be
directed toward the Will as the spring of action and the organ
of the Future. The result was that "the thought of making
freedom the sum and substance of philosophy emancipated
the human spirit in all its relationships," emancipated the
thinking ego for free speculation in thought-trains whose ulti-

mate goal was to "prove . . . that not only is the Ego all, but contrariwise too, all is Ego."[12]

What had appeared in a restrictive, tentative way in Pascal's personified concept of Mankind now began to proliferate to an incredible degree. The activities of men, whether thinking or acting, were all transformed into activities of personified concepts—which made philosophy both infinitely more difficult (the chief difficulty in Hegel's philosophy is its abstractness, its only occasional hints at the actual data and phenomena he has in mind) and incredibly more alive. It was a veritable orgy of sheer speculation, which, in sharp contrast with Kant's critical reason, was brimful of historical data in a disguised state of radical abstraction. Since the personified concept itself is supposed to act, it looks as though (in Schelling's words) philosophy has "raised itself to a higher standpoint," to a "higher realism" in which mere thought-things, Kant's *noumena,* dematerialized products of the thinking ego's reflection on actual data—historical data in Hegel, mythological or religious in Schelling—begin their curious disembodied ghostly dance whose steps and rhythms are neither regulated nor limited by any idea of reason.

It was in this region of pure speculation that the Will appeared during the short period of German Idealism. "In the final and highest instance," declared Schelling, "there is no other Being than Will. Will is primordial Being, and all predicates apply to it alone—groundlessness, eternity, independence of time, self-affirmation! All philosophy strives only to find this highest expression."[13] And quoting this passage in his *What Is Called Thinking?,* Heidegger at once adds: "The predicates, then, which metaphysical thought has since antiquity attributed to Being, Schelling finds in their final, highest . . . most perfected form in willing. *The Will in this willing does not mean here a capacity of the human soul,* however; the word 'willing' here designates the Being of beings as a whole" (italics added).[14] No doubt Heidegger is right; Schelling's Will is a metaphysical entity but, unlike the more common and older metaphysical fallacies, it is personified. In a different context and more precisely, Heidegger himself sums up the meaning of this personified Concept: the *false* "opinion [easily] arises that the human will is the origin of the will-to-will, while on the contrary, man is being willed by the Will-to-will without even experiencing the essence of such willing."[15]

With these words Heidegger resolutely turns against the subjectivism of the modern age as well as against phenomenological analyses, whose chief aim has always been to "save the phenomena" as given in consciousness. And what he turns to while entering on the "rainbow bridge of concepts" is German Idealism and its ingenuous exclusion of man and man's faculties in favor of personified concepts.

Nietzsche diagnosed the inspiration behind this post-Kantian German philosophy with unsurpassed clarity; he knew that philosophy only too well and finally went a similar, perhaps even more extreme way himself.

[German philosophy, said Nietzsche] is the most fundamental form of . . . homesickness there has ever been: the longing for the best that has ever existed. One is no longer at home anywhere; at last one longs back for that place in which alone one can be at home: the *Greek* world! But it is in precisely that direction that all bridges are broken—except the rainbow-bridges of concepts. . . . To be sure, one must be very light, very subtle, very thin to step across these bridges! But what happiness there is already in this will to spirituality, to ghostliness [*Geisterhaftigkeit*] almost! . . . One wants to go *back*, through the Church Fathers to the Greeks. . . . German philosophy is a piece of . . . will to Renaissance, will to go on with the discovery of antiquity, the digging up of ancient philosophy, above all of the pre-Socratics—the most deeply buried of all Greek temples! A few centuries hence, perhaps, one will judge that all German philosophy derives its real dignity from being a gradual reclamation of the soil of antiquity . . . we are growing more Greek by the day; at first, as is only fair, in concepts and evaluations, as Hellenizing ghosts, as it were. . . .[16]

No doubt the personified concept had its root in verifiable experience, but the pseudo-kingdom of disembodied spirits working behind men's backs was built out of homesickness for another world, in which man's spirit could feel at home.

This, then, is my justification for having omitted from our considerations that body of thought, German Idealism, in which sheer speculation in the realm of metaphysics perhaps reached its climax together with its end. I did not want to cross the "rainbow-bridge of concepts," perhaps because I am not homesick enough, in any event because I do not believe in a world, be it a past world or a future world, in which man's mind, equipped for withdrawing from the world of appearances, could or should ever be comfortably at home. Moreover, at least in the cases of Nietzsche and Heidegger, it was precisely a confrontation with the Will as a human faculty and not as an ontological category that prompted them first to repudiate the faculty and *then* turn about to put their confidence in this ghostly home of personified concepts which so obviously was "built" and decorated by the thinking, as opposed to the willing, ego.

14 *Nietzsche's repudiation of the Will*

In my discussion of the Will I have repeatedly mentioned two altogether different ways of understanding the faculty: as a faculty of *choice* between objects or goals, the *liberum arbitrium,* which acts as arbiter between given ends and deliberates freely about means to reach them; and, on the other hand, as our "faculty for beginning spontaneously a series in time" (Kant)[17] or Augustine's *"initium ut esset homo creatus est,"* man's capacity for beginning because he himself is a beginning. With the modern age's concept of Progress and its inherent shift from understanding the future as that which approaches us to that which we determine by the Will's projects, the instigating power of the Will was bound to come to the foreground. And so indeed it did, as far as we can tell from the common opinion of the time.

On the other hand, nothing is more characteristic of the beginnings of what we now call "existentialism" than the absence of any such optimistic overtones. According to Nietzsche, only "lack of historical sense," a lack that for him is "the original error of all philosophers,"[18] can explain that optimism: "Let us not be deceived! Time marches forward; we'd like to believe that everything that is in it also marches forward—that the development is one that moves forward." And as to Progress' correlate, the idea of mankind: " 'Mankind' does not advance; it does not even exist."[19]

In other words, though the universal suspicion at the beginning of the modern age had been powerfully neutralized, held in check, first by the very notion of Progress and then by its seeming embodiment and apogee in the French Revolution, this had proved to be only a delaying action, whose force eventually exhausted itself. If one wants to look on this development historically, one can only say that Nietzsche's thought-experiments—"such an experimental philosophy as I live anticipates experimentally even the possibilities of the most fundamental nihilism"[20]—at last completed what had begun with Descartes and Pascal in the seventeenth century.

Men, forever tempted to lift the veil of the future—with the aid of computers or horoscopes or the intestines of sacrificial animals—have a worse record to show in these "sciences" than in almost any other scientific endeavor. Still, if it were a matter of honest competition between futurologists in respect to our own time, the prize might well go to John Donne, a poet without any scientific ambitions, who in 1611 wrote in immediate reaction to what he knew was going on in the sciences (which for a long time would still be operating under the name of "natural philosophy"). He did not have to wait for Descartes, or Pascal, to draw all the conclusions from what he perceived.

> And new Philosophy calls all in doubt,
> The Element of fire is quite put out;
> The Sun is lost and th'earth, and no mans wit
> Can well direct him where to looke for it. . . .
> 'Tis all in pieces, all cohaerence gone;
> All just supply, and all Relation:
> Prince, Subject, Father, Sonne, are things forgot. . . .

And he ends with lamentations that needed roughly three hundred years to be heard again: "when thou knowst this, Thou knowst how ugly a monster . . . how wan a Ghost . . . how drie a Cinder this world is."[21]

It is against this historical background that we shall have

to consider the last two thinkers still close enough to the West's philosophical heritage to recognize in the Will one of the mind's important faculties. We start with Nietzsche and remember that he never wrote any book with the title "Will to Power," that the collection of fragments, notes, and aphorisms bearing this title was published posthumously, selected from a chaos of unconnected and often contradictory sayings. Each one of them is what all Nietzsche's mature writings actually are, namely, a thought-experiment, a literary genre surprisingly rare in our recorded history. The most obvious analogy is Pascal's *Pensées,* which share with Nietzsche's *Will to Power* a haphazardness of arrangement that has led later editors to try to *re*arrange them, with the rather annoying result that the reader has a good deal of trouble identifying and dating them.

We shall consider first a number of simple descriptive statements without metaphysical or general philosophical connotations. Most of them will sound rather familiar, but it will be better not to jump to the conclusion that we may be confronted here with bookish influences. To draw such inferences is especially tempting in the case of Heidegger because of his profound knowledge of medieval philosophy, on the one hand, and his insistence on the primacy of the future tense in *Being and Time* (which I have already spoken of), on the other. It is all the more noteworthy that in his discussion of the Will, which chiefly takes the form of an interpretation of Nietzsche, he nowhere mentions Augustine's discoveries in the *Confessions.* Hence what will sound familiar in the following is best ascribed to the peculiar characteristics of the willing faculty; even Schopenhauer's influence on the young Nietzsche we may disregard without great scruples. Nietzsche knew that "Schopenhauer spoke of the 'will'; but nothing is more characteristic of his philosophy than the absence of all genuine willing,"[22] and he saw correctly that the reason for this lay in a "basic misunderstanding of the *will* (as if craving, instinct, drive were the *essence* of the will)" whereas "the will is precisely that which treats cravings as their master and appoints to them their way and measure."[23]

For "to will is not the same as to desire, to strive for, to want: from all these it is distinguished through the element of

Command. . . . That something is commanded, this is inherent in willing."[24] Heidegger comments: "No characteristic phrase occurs more frequently in Nietzsche than . . . to will is to command; inherent in Will is the commanding thought."[25] It is no less characteristic that this commanding thought is directed only very rarely toward dominating others: command and obedience both occur in the mind—in a fashion strangely similar to Augustine's conception, of which Nietzsche certainly knew nothing.

He explains at some length in *Beyond Good and Evil:*

Somebody who wills gives orders to something *in* him that obeys. . . . The strangest aspect of this multiple phenomenon we call 'Will' is that we have but one word for it, and especially only one word for the fact that *we are in every given case at the same time those who issue the orders and those who obey them;* insofar as we obey, we experience the feelings of coercion, urging, pressing, resisting, which usually begin to manifest themselves immediately after the act of willing; insofar however . . . as we are in command . . . we experience a sensation of pleasure, and this all the more strongly as we are used to overcoming the dichotomy through the notion of the I, the Ego, and this in such a way that we take the obedience in ourselves for granted and therefore identify willing and performing, willing and acting [italics added].

This willing operation existing only in our minds overcomes the mental duality of the two-in-one that has become a battle between one who commands and one who is supposed to obey by identifying the "I" as a whole with the commanding part and anticipating that the other, the resisting part, will obey and do as it is told. "What is called 'freedom of the will' is essentially a passionate superiority toward a someone who must obey. 'I am free; "he" must obey'—the consciousness of this is the very willing."[26]

We would not expect Nietzsche to believe in divine grace as the healing power for the Will's duality. What *is* unexpected in the above description is that he detected in the "consciousness" of the struggle a kind of trick of the "I" that enables it to escape the conflict by identifying itself with the commanding part and to overlook, as it were, the unpleasant, paralyzing sentiments of being coerced and hence always on the point of resisting. Nietzsche often denounces this feeling of superiority as an illusion, albeit a wholesome one. In other passages, he accounts for the "strangeness" of the whole phenomenon by calling it an "oscillation [of the will] between yes and no," but he sticks to the feeling of the "I" 's superiority by identifying the oscillation with a kind of swinging from pleasure to pain. The pleasure, different in this as in other respects from Scotus' *delectatio*, is clearly the anticipated joy of the I-can inherent in the willing act itself, independent of performance, of the triumphal feeling we all know when we perform well, regardless of praise or audience. In Nietzsche, the point is that he numbers the negative slave-feelings of being coerced and of resisting or resenting among the necessary obstacles without which the Will would not even know its own power. Only by surmounting an inner resistance does the Will become aware of its genesis: it did not spring up to obtain power; power is its very source. Again in *Beyond Good and Evil*: " 'Freedom of the will' is the word for that manifold pleasurable condition of the willer *who is in command and at the same time* considers himself as one with the executor of the command—as such enjoying the triumph over the resistance, but possessed of the judgment that it is his will itself that is overcoming the resistance. In this fashion the willer adds the pleasurable feelings of executing . . . to his pleasurable feeling as Commander."[27]

This description, which takes the two-in-one of the Will, the resisting "I" and the triumphant "I," to be the source of the Will's power, owes its plausibility to the unexpected introduction of the pain-pleasure principle into the discussion: "to posit pleasure and displeasure as cardinal facts."[28] Just as the mere absence of pain can never cause pleasure, so the Will, if it did not have to overcome resistance, could never achieve power. Here, unwittingly following the ancient hedonist philosophies rather than the contemporary pleasure-pain calculus, Nietzsche relies in his description on the experience of *release* from pain—not on the mere absence of pain or the mere presence of pleasure. The intensity of the sensation of release is only matched by the intensity of the sensation of pain and is always greater than any pleasure unrelated to pain. The pleasure of drinking the most exquisite wine cannot be compared in intensity with the pleasure felt by a desperately thirsty man who obtains his first drink of water. In this sense there is a clear distinction between joy, independent of and unrelated to needs and desires, and pleasure, the sensuous lust of a creature whose body is alive to the extent that it is in need of something it does not have.

Joy, it seems, can only be experienced if one is wholly free of pain and desire; that is, it stands outside the pain-pleasure calculus, which Nietzsche despised because of its inbred utilitarianism. Joy—what Nietzsche called the Dionysian principle —comes from *abundance,* and it is true that all joy is a kind of luxury; it overcomes us, and we can indulge in it only after the needs of life have been satisfied. But this is not to deny the sensuous element in joy as well; abundance is still *life's* abundance, and the Dionysian principle in its sensuous lust turns to destruction precisely because abundance can afford destruction. In this respect is not the Will in the closest possible affinity with the life-principle, which constantly produces and destroys? Hence Nietzsche defines the Dionysian as "temporary identification with the principle of life (including the voluptuousness of the martyr)," as "Joy in the destruction . . . and at the sight of its progressive ruin . . . Joy in what is coming and lies in the future, which triumphs over existing things, however good."[29]

The Nietzschean shift from the I-will to the anticipated I-can, which negates the Paulinian I-will-and-I-can*not* and thereby all Christian ethics, is based on an unqualified Yes to Life, that is, on an elevation of Life as experienced outside all mental activities to the rank of supreme value by which everything else is to be evaluated. This is possible and plausible because there is indeed an I-can inherent in every I-will, as we saw in our discussion of Duns Scotus: *"Voluntas est potentia quia ipsa alquid potest"* ("The Will is a power because it *can* achieve something").[30] The Nietzschean Will, however, is not limited by its own inherent I-can; for instance, it can will eternity, and Nietzsche looks forward to a future that will produce the "superman," that is, a new human species strong enough to live in the thought of an "eternal recurrence." "We produced the weightiest thought—*now let us produce the being* to whom it will be easy and blessed! . . . To celebrate the future, not the past. To sing [*dichten*] the myth of the future."[31]

Life as the highest value cannot, of course, be demonstrated; it is a mere hypothesis, the assumption made by common sense that the will is free because without that assumption—as has been said over and over—no precept of a moral, religious, or juridical nature could possibly make sense. It is contradicted by the "scientific hypothesis" according to which—as Kant, notably, pointed out—every act, the moment it enters the world, falls into a network of causes, and thus appears in a sequence of occurrences explicable only in the context of causality. For Nietzsche, it is decisive that the common-sense hypothesis constitutes a "dominant sentiment from which we cannot liberate ourselves even if the scientific hypothesis were demonstrated."[32] But the identification of willing with living, the notion that our urge to live and our will to will are ultimately the same, has other and perhaps more serious consequences for Nietzsche's concept of power.

This may become clear when we turn to two leading metaphors in *The Gay Science,* one having to do with life and the other introducing the theme of "Eternal Recurrence"—the "basic idea of Zarathustra," as he called it in *Ecce Homo,* and the basic idea also of the posthumous aphorisms collected under the misleading, non-Nietzschean title *The Will to Power.* The first appears under the title "Will and Wave" (*Wille und Welle*):

How greedily this wave approaches, as if it were after something! How it crawls with terrifying haste into the inmost nooks of this labyrinthine cliff! . . . it seems that something of value, high value, must be hidden there.—And now it comes back, a little more slowly but still quite white with excitement; is it disappointed? Has it found what it looked for? Does it pretend to be disappointed?—But already another wave is approaching, still more greedily and savagely than the first, and its soul, too, seems to be full of secrets and the lust to dig up treasures. *Thus live waves— thus live we who will.* . . . Carry on as you like, roaring with overweening pleasure and malice—or dive again . . . and throw your infinite white mane of foam and spray over them: Everything suits me, for everything suits you so well, and *I am so well disposed toward you* for everything. . . . For . . . I know you and your secret, I know your kind! You and I—are we not of one kind?—You and I—do we not have one secret? [Italics added.][33]

Here at first it seems as though we were dealing with a perfect metaphor, a "perfect resemblance of two relations between totally dissimilar things."[34] The relation of the waves to the sea from which they erupt without intent or aim, creating a tremendous purposeless excitement, resembles and therefore illuminates the turmoil the Will excites in the household of the soul—always seemingly in quest of something till it quiets down, yet never extinguished, always ready for a new assault. The Will enjoys willing as the sea enjoys waves, for "rather than not will, man even wills *nothingness*."[35] Upon closer examination, however, it appears that something quite decisive has happened here to what was originally a typically Homeric metaphor. Those metaphors, we saw, were always irreversible: Looking upon the storms of the sea, you were reminded of your inward emotions; but those emotions did not tell you anything about the sea. In the Nietzschean metaphor, the two dissimilar things the metaphor is bringing together not only resemble each other, for Nietzsche they are identical; and the "secret" of which he is so proud is precisely his knowledge of this identity. Will and Wave are the same, and one is even tempted to assume that the experiences of the willing ego had made Nietzsche discover the turmoil of the sea.

In other words, the appearances of the world have become a mere *symbol* for inward experiences, with the consequence that the metaphor, originally designed to bridge the rift between the thinking or willing ego and the world of appearances, collapses. The collapse has come about not because of a superior weight given to the "objects" that confront human life but, rather, because of a partisanship for man's soul apparatus, whose experiences are understood to have absolute primacy. There are many passages in Nietzsche that point to this fundamental anthropomorphism. To cite only one example: "All the presuppositions of mechanistic theory [in Nietzsche identical with the "scientific hypothesis"]—matter, atom, gravity, pressure and stress—are not 'facts-in-themselves' but interpretations with the aid of psychical fictions."[36] Modern science has come to strangely similar suspicions in its speculative reflections on its own results: today's "astrophysicists . . . must reckon with . . . the possibility that their outer world is only our inner world turned inside out" (Lewis Mumford).

We now turn to our second story, which is actually not a metaphor or a symbol but a *parable,* the story of a thought-experiment that Nietzsche entitled *"Das grösste Schwergewicht,"* the thought that would weigh most heavily on you.

What, if some day or night a demon were to steal after you into your loneliest loneliness and say to you: "This life as you now live it, you will have to live once more and innumerable times more; and there will be nothing new in it, but every pain and every joy and every thought and sigh and everything unutterably small or great in your life will have to return to you, all in the same succession and sequence—even this spider and this moonlight between the trees, and even this moment and I myself. The eternal hourglass of existence is turned upside down again and again, and you with it, speck of dust!"

Would you not throw yourself down and gnash your teeth and curse the demon who spoke thus? Or have you once experienced a tremendous moment when you would have answered him: "You are a god and never have I heard anything more divine." If this thought gained possession of you, it would change you as you are or perhaps crush you. The question in each and every thing, "Do you desire this once more and innumerable times more?" would lie upon your actions as the greatest weight. Or *how well disposed would you have to become to yourself and to life to crave nothing more fervently* than this ultimate eternal confirmation and seal? [Italics added.][37]

No later version of the eternal-recurrence notion displays so unequivocally its main characteristic, namely, that it is not a theory, not a doctrine, not even a hypothesis, but a mere thought-experiment. As such, since it implies an experimental return to the ancient cyclical time concept, it seems to be in flagrant contradiction with any possible notion of the Will, whose projects always assume rectilinear time and a future that is unknown and therefore open to change. In the context of Nietzsche's own statements on the Will, and the shift he postulated from the I-will to an anticipated I-can, the only affinity between the two stories would seem to lie in the "tremendous moment" of overflowing "benevolence"—the being "well disposed to" Life—that obviously gave birth in each case to the thought.

If we see it in terms of his notion of the Will, this would be the moment when the I-can feeling is at its peak and spreads a general "feeling of strength" (*Kraftgefühl*). That emotion, as Nietzsche observes, often arises in us "even before the deed, occasioned by the idea of what is to be done (as at the sight of an enemy or an obstacle to which we feel ourselves equal)." To the operating will this emotion is of little consequence; it is "always an accompanying feeling," to which we wrongly ascribe the "force of action," the quality of a causative agent. "Our belief in causality is belief in force and effect; a transference from our experience [in which] we identify force and the feeling of force."[38] Hume's famous discovery that the relation between cause and effect rests on belief engendered by custom and association, and not on knowledge, was made afresh, and in many variations, by Nietzsche, who was unaware of having had a predecessor.

His own examination is more searching and more critical because, in the place of Hume's utility calculus and his "moral sentiment," he puts the experience of an I-will which is followed by an effect, that is, he uses the fact that man is conscious of himself as a causative agent even before he has done anything. But Nietzsche does not believe that this renders the Will less irrelevant; for Nietzsche as well as for Hume, free will is an illusion inherent in human nature, an illusion which philosophy, a critical examination of our faculties, will cure us of. Except that for Nietzsche the moral consequences of the cure are decidedly more serious.

If we can no longer ascribe "the value of an action . . . to the *intention*, the purpose for the sake of which one has acted or lived . . . [if] the absence of intention and purpose in events comes more and more to the foreground of consciousness," the conclusion seems inevitable that "Nothing has any meaning," for "this melancholy sentence means 'All meaning lies in intention, and if intention is altogether lacking, then meaning is altogether lacking too.' " Hence: "Why could 'a purpose' not be an epiphenomenon in the series of changes of effective forces that bring forth purposive action—a pale image in our consciousness . . . a symptom of occurrences, *not* their cause?—But with this we have criticized the *will itself:* is it not an illusion to take for a cause that which rises to consciousness as an act of will?" (Italics added.)[39]

The fact that this passage is contemporaneous with the passages about "Eternal Recurrence" justifies us in asking whether and how these two thoughts can be, if not reconciled, at any rate conceived in such a way that they will not clash head on with each other. Let us first comment very briefly on the few important non-speculative but, rather, descriptive statements made by Nietzsche on the Will.

There is, first—what seems obvious but had never been pointed out before—that "the Will cannot will backward"; it cannot stop the wheel of time. This is Nietzsche's version of the I-will-and-I-can*not*, for it is precisely this willing-backward that the Will wills and intends. From that impotence Nietzsche derives all human evil—resentment, the thirst for vengeance (we punish because we cannot undo what has been done), the thirst for the power to dominate others. To this "genealogy of morals," we could add that the Will's impotence persuades men to prefer looking backward, remembering and thinking, because, to the backward glance, everything that is *appears* to be necessary. The repudiation of willing liberates man from a responsibility that would be unbearable if nothing that was done could be undone. In any case, it was probably the Will's clash with the past that made Nietzsche experiment with Eternal Recurrence.

Second, the concept "will-to-power" is redundant: the Will generates power by willing, hence the will whose objective is humility is no less powerful than the will to rule over others. The willing act itself is already an act of potency, an indication of strength (the "feeling of strength," *Kraftgefühl*) that goes beyond what is required to meet the needs and demands of everyday life. If there is a simple contradiction in Nietzsche's thought-experiments, it is the contradiction between the Will's factual impotence—it wills but cannot will backward—and this feeling of strength.

Third, the Will—whether it wills backward and senses its impotence or wills forward and senses its strength—transcends the sheer givenness of the world. This transcendence is gratuitous and corresponds to the overwhelming superabundance of Life. Hence the Will's authentic goal is abundance: "By the words 'freedom of the Will' we signify this feeling of a surplus of strength," and the feeling is more than a mere illusion of consciousness because it does correspond with the superabundance of life itself. Hence one could understand all of Life as a Will-to-power. "Only where there is life is there also will: not will to life but . . . will to power."[40] For one could very well explain "nourishment" as the "consequence of insatiable appropriation, of the will to power, [and] 'procreation' [as] the crumbling that supervenes when the ruling cells are incapable of organizing that which has been appropriated."[41]

This transcending, which is inherent in willing, Nietzsche calls "Overcoming." It is possible because of abundance: the activity itself is seen as creativity, and the "virtue" that corresponds to this whole complex of ideas is Generosity—the overcoming of the thirst for vengeance. It is the extravagance and "recklessness [*Übermut*] of an overflowing, spendthrift will" that opens up a future beyond all past and present. *Surplus*, according to Nietzsche as well as to Marx (the sheer fact of a surplus of labor force left over after the requirements for the preservation of individual life and of species survival have been met), constitutes the *conditio-per-quam* of all culture. The so-called superman is man insofar as he is able to transcend, "overcome," himself. But this overcoming, we should not forget, is a merely mental exercise: to "recreate all 'it was' into a 'thus I willed it'—that alone should I call redemption."[42] For "Man seeks . . . a world that is not self-contradictory, not deceptive, does not change, a *true* world. . . ." Man, as he is now when he is honest, is a nihilist, namely, "a man who judges of the world as it is that it ought *not* to be, and of the world as it ought to be that it does not exist. . . . [To overcome nihilism one needs] the strength to reverse values and to deify . . . the apparent world as the only world, and to call them good."[43]

Clearly, what is needful is not to change the world or men but to change their way of "evaluating" it, their way, in other words, of thinking and reflecting about it. In Nietzsche's words, what must be overcome are the philosophers, those whose "life is an experiment of cognition";[44] they must be taught how to cope. Had Nietzsche developed these thoughts into a systematic philosophy, he would have fashioned a kind of greatly enriched Epictetian doctrine, teaching once more the "art of living one's own life," whose psychologically power-full trick consists in *willing* that to happen which happens any-how.[45]

But the point is that Nietzsche, who knew and estimated Epictetus very highly, did not stop with the discovery of the Will's mental omnipotence. He embarked on a construction of the given world that would make sense, be a fitting abode for a creature whose "strength of will [is great enough] to do without meaning in things . . . [who] can endure to live in a meaningless world."[46] "Eternal Recurrence" is the term for this final redeeming thought inasmuch as it proclaims the *"Innocence* of all Becoming" (*die Unschuld des Werdens*) and with that its inherent aimlessness and purposelessness, its freedom from guilt and responsibility.

"Innocence of Becoming" and "Eternal Recurrence" are not drawn from a mental faculty; they are rooted in the indisput-able *fact* that we indeed are "thrown" into the world (Heideg-ger), that no one has asked us if we wished to be here or wished to be as we are. For all we know or can ever know, "no one is responsible for man's being there at all, for his being such-and-such, or for his being in these circumstances or in this environment." Hence, the basic insight into the essence of Being is "that *there are no moral facts* at all," an insight Nietz-sche, as he said, "was the first to formulate." Its consequences are very great, not only because Christianity and its concept of a " 'moral world-order' infects the innocence of becoming by means of 'punishment' and 'guilt' [and therefore can be seen as] a metaphysics of the hangman," but because, with the elimination of intent and purpose, of somebody who can "be held responsible," causality itself is eliminated; nothing can be "traced back" to a cause once the *"causa prima"* is eliminated.[47]

With the elimination of cause and effect, there is no longer any sense in the rectilinear structure of Time whose past is always understood as the cause of the present, whose present is the tense of intention and preparation of our projects for the future, and whose future is the outcome of both. Besides, that time construct crumbles under the weight of the no less factual insight that "Everything passes," that the future brings only what *will have been,* and therefore that everything that is "deserves to pass away."[48] Just as every I-will, in its identification with the commanding part of the two-in-one, triumphantly anticipates an I-can, so expectation, the mood with which the Will affects the soul, contains within itself the melancholy of an and-this-too-*will-have-been,* the foreseeing of the future's past, which reasserts the Past as the dominant tense of Time. The only redemption from this all-devouring Past is the thought that everything that passes returns, that is, a cyclical time construct that makes Being swing within itself.

And is not Life itself construed so, does not one day follow upon the next, season succeed season by repeating itself in eternal sameness? Is not this world view much "truer" to reality as we know it than the world view of the philosophers? "If the motion of the world aimed at a final state, that state would have been reached. The sole fundamental fact, however, is that it does not aim at a final state; and every philosophy and scientific hypothesis . . . which necessitates such a final state is *refuted* by this fundamental fact. I seek a conception of the world that takes this fact into account. Becoming must be explained without recourse to final intentions; Becoming must appear justified at every moment (or incapable of being evaluated; which amounts to the same thing); the present must absolutely not be justified by reference to a future, nor the past by reference to the present. . . ." Nietzsche then summarizes: "1. Becoming does not aim at a *final state,* does not flow into 'being.' 2. Becoming is not a merely *apparent state;* perhaps the world of beings is mere appearance. 3. Becoming is of [equal value at] every moment . . . in other words, it has no value at all, for anything against which to measure it . . . is lacking. *The total value of the world cannot be evaluated.*"[49]

In the turmoil of aphorisms, remarks, and thought-experiments that constitute the posthumous collection entitled *The Will to Power* the importance of this last passage, which I have quoted at some length, is difficult to spot. Judging by internal evidence, I am inclined to think of it as Nietzsche's last word on the subject; and this last word clearly spells a repudiation of the Will and the willing ego, whose internal experiences have misled thinking men into assuming that there are such things as cause and effect, intention and goal, in reality. The superman is one who has overcome these fallacies, whose insights are strong enough either to resist the promptings of the Will or to turn his own will around, redeem it from all oscillations, quiet it to that stillness where "looking away" is "the only negation,"[50] because nothing is left but the "wish to be a Yes-sayer," to bless everything there is for being, "to bless and say Amen."[51]

15 *Heidegger's Will-not-to-will*

Neither the word "willing" nor the word "thinking" occurs in Heidegger's early work before the so-called reversal (*Kehre*) or "turn-about" that took place in the mid-thirties; and Nietzsche's name is nowhere mentioned in *Being and Time.*[52] Hence Heidegger's position on the faculty of the Will, culminating in his passionate insistence on willing "*not* to will"—which of course has nothing to do with the Will's oscillation between *velle* and *nolle*, willing and nilling—arises directly from his extremely careful investigation of Nietzsche's work, to which, after 1940, he returns time and again. Still, the two volumes of his *Nietzsche*, which were published in 1961, are in certain respects the most telling; they contain lecture courses from the years 1936 to 1940, that is, the very years when the "reversal" actually occurred and therefore had not yet been subjected to Heidegger's own interpretations. If in reading these two volumes one ignores Heidegger's later re-interpretation (which came out before the *Nietzsche*), one is tempted to

date the "reversal" as a concrete autobiographical event precisely between volume I and volume II; for, to put it bluntly,
the first volume explicates Nietzsche by going along with him,
while the second is written in a subdued but unmistakable
polemical tone. This important change of mood has been observed, as far as I know, only by J. L. Mehta, in his excellent
book on *The Philosophy of Martin Heidegger*,[53] and less decisively by Walter Schulz. The relevance of this dating seems
evident: what the reversal originally turns against is primarily
the will-to-power. In Heidegger's understanding, the will to
rule and to dominate is a kind of original sin, of which he
found himself guilty when he tried to come to terms with his
brief past in the Nazi movement.

When he later announced publicly—for the first time in the
Letter on Humanism (1949)[54]—that there had been a "reversal," for years in fact, in a larger sense, he had been re-
casting his views on the whole of history from the Greeks to
the present and focusing primarily not on the Will but on the
relation between Being and Man. Originally during those
years, the "reversal" had been a turning against the self-assertion of man (as proclaimed in the famous speech delivered
when he became rector of Freiburg University in 1933[55]),
symbolically incarnated in Prometheus, "the first philosopher,"
a figure nowhere else mentioned in his work. Now it turned
against the alleged subjectivism of *Being and Time* and the
book's primary concern with man's existence, his mode of being.

To put the matter in a rough and oversimplified way: while
Heidegger had always been concerned with "the question of
the meaning of Being," his first, "provisional," goal had been to
analyze the being of man as the only entity that can ask the
question because it touches his own being; hence, when man
raises the question What is Being?, he is thrown back upon
himself. But when, thrown back upon himself, he raises the
question Who is Man?, it is Being, on the contrary, that moves
into the foreground; it is Being, as now emerges, that bids
man to think. ("Heidegger was forced to move away from the
original approach of *Being and Time;* instead of seeking to
approach Being through the openness and transcendence in-

herent in man, he now tries to define man in terms of Being."⁵⁶) And the first demand Being makes of man is to think out the "ontological difference," that is, the difference between the sheer isness of beings and the Being of this isness itself, the Being of Being. As Heidegger himself states it in the *Letter on Humanism:* "To put it simply, thinking is thinking of Being, where the 'of' has a double meaning. Thinking is of Being, insofar as, being brought to pass by Being, it belongs to Being. At the same time it is thinking of Being insofar as, belonging to Being, it listens to Being."⁵⁷ Man's listening transforms the silent claim of Being into speech, and "language is the language of Being as the clouds are the clouds of the sky."⁵⁸

The "reversal" in this sense has two important consequences that have hardly anything to do with the repudiation of the Will. First, Thinking is no longer "subjective." To be sure, without being thought by man, Being would never become manifest; it depends upon man, who offers it an abode: "language is the abode of Being." But what man thinks does not arise from his own spontaneity or creativity; it is the obedient response to the command of Being. Second, the entities in which the world of appearances is given to man distract man from Being, which hides behind them—very much as the trees hide the forest that nevertheless, seen from outside, is constituted by them.

In other words, "Oblivion of Being" (*Seinsvergessenheit*) belongs to the very nature of the relation between Man and Being. Heidegger now is no longer content to eliminate the willing ego in favor of the thinking ego—maintaining, for instance, as he still does in the *Nietzsche,* that the Will's insistence on the future forces man into *oblivion* of the past, that it robs thinking of its foremost activity, which is *an-denken,* remembrance: "The Will has never owned the beginning, has left and abandoned it essentially through forgetting."⁵⁹ Now he desubjectivizes thinking itself, robs it of its Subject, man as a thinking being, and transforms it into a function of Being, in which all "efficacy rests . . . flowing from there towards the essent [*das Seiende*]," thereby determining the actual course of the world. "Thinking, in turn, lets itself be claimed by Being [that is the actual meaning of what happens through the essents], in order to give utterance to the truth of Being."[60] This re-interpretation of the "reversal," rather than the reversal itself, determines the entire development of Heidegger's late philosophy. Contained in a nutshell in the *Brief über den Humanismus,* which interprets *Being and Time* as a necessary anticipation of and preparation for the "reversal," it centers on the notion that to think, namely, "to say the unspoken word of Being," is the only authentic "doing" (*Tun*) of man; in it, the "History of Being" (*Seinsgeschichte*), transcending all mere human acts and superior to them, actually comes to pass. This thinking reminisces insofar as it hears the voice of Being in the utterances of the great philosophers of the past; but the past comes to it from the opposite direction, so that the "descent" (*Abstieg*) into the past coincides with the patient, thoughtful expectation of the arrival of the future, the "*avenant.*"[61]

We start with the original reversal. Even in the first *Nietzsche* volume, where Heidegger carefully follows Nietzsche's descriptive characterizations of the Will, he uses what later appears as the "ontological difference": the distinction between the Being of Being and the isness (*Seiendheit*) of entities. According to this interpretation, the will-to-power signifies the isness, the chief mode in which everything that is actually *is.* In this aspect, the Will is understood as a mere function of the life process—"world comes into being through the carrying out of the life process"[62]—whereas "Eternal Recurrence" is seen as Nietzsche's term for the Being of Being, through which time's transient nature is eliminated and Becoming, the medium of the will-to-power's purposiveness, receives the seal of Being. "Eternal Recurrence" is the most affirmative thought because it is the negation of the negation. In that perspective, the will-to-power is no more than a biological urge that keeps the wheel rolling and is transcended by a Will that goes beyond the mere life instinct in saying "Yes" to Life. In Nietzsche's view, as we saw, "Becoming has no goal; it does not end in 'Being.' . . . Becoming is of equal value at every moment:

. . . in other words, it has no value, for there is nothing by which value could be measured and in respect to which the word 'value' would make sense."[63]

As Heidegger sees it, the real contradiction in Nietzsche is not due to the seeming opposition between the will-to-power, which, being goal-directed, presupposes a rectilinear time concept, and Eternal Recurrence, with its cyclical time concept. It lies, rather, in Nietzsche's "transvaluation of values," which, according to Nietzsche himself, could make sense only in the framework of the will-to-power but which he nevertheless saw as the ultimate consequence of the "Eternal Recurrence" thought. In other words, in the last analysis, it was the will-to-power, "in itself value-positing," that determined Nietzsche's philosophy of the Will. The will-to-power finally "evaluates" an eternally recurring Becoming as the sole way out of the meaninglessness of life and world, and this transposition is not only a return to "the subjectivity of which the distinctive mark is evaluative thinking,"[64] but also suffers from the same lack of radicalism characteristic of Nietzsche's inverted Platonism, which, by putting things upside down or downside up, still keeps intact the categorical framework in which such reversals can operate.

Heidegger's strictly phenomenological analyses of the Will in volume I of his *Nietzsche* closely follow his early analyses of the self in *Being and Time*, except that the Will takes the place ascribed to Care in the earlier work. We read: "Self-observation and self-examination never bring the self to light or show how we are ourselves. But by willing, and also by nilling, we do just that; we appear in a light that itself is lighted by the act of willing. To will always means: to bring oneself to one's self. . . . Willing, we encounter ourselves as who we are authentically. . . ."[65] Hence, "to will is essentially to will one's own self, but not a merely given self that is as it is, but the self that wants to become what it is. . . . The will to get away from one's self is actually an act of nilling."[66] We shall see later that this return to the concept of the self of *Being and Time* is not without importance for the "reversal," or "change of mood," manifest in the second volume.

In the second volume, the emphasis shifts decisively from

the thought of "Eternal Recurrence" to an interpretation of the Will as almost exclusively will-to-power, in the specific sense of a will to rule and dominate rather than as an expression of the life instinct. The notion of volume I, that every act of willing, by virtue of being a command, generates a counter-will (*Widerwillen*)—that is, the notion of a necessary obstacle in every act of willing, which first must overcome a non-willing —is now generalized into an inherent characteristic of every act of making. For a carpenter, for instance, the wood constitutes the obstacle "against which" he works when he forces it to become a table.[67] This again is generalized: every object by virtue of being an "object"—and not merely a thing, independent of human evaluation, calculation, and making—is there to be overcome by a subject. The will-to-power is the culmination of the modern age's subjectivization; all of man's faculties stand under the Will's command. "The Will is to will to be master. . . . [It is] fundamentally and exclusively: Command. . . . In the command the one who issues the command obeys . . . himself. Thus the commanding [self] is its own superior."[68]

Here the concept of the Will indeed loses the biological characteristics that play such an important role in Nietzsche's understanding of the Will as a mere symptom of the life instinct. It is in the nature of power—and no longer in the nature of life's superabundance and surplus—to spread and expand: "Power exists only insofar as its power increases and insofar as [the will-to-power] commands this increase." The Will urges itself on by issuing orders; not life but "the will-to-power is the essence of power. This essence, and never a [limited] amount of power, remains the goal of the Will, inasmuch as Will can exist only in relation to power. This is why the Will necessarily needs this goal. It is also why a terror of the void essentially permeates all willing. . . . Seen from the perspective of the Will . . . [nothingness] is the extinction of the Will in not-willing. . . . Hence . . . [quoting Nietzsche] our will 'would rather will nothingness than not will.' . . . 'To will nothingness' here means *to will . . . the negation, the destruction, the laying waste*" [italics added].[69]

Heidegger's last word on this faculty concerns the Will's

destructiveness, just as Nietzsche's last word concerned its "creativity" and superabundance. This destructiveness manifests itself in the Will's obsession with the future, which forces men into *oblivion*. In order to will the future in the sense of being the future's master, men must forget and finally destroy the past. From Nietzsche's discovery that the Will cannot "will backwards," there follow not only frustration and resentment, but also the positive, active will to annihilate what was. And since everything that is real has "become," that is, incorporates a past, this destructiveness ultimately relates to everything that is.

Heidegger sums it up in *What Is Called Thinking?*: "Faced with what 'was,' willing no longer has anything to say. . . . The 'it was' resists the Will's willing . . . the 'it was' is revolting and contrary to the Will. . . . But by means of this revulsion, the contrary takes root within willing itself. Willing . . . suffers from it—that is, the Will suffers from itself . . . from . . . the by-gone, the past. But what is past stems from the passing. . . . Thus the Will itself wills passing. . . . The Will's revulsion against every 'it was' appears as *the will to make everything pass away*, hence to will that everything deserve passing away. The revulsion arising in the Will is then the will against everything that passes—*everything*, that is, that comes to be out of a coming-to-be, and that *endures"* (italics added).[70]

In this radical understanding of Nietzsche, the Will is essentially destructive, and it is against that destructiveness that Heidegger's original reversal pits itself. Following this interpretation, technology's very nature is the will to will, namely, to subject the whole world to its domination and rulership, whose natural end can only be total destruction. The alternative to such rulership is "letting be," and letting-be as an activity is thinking that obeys the call of Being. The mood pervading the letting-be of thought is the opposite of the mood of purposiveness in willing; later, in his re-interpretation of the "reversal," Heidegger calls it *"Gelassenheit,"* a calmness that corresponds to letting-be and that "prepares us" for "a thinking that is not a willing."[71] This thinking is "beyond the distinction between activity and passivity" because it

is beyond the "domain of the Will," that is, beyond the category of causality, which Heidegger, in agreement with Nietzsche, derives from the willing ego's experience of causing effects, hence from an illusion produced by consciousness.
The insight that thinking and willing are not just two different faculties of the enigmatic being called "man," but are opposites, came to both Nietzsche and Heidegger. It is their version of the deadly conflict that occurs when the two-in-one of consciousness, actualized in the silent dialogue between me and myself, changes its original harmony and friendship into an ongoing conflict between will and counter-will, between command and resistance. But we have found testimony to this conflict throughout the history of the faculty.

The difference between Heidegger's position and those of his predecessors lies in this: the mind of man, claimed by Being in order to transpose into language the truth of Being, is subject to a *History* of Being (*Seinsgeschichte*), and this History determines whether men respond to Being in terms of willing or in terms of thinking. It is the *History* of Being, at work behind the backs of acting men, that, like Hegel's World Spirit, determines human destinies and reveals itself to the thinking ego if the latter can overcome willing and actualize the letting-be.

At first glance, this may look like another, perhaps a bit more sophisticated, version of Hegel's ruse of reason, Kant's ruse of nature, Adam Smith's invisible hand, or divine Providence, all forces invisibly guiding the ups and downs of human affairs to a predetermined goal: freedom in Hegel, eternal peace in Kant, harmony between the contradictory interests of a market economy in Adam Smith, ultimate salvation in Christian theology. The notion itself—namely, that the actions of men are inexplicable by themselves and can be *understood* only as the work of some hidden purpose or some hidden actor—is much older. Plato could already "imagine that each of us living creatures is a puppet made by gods, possibly as a plaything, possibly with some more serious purpose," and imagine that what we take for causes, the pursuit of pleasure and the avoidance of pain, are but "the strings by which we are worked."[72]

We hardly need a demonstration of historical influences to comprehend the stubborn resiliency of the idea, from Plato's airy fiction to Hegel's mental construct—which was the result of an unprecedented re-thinking of world history that deliberately eliminated from the factual record everything "merely" factual as accidental and non-consequential. The simple truth is that no man can act alone, even though his motives for action may be certain designs, desires, passions, and goals of his own. Nor can we ever achieve anything wholly according to plan (even when, as *archōn,* we successfully lead and initiate and hope that our helpers and followers will execute what we begin), and this combines with our consciousness of being *able* to cause an effect to give birth to the notion that the actual outcome must be due to some alien, supernatural force which, undisturbed by human plurality, has provided for the end result. The fallacy is similar to the fallacy Nietzsche detected in the notion of a necessary "progress" of Mankind. To repeat: " 'Mankind' does not advance, it does not even exist. . . . [But since] time marches forward, we'd like to believe that everything that is in it also marches forward—that the development is one that moves forward."[73]

Certainly Heidegger's *Seinsgeschichte* cannot fail to remind us of Hegel's World Spirit. The difference, however, is decisive. When Hegel saw "the World Spirit on horseback" in Napoleon at Jena, he knew that Napoleon himself was unconscious of being the incarnation of the Spirit, knew that he acted out of the usual human mixture of short-term goals, desires, and passions; for Heidegger, however, it is Being itself that, *forever changing,* manifests itself in the thinking of the actor so that *acting and thinking* coincide. "If to act means to give a hand to the essence of Being, then thinking is actually acting. That is, preparing [building an abode] for the essence of Being in the midst of entities by which Being transposes itself and its essence into speech. Without speech, mere doing lacks the dimension in which it can become effective and follow directions. Speech, however, is never a simple expression of thinking, feeling, or willing. Speech is the original dimension in which the human being is able to respond to Being's claim and, responding, belong to it. Thinking is the actualization of that original correspondence."[74]

In terms of a mere reversal of viewpoints, one would be tempted to see in Heidegger's position the justification of Valéry's aphoristic reversal of Descartes: " *'L'homme pense, donc je suis'—dit l'univers"* ("Man thinks, therefore I am, says the universe").[75] The interpretation is indeed tempting since Heidegger would certainly agree with Valéry's "*Les événe-ments ne sont que l'écume des choses"* ("Events are but the foam of things"). He would not agree, however, with Valéry's assumption that what really is—the underlying reality whose surface is mere foam—is the stable reality of a substantial, ultimately unchanging Being. Nor, either before or after the "reversal," would he have agreed that "the new is by definition the perishable part of things" ("*Le nouveau est, par définition, la partie périssable des choses").*[76]

Ever since he re-interpreted the reversal, Heidegger has insisted on the continuity of his thought, in the sense that *Being and Time* was a necessary preparation that already contained in a provisional way the main direction of his later work. And indeed this is true to a large extent, although it is liable to de-radicalize the later reversal and the consequences obviously implicit in it for the future of philosophy. Let us begin with the most startling consequences, to be found in the later work itself, to wit, first, the notion that solitary thinking in itself constitutes the only relevant action in the factual record of history, and second, that thinking is the same as thanking (and not just for etymological reasons). Having done this, we shall try to follow the development of certain key terms in *Being and Time* and see what happens to them. The three key terms I propose are Care, Death, and Self.

Care—in *Being and Time*, the fundamental mode of man's existential concern with his own being—does not simply disappear in favor of the Will, with which it obviously shares a certain number of characteristics; it changes its function radically. It all but loses its relatedness to itself, its concern with man's own being, and, along with that, the mood of "anxiety" caused when the world into which man is "thrown" reveals itself as "nothingness" for a being that knows its own mortality—*"das nackte Dass im Nichts der Welt,"* "the naked That in the Nothingness of the world."[77]

The emphasis shifts from *Sorge* as worry or concern with itself to *Sorge* as *taking* care, and this not of itself but of Being. Man who was the "caretaker" (*Platzhalter*) of Nothing and therefore open to the disclosure of Being now becomes the "guardian" (*Hüter*) or "shepherd" (*Hirte*) of Being, and his speech offers Being its abode.

Death, on the other hand, which originally was actual for man only as the utmost possibility—"if it were actualized [for instance, in suicide], man obviously would lose the possibility he has of existing in the face of death"[78]—now becomes the "shrine" that "collects," "protects," and "salvages" the essence of mortals, who are mortals not because their life has an end but because to-be-dead still belongs to their innermost being.[79] (These strange-sounding descriptions refer to well-known experiences, testified to, for instance, by the old adage *de mortuis nil nisi bonum*. It is not the dignity of death as such that puts us in awe but, rather, the curious change from life to death that overtakes the personality of the dead. In remembrance—the way living mortals think of their dead—it is as though all non-essential qualities perished with the disappearance of the body in which they were incarnated. The dead are "enshrined" in remembrance like precious relics of themselves.)

Finally there is the concept of the *Self*, and it is this concept whose change in the "reversal" is the most unexpected and the most consequential. In *Being and Time,* the term "Self" is the "answer to the question Who [is man]?" as distinguished from the question of What he is; the Self is the term for man's existence as distinguished from whatever qualities he may possess. This existence, the "authentic being a Self," is derived polemically from the "Them." (*"Mit dem Ausdruck 'Selbst' antworten wir auf die Frage nach dem Wer des Daseins. . . . Das eigentliche Selbstsein bestimmt sich als eine existenzielle Modifikation des Man."*)[80] By modifying the "They" of everyday life into "being oneself," human existence produces a *"solus ipse,"* and Heidegger speaks in this context of an "existential solipsism," that is, of the actualization of the *principium individuationis*, an actualizing we have encountered in other philosophers as one of the essential functions of the Will. Heidegger had originally ascribed it to Care, his early term for man's organ for the future.[81]

To underline the similarity of Care (before the "reversal") and Will in a modern setting, we turn to Bergson, who—certainly not influenced by earlier thinkers but following the immediate evidence of consciousness—had posited, only a few decades before Heidegger, the co-existence of two selves, the one social (Heidegger's "They") and the other "fundamental" (Heidegger's "authentic"). The Will's function is "to recover this fundamental self" from "the requirements of social life in general and language in particular," namely the language ordinarily spoken in which every word already has a "social meaning."[82] It is a cliché-ridden language, needed for communication with others in an "external world quite distinct from [ourselves], which is the common property of all conscious beings." Life in common with others has created its own kind of speech that leads to the formation of "a second self . . . which obscures the first." The task of philosophy is to lead this social self back "to the real and concrete self . . . whose activity cannot be compared to that of any other force," because this force is sheer *spontaneity* of which "each of us has immediate knowledge" obtained only by the immediate observation of oneself by oneself.[83] And Bergson, quite in line with Nietzsche and also, as it were, in tune with Heidegger, sees the "proof" of this spontaneity in the fact of artistic creativity. The coming into existence of a work of art cannot be explained by antecedent causes as though what is now actual has been latent or potential before, whether in the form of external causes or inner motives: "When a musician composes a symphony, was his work possible before being real?"[84] Heidegger is quite in line with the general position when he writes in volume I of his *Nietzsche* (i.e., before the "reversal"): "To will always means: to bring oneself to one's self. . . . Willing, we encounter ourselves as who we are authentically. . . ."[85]

Yet this is as much of an affinity between Heidegger and his immediate predecessors as can be claimed. Nowhere in *Being and Time*—except for a peripheral remark about poetic speech "as possible disclosure of existence"[86]—is artistic creativity mentioned. In volume I of the *Nietzsche,* the tension and close relationship between poetry and philosophy, the poet and the philosopher, is twice noticed but not in either the Nietzschean or the Bergsonian sense of sheer creativity.[87] On the contrary, the Self in *Being and Time* becomes manifest in "the voice of conscience," which calls man back from his everyday entanglement in the *"man"* (German for "one" or "they") and what conscience, in its call, discloses as human "guilt," a word (*Schuld*) that in German means both being guilty of (responsible for) some deed and having debts in the sense of owing somebody something.[88]

The main point in Heidegger's "idea of guilt" is that human existence is guilty to the extent that it "factually exists"; it does not "need to become guilty of something through omissions or commissions; [it is only called upon] to actualize authentically the 'guiltiness' which it is anyhow."[89] (It apparently never occurred to Heidegger that by making all men who listen to the "call of conscience" equally guilty, he was actually proclaiming universal innocence: where everybody is guilty, nobody is.) This existential culpability—given by human existence—is established in two ways. Inspired by Goethe's "One who acts always becomes guilty," Heidegger shows that every action, by actualizing a single possibility, at one stroke kills all the others among which it had to choose. Every commitment entails a number of defaults. More important, however, the concept of "being thrown into the world" already implies that human existence *owes* its existence to something that it is not itself; by virtue of its very existence it is indebted: *Dasein*—human existence inasmuch as it *is*—"has been thrown; it is there, but *not* brought into the there by itself."[90]

Conscience demands that man accept that "indebtedness," and acceptance means that the Self brings itself to a kind of "acting" (*handeln*) which is polemically understood as the opposite of the "loud" and visible actions of public life—the mere froth on what truly is. This acting is silent, a "letting one's own self act in its indebtedness," and this entirely inner "action" in which man opens himself to the authentic actuality of being thrown,[91] can exist only in the activity of thinking. That is probably why Heidegger, throughout his whole work, "on purpose avoided"[92] dealing with action. What is most surprising in his interpretation of conscience is the vehement denunciation of "the ordinary interpretation of conscience" that has always understood it as a kind of soliloquy, the "soundless dialogue of me and myself." Such a dialogue, Heidegger maintains, can be explained only as an inauthentic attempt at self-justification against the claims of the "Them." This is all the more striking because Heidegger, in a different context—and, it is true, only marginally—speaks of "the voice of the friend that every *Dasein* [human existence] carries with it."[93]

No matter how strange and, in the last analysis, unaccounted for by phenomenological evidence Heidegger's analysis of conscience may prove to be, the tie with the sheer facts of human existence implicit in the concept of a primordial indebtedness certainly contains the first hint of his later identification of thinking and thanking. What the call of conscience actually achieves is the recovery of the individualized (*vereinzeltes*) self from involvement in the events that determine men's everyday activities as well as the course of recorded history—*l'écume des choses*. Summoned back, the self is now turned to a thinking that expresses gratitude that the "naked That" has been given at all. That the attitude of man, confronted with Being, should be *thanking* can be seen as a variant of Plato's *thaumazein*, the beginning principle of philosophy. We have dealt with that *admiring* wonder, and to find it in a modern context is neither striking nor surprising; we have only to think of Nietzsche's praise of the "Yes-sayers" or turn our attention from academic speculations to some of this century's great poets. They at least show how suggestive such affirmation can be as a solution for the apparent meaninglessness of an entirely secularized world. Here are two lines by the Russian Osip Mandelstam, written in 1918:

> We will remember in Lethe's cold waters
> That earth for us has been worth a thousand heavens.

These verses can easily be matched by a number of lines by
Rainer Maria Rilke in the *Duino Elegies*, written at about the
same time; I shall quote a few:

> *Erde du liebe, ich will. Oh glaub es bedürfte*
> *Nicht deiner Frühlinge mehr, mich dir zu gewinnen.*
> *Einer, ach ein einziger ist schon dem Blute zu viel.*
> *Namenlos bin ich zu dir entschlossen von weit her,*
> *Immer warst du im recht. . . .*

> Earth, you darling, I will. Oh, believe me, you need
> Your spring-times no longer to win me; a single one,
> Just one, is already more than my blood can endure.
> I've now been unspeakably yours for ages and ages.
> You were always right. . . .
>
> Ninth Elegy

And finally, as a reminder, I cite again what W. H. Auden
wrote some twenty years later:

> That singular command
> I do not understand,
> *Bless what there is for being,*
> Which has to be obeyed, for
> What else am I made for,
> Agreeing or disagreeing?

Perhaps these examples of non-academic testimony to the
dilemmas of the last stage of the modern age can explain the
great appeal of Heidegger's work to an elite of the intellectual
community despite the almost unanimous antagonism it has
aroused in the universities ever since the appearance of *Being
and Time.*

But what is true of the coincidence of thinking and thanking is hardly true of the merging of acting and thinking. With
Heidegger, this is not just the elimination of the subject-object
split in order to desubjectivize the Cartesian Ego, but actual
fusion of the changes in the "History of Being" (*Seinsgeschichte*) with the activity of thinking in the thinkers. "Being's
History" secretly inspires and guides what happens on the
surface, while the thinkers, hidden by and protected from the
"Them," respond and actualize Being. Here the personified
concept whose ghostlike existence brought about the last great

enlivenment of philosophy in German Idealism has become fully incarnated; there is a Somebody who *acts out* the hidden meaning of Being and thus provides the disastrous course of events with a counter-current of wholesomeness.

This Somebody, the thinker who has weaned himself from willing to "letting-be," is actually the "authentic Self" of *Being and Time*, who now listens to the call of Being instead of the call of Conscience. Unlike the Self, the thinker is not summoned by himself to his Self; still, to "hear the call authentically signifies once again bringing oneself into factually acting" (*"sich in das faktische Handeln bringen"*).[94] In this context the "reversal" means that the Self no longer acts in itself (what has been abandoned is the *In-sich-handeln-lassen des eigensten Selbst*[95]) but, obedient to Being, enacts by sheer thinking the counter-current of Being underlying the "foam" of beings—the mere appearances whose current is steered by the will-to-power.

The "They" reappear here, but their chief characteristic is no longer "idle talk" (*Gerede*); it is the destructiveness inherent in willing.

What has brought about this change is a decisive radicalization of both the age-old tension between thinking and willing (to be resolved by the "Will-not-to-will") and of the personified concept, which appeared in its most articulate form in Hegel's "World Spirit," that ghostly Nobody that bestows meaning on what factually, but in itself meaninglessly and contingently, *is*. With Heidegger, this Nobody, allegedly acting behind the backs of acting men, has now found a flesh-and-blood incarnation in the existence of the thinker, who acts while he does nothing, a person, to be sure, and even identifiable as "Thinker"—which, however, does not signify his return into the world of appearances. He remains the *"solus ipse"* in "existential solipsism," except that now the fate of the world, the History of Being, has come to depend on him.

Thus far we have been following Heidegger's own repeated demands to pay due attention to the continuous development of his thinking ever since *Being and Time*, despite the "reversal" that took place in the middle thirties. We have relied, too, on his own interpretations of the reversal during the later thirties and early forties—interpretations closely and coherently borne out by his numerous publications of the fifties and sixties. But there is another, perhaps even more radical, interruption in his life as well as his thought to which, as far as I know, no one, Heidegger included, has paid public attention.

This interruption coincided with the catastrophic defeat of Nazi Germany and his own serious difficulties with the academic community and the occupation authorities immediately thereafter. For a period of roughly five years he was so effectively silenced that among his published works there exist only two longer essays—the *Letter on Humanism,* written in 1946 and published in Germany and France in 1947, and "The Anaximander Fragment" ("*Der Spruch des Anaximander*"), also written in 1946 and published as the last essay of *Holzwege* in 1950.

Of these, the *Letter on Humanism* contains an eloquent summing-up and immense clarification of the interpretive turn he had given the original reversal, but "The Anaximander Fragment" is of a different character: it presents an altogether new and unexpected outlook on the whole posing of the problem of Being. The main theses of this essay, which I shall now try to outline, were never followed up or fully explicated in his later work. He does mention, in a note to its publication in the *Holzwege,* that the essay was taken from a "treatise" *(Abhandlung)* written in 1946, which unfortunately has never been published.

To me it seems obvious that this new outlook, so isolated from the rest of his thought, must have emerged from another change of "mood," no less important than the change that happened between the first and the second volumes of the work on Nietzsche—the turn from the "Will-to-Power" as Will-to-will to the new *Gelassenheit,* the serenity of "letting-be" and the paradoxical "Will-not-to-will." The changed mood reflected Germany's defeat, the "point zero" (as Ernst Jünger called it) that for a few years seemed to promise a new beginning. In Heidegger's version: "Do we stand in the very twilight of the most monstrous transformation our planet has ever undergone . . . ? [Or] do we gaze into the evening of a night which heralds another dawn? . . . *Are* we the latecomers . . . at

the same time precursors of the dawn of an altogether different age, which has already left our contemporary historiologi-
cal representations of history behind?"⁹⁶

It was the same mood that Jaspers expressed at a famous
symposium in Geneva in the same year: "We live as though
we stood knocking at gates that are still closed. . . . What
happens today will perhaps one day found and establish a
world."⁹⁷ This mood of hope disappeared quickly in the
rapidity of German economic and political recovery from
"point zero"; confronted with the reality of Adenauer's Germany, neither Heidegger nor Jaspers ever expounded systematically what must very soon have appeared to them as a
complete misreading of the new era.

Still, in Heidegger's case, we do have the Anaximander
essay with its haunting hints at another possibility of ontological speculation, hints that are half hidden in the highly technical philological considerations of the Greek text (which is
rather obscure and probably corrupt), and from them I shall
risk an exegesis of this fascinating variant of his philosophy. In
Heidegger's literal and provisional translation the short Greek
text reads: "But that from which things arise [*genesis*] also
gives rise to their passing away [*phthora*], according to what is
necessary; for things render justice [*dikēn didonai*] and pay
penalty [*tisin*] to one another for their injustice [*adikia*], according to the ordinance of time."⁹⁸ The subject, then, is the
coming-to-be and passing-away of everything that is. While
whatever is *is,* it "lingers" in the present "between a twofold
absence," its arrival and its departure. During the absences it
is hidden; it is unconcealed only for the short duration of its
appearance. Living in a world of appearances, all we know or
can know is a "movement which lets every emerging being
abandon concealment and go forward into unconcealment,"
lingering there for a while, till it "in its turn abandons unconcealment, departing and withdrawing into concealment."⁹⁹

Even this non-speculative, strictly phenomenological description is clearly at variance with Heidegger's usual teaching
of an ontological difference according to which *a-lētheia*, truth
understood as Un-hiddenness or Unconcealment, is always on
the side of Being; in the world of appearances, Being reveals

itself only in the thinking response of man in terms of language. In the words of the *Letter on Humanism,* "Language is the house of Being" (*"Die Sprache* [*ist*] *zumal das Haus des Seins und die Behausung des Menschenwesens"*).[100] In the exegesis of the Anaximander fragment, unconcealment is not truth; it belongs to the beings that arrive from and depart into a hidden Being. What can hardly have caused but certainly facilitated this reversal is the fact that the Greeks, especially the pre-Socratics, often thought of Being as *physis* (nature), whose original meaning is derived from *phyein* (to grow), that is, to come to light out of darkness. Anaximander, says Heidegger, thought of *genesis* and *phthora* in terms of *physis,* "as ways of luminous rising and declining."[101] And *physis,* according to a much quoted fragment of Heraclitus, "likes to hide."[102]

Although Heidegger does not mention the Heraclitus fragment in the Anaximander essay, its main theses read as though it had been inspired by Heraclitus rather than by Anaximander. Of central importance is the speculative content; there the relation in the ontological difference is reversed, and this is spelled out in the following sentences: "The unconcealment of beings, the brightness granted them [by Being], obscures the light of Being"; for *"as it reveals itself in beings, Being withdraws"* (*"Das Sein entzieht sich indem es sich in das Seiende entbirgt"*).[103] The sentence I have italicized is stressed in the text by being emphatically repeated. Its immediate plausibility in the German original rests entirely on the linguistically cognate relation of *verbergen* (hide, conceal) with *bergen* (shield and shelter) and *entbergen* (disclose). If we try to explicate the speculative content of that cognateness as construed by Heidegger, we may sum it up as follows: the coming and going, appearing and disappearing, of beings always begins with a disclosure that is an *ent-bergen,* the loss of the original shelter (*bergen*) that had been granted by Being; the being then "lingers for a while" in the "brightness" of disclosure, and ends by returning to the sheltering shield of Being in its concealment: "Presumably, Anaximander spoke of *genesis* and *phthora* [generation and decline] . . . [that is] *genesis estin* (which is the way I should like to read it) and *phthora ginetai,* 'coming-to-be *is,*' and 'passing-away comes to be.' "[104]

In other words, undoubtedly there is such a thing as becoming; everything we know has become, has emerged from some previous darkness into the light of day; and this becoming remains its law while it lasts: its lasting is at the same time its passing-away. Becoming, the law that rules beings, is now the opposite of Being; when, in passing-away, becoming ceases, it changes again into that Being from whose sheltering, concealing darkness it originally emerged. In this speculative context, the ontological difference consists of the difference between Being in the strong durative sense and becoming. It is through withdrawal that "Being holds to its truth" and shields it; it shields it against the "brightness" of beings that "obscures the light of Being" even though, originally, Being has granted this brightness. This leads to the seemingly paradoxical statement "As [Being] provides the unconcealment of beings, it [establishes] the concealment of Being."[105]

In the course of this speculation, the reversal of Heidegger's common approach to the "quest for Being" (*die Seinsfrage*) and "the oblivion of Being" (*Seinsvergessenheit*) becomes manifest. It is no longer genuine inauthenticity or any other particularity of human existence that causes man to "forget" Being in his abandonment to the "*man*" (German for the plurality of "Them"); nor does he do so because he is distracted by the sheer superabundance of mere entities. "Oblivion of Being belongs to the self-veiling essence of Being . . . the history of Being [and not the history of men in philosophy in general or metaphysics in particular] begins with the oblivion of Being, since Being—together with its essence, its distinction from beings—keeps to itself."[106] Through Being's withdrawal from the realm of beings, these entities, whose unconcealment has been caused by it, are set "adrift in errancy," and this *errancy* constitutes "the realm of error . . . the space in which history unfolds. . . . *Without errancy there would be no connection from destiny to destiny: there would be no history*" (italics added).[107]

To sum up: We are still confronted with the ontological difference, the categorical separation of Being and beings, but this separation has acquired, as it were, a kind of history with a beginning and an end. In the beginning, Being discloses itself in beings, and the disclosure starts two opposite movements: Being withdraws into itself, and beings are "set adrift" to constitute the "realm (in the sense of a prince's realm) of error." This realm of error is the sphere of common human history, where factual destinies are connected and form a coherent shape through "erring." In that scheme, there is no place for a "History of Being" (*Seinsgeschichte*) enacted behind the backs of acting men; Being, sheltered in its concealment, has no history, and "every epoch of world history is an epoch of errancy." However, the very fact that the time continuum in the historical realm is broken up into different eras indicates that the casting adrift of entities also occurs in epochs, and in Heidegger's scheme there seems to exist a privileged moment, the transitional moment from one epoch to the next, from destiny to destiny, when Being qua Truth breaks into the continuum of error, when the "epochal essence of Being lays claim to the ecstatic nature of *Da-sein*."[108] To this claim, thinking can respond, recognizing "the claim to destiny": that is, the spirit of a whole age may become "mindful of what is destined" instead of getting lost in the erring particularities of human day-to-day affairs.

Nowhere in this context does Heidegger mention a connection between thinking and thanking and he is quite aware of the possible pessimistic, "not to say nihilistic," conclusions to be drawn from an interpretation that would fit only too well with Burckhardt's and Nietzsche's understanding of the Greek experience at its deepest level.[109] Also, it may be worth noting that here he seems not at all interested in stressing the tension of the very close relation between philosophy and poetry. Instead he concludes the essay with something he has said nowhere else: "If the essence of man consists in thinking the truth of Being [N.B., now a Being that has withdrawn, that veils and hides itself], then thinking must poetize on the riddle of Being" ("*am Rätsel des Seins dichten*").[110]

I have mentioned in passing the radical change the concept of death underwent in Heidegger's late writings, where death appears as the ultimate savior of man's essence, the *Gebirg des Seins in dem Spiel der Welt*, the "shelter of Being in the play of the world."[111] And I have tried to explicate and, in a way, justify the strangeness of this by some well-known testimony to certain familiar experiences which, as far as I know, have never been conceptualized. In the Anaximander essay, the word "death" does not occur, but the concept is of course transparently present in the notion of life between two absences, before it arrives in birth and after it passes away in death. And here we do have a conceptual clarification of death as the shelter for the essence of human existence, whose temporal, transitory presence is understood as the lingering between two absences and a sojourn in the realm of errancy. For the source of this "erring"—and here of course we can see to what an extent this variant remains a mere variation of Heidegger's basic and enduring philosophical convictions—is the fact that a being that "lingers a while in presence" between two absences and has the ability to transcend its own presence can be said to be actually "present [only] insofar as it lets itself belong to the non-present."[112]

It has a chance of achieving that if it seizes on the epochal moment in the transition between epochs when historical destinies change and the truth underlying the next era of errancy becomes manifest to thought. The Will as destroyer appears here, too, though not by name; it is the "craving to persist," "to hang on," the inordinate appetite men have "to cling to themselves." In this way they do more than just err: "Lingering as persisting . . . is an insurrection on behalf of sheer endurance."[113] The insurrection is directed against "order" (*dikē*); it creates the "disorder" (*adikia*) permeating the "realm of errancy."

These statements take us back to familiar territory, as becomes evident when we read that the disorder is "tragic" and not a thing for which man can be made accountable. To be sure, there is no longer any "call of conscience" summoning man back to his authentic self, to the insight that, no matter what he has done or omitted to do, he was already *schuldig* ("guilty") since his existence was a debt he "owed" after having been thrown into the world. But, just as, in *Being and Time*, this "guilty" self could salvage itself by anticipating its death, so here the "erring" *Dasein*, while "lingering a while" in the present realm of errancy, can, through the thinking activity, join itself to what is absent. There is the difference, though, that here the absent (Being in its enduring withdrawal) has no history in the realm of errancy, and thinking and acting do not coincide. To act is to err, to go astray. We should consider, too, how the early definition of being-guilty as a primary trait of *Dasein,* independent of any specific act, has been replaced by "erring" as the decisive mark of all human history. (Both formulations, incidentally, for the German reader are curiously reminiscent of Goethe's *"Der Handelnde wird immer schuldig"* and *"Es irrt der Mensch solang er strebt."*[114])

To these distinct self-echoes we may then add the following sentences from the Anaximander essay: "Every thinker is dependent upon the address of Being. The extent of this dependence determines the freedom from irrelevant influences"[115] —by which Heidegger clearly means the factual day-to-day events brought about by erring men. When we put these correspondences together, it does seem as though we are dealing here with a mere variation of Heidegger's basic teaching.

However that may be, it is obvious that my present interpretation is tentative in the extreme; it cannot possibly be a substitute for the unpublished treatise of which the Anaximander essay was originally a part. In our present state of textual knowledge the whole thing remains very doubtful. But whether we see it as a variant or a variation, Heidegger's denunciation of the instinct of self-preservation (common to all living things) as a willful rebellion against the "order" of Creation as such is so rare in the history of ideas that I should like to quote here the only similar utterance of which I am aware, three little-known lines of Goethe in a poem written about 1821 under the title *"Eins und Alles":*

> *Das Ewige regt sich fort in allen:*
> *Denn alles muss in Nichts zerfallen,*
> *Wenn es im Sein beharren will.*

> The Eternal works and stirs in all;
> For all must into Nothing fall,
> If it will persist in Being.

16 *The abyss of freedom and the* novus ordo seclorum

Very early in these deliberations I warned of an inevitable flaw in all critical examinations of the willing faculty. It is a rather obvious one but easy to overlook in discussing the particular arguments and counter-arguments: simply that every *philosophy* of the Will is conceived and articulated not by men of action but by philosophers, Kant's "professional thinkers," who in one way or another are committed to the *bios theōrēti-kos* and therefore by nature more inclined to "interpret the world" than to "change it."

Of all the philosophers and theologians we have consulted, only Duns Scotus, we found, was ready to pay the price of contingency for the gift of freedom—the mental endowment we have for beginning something new, of which we know that it could just as well not be. No doubt the philosophers have always been more "pleased" with necessity than with freedom because for their business they needed a *tranquillitas animae* (Leibniz), a peace of mind, which—relying on Spinoza's *acquiescentia sibi*, one's agreement with oneself—could be effectively guaranteed only by an acquiescence in the arrangement of the world. The same self that the thinking activity disregards in its withdrawal from the world of appearances is asserted and ensured by the Will's reflexivity. Just as thinking prepares the self for the role of spectator, willing fashions it into an "enduring I" that directs all particular acts of volition. It creates the self's *character* and therefore was sometimes understood as the *principium individuationis*, the source of the person's specific identity.

Yet it is precisely this individuation brought about by the Will that breeds new and serious trouble for the notion of freedom. The individual, fashioned by the will and aware that it could be different from what it is (character, unlike bodily appearance or talents and abilities, is not given to the self at birth) always tends to assert an "I-myself" against an indefinite "they"—all the others that I, as an individual, am *not*. Nothing indeed can be more frightening than the notion of solipsistic freedom—the "feeling" that my standing apart, isolated from everyone else, is due to free will, that nothing and nobody can be held responsible for it but me myself. The will with its projects for the future challenges the belief in necessity, the acquiescence in the arrangement of the world which it calls complacency. Yet isn't it clear to everyone that the world is not, and has never been, what it *ought* to be? And who knows, or has ever known, what this "ought" should be? The "ought" is utopian; it has no proper *topos* or place in the world. Isn't trust in necessity, the conviction that everything is as "it was to be," infinitely preferable to freedom bought at the price of contingency? Under these circumstances, doesn't freedom look like a euphemism for the burnt-over area marked by the "forsakenness with which [human existence, the *Dasein*] has been abandoned to itself" (*"die Verlassenheit in der Überlassenheit an es selbst"*)?[116]

These difficulties and anxieties are caused by the Will insofar as it is a mental faculty, hence reflexive, recoiling upon itself—*volo me velle, cogito me cogitare*—or, to put it in Heideggerian terms, by the fact that, existentially speaking, human existence has been "abandoned to itself." Nothing of the sort disturbs our intellect, the mind's capability of cognition and its trust in truth. The cognitive abilities, like our senses, do not recoil upon themselves; they are totally intentional, namely, totally absorbed by the intended object. Hence at first glance it is surprising to find a similar bias against freedom in the great scientists of our century. As we know, they became greatly disturbed when their demonstrable discoveries in astrophysics, as well as in nuclear physics, gave rise to the suspicion that we live in a universe which, in Einstein's words, is ruled by a God who "plays dice" with it or, as Heisenberg suggested, that what we regard as the "outer world [may be] only our inner world turned inside out" (Lewis Mumford).

Such thoughts and after-thoughts are, of course, not scientific statements; they do not claim to deliver demonstrable truths or tentative theorems that their authors can hope to translate eventually into propositions susceptible of proof. They are reflections inspired by a quest for meaning and therefore no

The abyss of freedom and the novus ordo seclorum

less speculative than other products of the thinking ego. Einstein himself, in a much quoted remark, very clearly drew the line between cognitive statements and speculative propositions: "The most incomprehensible fact of nature is the fact that nature is comprehensible." Here we can almost watch how the thinking ego intrudes on the cognitive activity, interrupts and halts it by its reflections. It puts itself "out of order" with the scientist's ordinary activity by recoiling upon itself and musing on the fundamental incomprehensibility of what he is doing—an incomprehensibility that remains a riddle worth thinking about even though it cannot be solved.

Such reflections may yield various "hypotheses," and some may even turn out to yield knowledge when tested; in any case, their quality and weight will depend on the cognitive achievements of their authors. Still, it is hardly deniable that the reflections of the great founders of modern science—Einstein, Planck, Bohr, Heisenberg, Schrödinger—have brought about a "crisis in the foundations of modern science" (*Grundlagenkrise*), "and their central question" (What must the world be like in order that man may know it?) "is as old as science itself and it remains unanswered."[117]

It seems only natural that this generation of founders, on whose discoveries modern science was based and whose reflections on what they were doing have brought about the "crisis in the foundations," should have been followed by several generations of less distinguished epigones who find it easier to answer unanswerable questions because they are less aware of the line separating their ordinary activities from their reflections on them. I have spoken of the orgy of speculative thinking that succeeded Kant's liberation of reason's need to think beyond the intellect's cognitive capacity, the games played by German Idealists with personified concepts and the claims made for scientific validity—a far remove from Kant's "critique."

From the point of view of scientific truth, the Idealists' speculations were pseudo-scientific; now, at the opposite end of the spectrum, something similar seems to be going on. Materialists play the game of speculation with the help of computers, cybernetics, and automation; their extrapolations produce, not ghosts like the game of the Idealists, but materializations like those of spiritualist séances. What is so very striking in these materialist games is that their results resemble the concepts of the Idealists. Thus Hegel's "World Spirit" has recently found materialization in the construction of a "nervous system" fashioned on the model of a Giant Computer: Lewis Thomas[118] proposes to understand the world-wide community of human beings in the form of a Giant Brain, exchanging thoughts so rapidly "that the brains of mankind often appear functionally to be undergoing fusion." With mankind as its "nervous system," the whole earth thus "becomes . . . a breathing organism of finely meshed parts," all growing under the "protective membrane" of the planet's atmosphere.[119]

Such notions are neither science nor philosophy, but science fiction; they are widespread and demonstrate that the extravagances of materialist speculation are quite equal to the follies of Idealist metaphysics. The common denominator of all these fallacies, materialist or Idealist, apart from being historically derived from the notion of Progress and its concomitant, the undemonstrable entity called Mankind, is that they fulfill the same emotional function. In Lewis Thomas' words, they do away with "the whole dear notion of one's own self—the marvelous old free-willed, free-enterprising, autonomous, independent, isolated island of a Self," which is "a myth."[120] The proper name of this myth, which we are admonished from all sides to get rid of, is Freedom.

Professional thinkers, whether philosophers or scientists, have not been "pleased with freedom" and its ineluctable randomness; they have been unwilling to pay the price of contingency for the questionable gift of spontaneity, of being able to do what could also be left undone. Let us put them aside therefore and fasten our attention on men of action, who ought to be committed to freedom because of the very nature of their activity, which consists in "changing the world," and not in interpreting or knowing it.

Conceptually speaking, we turn from the notion of philosophical freedom to political liberty, an obvious difference which, as far as I know, only Montesquieu spoke of, and that in passing, when he used philosophical freedom as a backdrop against which political liberty could be more sharply outlined. In a chapter entitled *"De la liberté du citoyen"* ("Of the citizen's liberty") he said: *"La liberté philosophique consiste dans l'exercise de sa volonté, ou du moins (s'il faut parler dans tous les systèmes) dans l'opinion où l'on est que l'on exerce sa volonté. La liberté politique consiste dans la sûreté, ou du moins dans l'opinion que l'on a de sa sûreté"*—"Philosophic liberty consists in the exercise of the will, or at least (if we must take account of all systems) in the opinion that we exert our will. Political liberty consists in safety, or at least in the opinion of being safe."[121] The citizen's political liberty is "that tranquillity of mind that comes from the opinion that everybody has of his safety; and in order to be in possession of this liberty the government must be such that one citizen could not be afraid of another."[122]

Philosophic freedom, the freedom of the will, is relevant only to people who live outside political communities, as solitary individuals. Political communities, in which men become citizens, are produced and preserved by laws, and these laws, made by men, can be very different and can shape various forms of government, all of which in one way or another constrain the free will of their citizens. Still, with the exception of tyranny, where one arbitrary will rules the lives of all, they nevertheless open up some space of freedom for action that actually sets the constituted body of citizens in motion. The principles inspiring the actions of the citizens vary in accordance with the different forms of government, but they are all, as Jefferson rightly called them, "energetic principles";[123] and political freedom *"ne peut consister qu'à pouvoir faire ce que l'on doit vouloir et à n'être point contraint de faire ce que l'on ne doit pas vouloir"*—"can consist only in the power of doing what we ought to will and in not being constrained to do what we ought not to will."[124]

The emphasis here is clearly on Power in the sense of the I-can; for Montesquieu, as for the ancients, it was obvious that an agent could no longer be called free when he lacked the capacity to do what he wanted to do, whether this was due to exterior or interior circumstances. Moreover, the Laws which, according to Montesquieu, transform free and lawless individ- uals into citizens are not God's Ten Commandments or the voice of conscience or reason's *lumen rationale* enlightening all men alike, but man-made *rapports,* "relations," which, since they concern the changeable affairs of mortal men—as dis- tinguished from God's eternity or the immortality of the cos- mos—must be "subject to all the accidents that can happen and vary in proportion as the will of man changes."[125] For Montesquieu, as for pre-Christian antiquity and for the men who at the end of the century founded the American Republic, the words "power" and "liberty" were almost synonymous. Freedom of movement, the power of moving about unchecked by disease or master, was originally the most elementary of all liberties, their very prerequisite.

Thus political freedom is distinct from philosophic freedom in being clearly a quality of the I-can and not of the I-will. Since it is possessed by the citizen rather than by man in general, it can manifest itself only in communities, where the many who live together have their intercourse both in word and in deed regulated by a great number of *rapports*—laws, customs, habits, and the like. In other words, political freedom is possible only in the sphere of human plurality, and on the premise that this sphere is not simply an extension of the dual I-and-myself to a plural We. Action, in which a We is always engaged in changing our common world, stands in the sharpest possible opposition to the solitary business of thought, which operates in a dialogue between me and myself. Under exceptionally propitious circumstances that dialogue, we have seen, can be extended to another insofar as a friend is, as Aristotle said, "another self." But it can never reach the We, the true plural of action. (An error rather prevalent among modern philosophers who insist on the importance of communication as a guarantee of truth—chiefly Karl Jaspers and Martin Buber, with his I-thou philosophy—is to believe that the intimacy of the dialogue, the "inner action" in which I "appeal" to myself or to the "other self," Aristotle's friend, Jaspers' beloved, Buber's Thou, can be extended and become paradigmatic for the political sphere.)

This We arises wherever men live together; its primal form

is the family; and it can be constituted in many different ways, all of which rest ultimately on some form of consent, of which obedience is only the most common mode, just as disobedience is the most common and least harmful mode of dissent. Consent entails the recognition that no man can act alone, that men if they wish to achieve something in the world must act in concert, which would be a platitude if there were not always some members of the community determined to disregard it and who in arrogance or in despair try to act alone. These are tyrants or criminals, depending on the final goal they aim at; what they have in common and what sets them apart from the rest of the community is that they put their trust in the use of the instruments of violence as a substitute for power. This is a tactic that only works for the short-range goals of the criminal, who after completing his crime can and must return to membership in the community; the tyrant, on the other hand, always a sheep in wolf's clothing, can last only by usurping the rightful seat of leadership, which makes him dependent on helpers to see his self-willed projects through. Unlike the mind's will power to affirm or negate, whose ultimate practical guarantee is suicide, political power, even if the tyrant's supporters consent to terror—that is, the use of violence—is always limited power, and since power and freedom in the sphere of human plurality are in fact synonyms, this means also that political freedom is always limited freedom.

Human plurality, the faceless "They" from which the individual Self splits to be itself alone, is divided into a great many units, and it is only as a member of such a unit, that is, of a community, that men are ready for action. The manifoldness of these communities is evinced in a great many different forms and shapes, each obeying different laws, having different habits and customs, and cherishing different memories of its past, i.e., a manifoldness of traditions. Montesquieu was probably right in assuming that each such entity moved and acted according to a different inspiring principle, recognized as the ultimate standard for judging the community's deeds and misdeeds—virtue in republics, honor and glory in monarchies, moderation in aristocracies, fear and suspicion in tyrannies—except that this enumeration, guided by the oldest distinction between forms of government (as the rule of one, of a few, of the best, or of all) is of course pitifully inadequate to the rich diversity of human beings living together on the earth.

The only trait that all these various forms and shapes of human plurality have in common is the simple fact of their genesis, that is, that at some moment in time and for some reason a group of people must have come to think of themselves as a "We." No matter how this "We" is first experienced and articulated, it seems that it always needs a beginning, and nothing seems so shrouded in darkness and mystery as that "In the beginning," not only of the human species as distinguished from other living organisms, but also of the enormous variety of indubitably human societies.

The haunting obscurity of the question has hardly been illuminated by recent biological, anthropological, and archaeological discoveries, whatever success they have had in extending the time span which separates us from an ever more distant past. And it is unlikely that any factual information will ever throw light on the bewildering maze of more or less plausible hypotheses, all of which suffer from the incurable suspicion that their very plausibility and probability may well turn out to be their undoing since our whole real existence—the genesis of the earth, the development of organic life on it, the evolution of man out of the countless animal species—occurred against statistically overwhelming probabilities. All that is real in the universe and in nature once was an "infinite" improbability. In the everyday world where we spend our own exiguous quotient of reality we can only be sure of a shrinkage of time behind us that is no less decisive than the shrinkage of spatial distances on the earth. What only a few decades ago, remembering Goethe's "three thousand years" (*"Wer nicht von dreitausend Jahren / Sich weiss Rechenschaft zu geben, / Bleib im Dunkel, unerfahren / Mag von Tag zu Tage leben"*), we still called antiquity is much closer to us today than it was to our ancestors.

This predicament of not-knowing is all too likely never to be resolved, corresponding, as it does, to other manifest limitations inherent in the human condition, which sets definite insurmountable boundaries to our thirst for knowledge—for example, we know *of* the immensity of the universe and nevertheless we shall never be able to know it—and the best we can do in the quandary is turn to the legendary tales that in our tradition have aided former generations to come to grips with the mysterious "In the beginning." I mean the foundation legends, which clearly had to do with a time antecedent to any form of government and to any particular principles that set governments in motion. Yet the time they dealt with was human time, and the beginning they recounted was not a divine creation but a man-made set of occurrences that memory could reach through an imaginative interpretation of old tales.

The two foundation legends of Western civilization, the one Roman and the other Hebrew (nothing comparable, Plato's *Timaeus* notwithstanding, ever existed in Greek antiquity), are utterly different from each other, except that both arose among a people that thought of its past as a story whose beginning was known and could be dated. The Jews knew the year of the creation of the world (and reckon time to this very day from it), and the Romans, as contrasted with the Greeks, who reckoned time from Olympiad to Olympiad, knew (or believed they knew) the year of the foundation of Rome and reckoned time accordingly. Much more striking, and fraught with much more serious consequences for our tradition of political thought, is the astounding fact that both legends (in sharp contradiction with the well-known principles allegedly inspiring political action in constituted communities) hold that in the case of foundation—the supreme act in which the "We" is constituted as an identifiable entity—the inspiring principle of action is love of freedom, and this both in the negative sense of liberation from oppression and in the positive sense of the establishment of Freedom as a stable, tangible reality.

Both the difference and the connection between the two— the freedom that comes from being liberated and the freedom that arises out of the spontaneity of beginning something new —are paradigmatically represented in the two foundation legends that have acted as guides for Western political thought. We have the Biblical story of the exodus of Israeli tribes from Egypt, which preceded the Mosaic legislation constituting the Hebrew people, and Virgil's story of the wanderings of Aeneas, which led to the foundation of Rome—*"dum conderet urbem,"* as Virgil defines the content of his great poem even in its first lines. Both legends begin with an act of liberation, the flight from oppression and slavery in Egypt and the flight from burning Troy (that is, from annihilation); and in both instances this act is told about from the perspective of a new freedom, the conquest of a new "promised land" that offers more than Egypt's fleshpots and the foundation of a new City that is prepared for by a war destined to undo the Trojan war, so that the order of events as laid down by Homer could be reversed. Virgil's reversal of Homer is deliberate and complete.[126] This time it is Achilles in the guise of Turnus ("Here too shalt thou tell that a Priam found his Achilles") who flees and is killed by Hector in the guise of Aeneas; in the center, "the source of all that woe" is again a woman, but this time she is a bride (Lavinia) and not an adulteress; and the end of the war is not triumph for the victor and utter destruction for the vanquished but a new body politic—"both nations unconquered join treaty under equal laws forever."

No doubt if we read these legends as tales, there is a world of difference between the aimless desperate wanderings of the Israeli tribes in the desert after the Exodus and the marvelously colorful tales of the adventures of Aeneas and his fellow Trojans; but to the men of action of later generations who ransacked the archives of antiquity for paradigms to guide their own intentions, this was not decisive. What was decisive was that there was a *hiatus* between disaster and salvation, between liberation from the old order and the new freedom, embodied in a *novus ordo saeclorum,* a "new order of the ages" with whose rise the world had structurally changed.

The legendary hiatus between a no-more and a not-yet clearly indicated that freedom would not be the automatic result of liberation, that the end of the old is not necessarily the beginning of the new, that the notion of an all-powerful time continuum is an illusion. Tales of a transitory period—

The abyss of freedom and the novus ordo seclorum

from bondage to freedom, from disaster to salvation—were all the more appealing because the legends chiefly concerned the deeds of great leaders, persons of world-historic significance who appeared on the stage of history precisely during such gaps of historical time. All those who, pressed by exterior circumstances or motivated by radical utopian thought-trains, were not satisfied to change the world by the gradual reform of an old order (and this rejection of the gradual was precisely what transformed the men of action of the eighteenth century, the first century of a fully secularized intellectual elite, into the men of the revolutions) were almost logically forced to accept the possibility of a hiatus in the continuous flow of temporal sequence.

We remember Kant's embarrassment in "dealing . . . with a power of spontaneously beginning a series of successive things or states," i.e., with an *"absolute* beginning," which, because of the unbreakable sequence of the time continuum, will nevertheless always remain "the continuation of a preceding series."[127] The word "revolution" was supposed to dissolve this embarrassment when, during the last decades of the eighteenth century, it changed its old astronomical meaning and came to signify an unprecedented event. In France this even led to a short-lived "revolution" of the calendar: in October 1793, it was decided that the proclamation of the Republic was a new beginning of human history; as this had happened in September 1792, the new calendar declared September 1793 to be the inauguration of the Year Two. This attempt to localize an absolute beginning in time was a failure, and probably not only because of the strong anti-Christian cast of the new calendar (all Christian holidays, including Sunday, were abolished, and a fictitious division of a thirty-day month into units of ten days was instituted; the tenth day of each decade was to replace the weekly Sunday as a day of rest). Its usage fizzled out around 1805, a date hardly remembered even by professional historians.

In the case of the American Revolution, the old legendary notion of a temporal hiatus between the old order and a new era seemed much better suited than a calendar "revolution" to bridge the gap between a time continuum of ordered succession and the spontaneous start of something new. Indeed, it would be tempting to use the rise of the United States of America as a historical example of the truth of old legends, like a verification of Locke's "in the beginning all the world was America." The colonial period would be interpreted as the transition period from bondage to freedom—the hiatus between leaving England and the Old World and the establishment of freedom in the New.

The parallel with the tales is astoundingly close: in both instances the act of foundation had come about through the deeds and the sufferings of exiles. This is true even of the Biblical tale as told in Exodus; Canaan, the promised land, is by no means the original Jewish home, but the land of the Jews' former "sojourn" (Exodus 6:4). Virgil insists still more strongly on the theme of exile: Aeneas and his companions were "driven . . . to distant places of exile in waste lands," weeping at leaving "the shores and the havens . . . where once was Troy," exiles "uncertain whither the fates carry us or where a resting-place is given."[128]

The founders of the American Republic were well acquainted with Roman as well as Biblical antiquity and they may have taken from the old legends the decisive distinction between mere liberation and actual freedom, but nowhere do they use the hiatus as a possible basis for explaining what they were doing. There was a simple factual reason for that: though the land eventually was to become a "resting-place" for many and an asylum for exiles, they themselves had not settled there as exiles but as colonists. Up to the last, when conflict with England proved to be inevitable, they had no trouble recognizing the political authority of the mother-country. They prided themselves on being British subjects, until the momentum of their rebellion against an unjust government—"taxation without representation"—had carried them into a full-fledged "revolution," a change in the form of government itself, and the constitution of a Republic as the only government, they now felt, fit to rule in the land of the free.

The abyss of freedom and the novus ordo seclorum

This was the moment when those who had started as men of action and had been transformed into men of revolution changed Virgil's great line *"Magnus ab integro saeclorum nascitur ordo"* ("the great order of the ages is [re]born as it was in the beginning")[129] to the *Novus Ordo Seclorum* (the *"new* order"), which we still find on our dollar bills. For the Founding Fathers, the variation implied an admission that the great effort to reform and restore the body politic to its initial integrity (to found "Rome anew") had led to the entirely unexpected and very different task of constituting something entirely new—founding a "new Rome."

When men of action, men who wanted to change the world, became aware that such a change might actually postulate a new order of the ages, the start of something unprecedented, they began to look to history for help. They set about rethinking such thought-things as the Pentateuch and the *Aeneid,* foundation legends that might tell them how to solve the problem of beginning—a problem because beginning's very nature is to carry in itself an element of complete arbitrariness. It was only now that they confronted the abyss of freedom, knowing that whatever would be done now could just as well have been left undone and believing, too, with clarity and precision, that once something is done it cannot be undone, that human memory telling the story will survive repentance as well as destruction.

This applies only to the realm of action, the "many-in-one of human beings,"[130] that is, to communities where the "We" is properly established for its journey through historical time. The foundation legends, with their hiatus between liberation and the constitution of freedom, indicate the problem without solving it. They point to the *abyss* of nothingness that opens up before any deed that cannot be accounted for by a reliable chain of cause and effect and is inexplicable in Aristotelian categories of potentiality and actuality. In the normal time continuum every effect immediately turns into a cause of future developments, but when the causal chain is broken— which occurs after liberation has been achieved, because liberation, though it may be freedom's *conditio sine qua non,* is never the *conditio per quam* that causes freedom—there is nothing left for the "beginner" to hold on to. The thought of an absolute beginning—*creatio ex nihilo*—abolishes the sequence of temporality no less than does the thought of an absolute end, now rightly referred to as "thinking the unthinkable."

We know the Hebrew solution for this perplexity. It assumes a Creator-God who creates time along with the universe and who as legislator remains outside His creation, and outside of time as the One "who is who he is" (the literal translation of "Jehovah" is "I am who I am") "from eternity to eternity." This concept of eternity, having been framed by a temporal creature, is the absolute of temporality. It is what is left of time when time is "absolved"—liberated from its relativeness—time as it would appear to an outside observer not subject to its laws and by definition unrelated by virtue of his Oneness. To the extent that the universe and everything in it can be traced back to the region of this absolute One-ness, the One-ness is rooted in something that may be beyond the reasoning of temporal men but still possesses a kind of rationale of its own: it can *explain,* give a logical account of, the existentially inexplicable. And the need for explanation is nowhere stronger than in the presence of an unconnected new event breaking into the continuum, the sequence of chronological time.

This seems to be why men who were much too "enlightened" to still believe in the Hebrew-Christian Creator-God turned with rare unanimity to pseudo-religious language when they had to deal with the problem of foundation as the beginning of a "new order of the ages." We have the "appeal to God in Heaven," deemed necessary by Locke for all who embarked on the novelty of a community emerging from "the state of nature"; we have Jefferson's "laws of nature and nature's God," John Adams' "great Legislator of the Universe," Robespierre's "immortal Legislator," his cult of a "Supreme Being."

Their explanations clearly work by analogy: just as God "in the beginning created the heavens and the earth," remaining outside His Creation and prior to it, so the human legislator—created in God's own image and therefore able to imitate God—when he lays the *foundations* of a human community, creates

The abyss of freedom and the novus ordo seclorum

the condition for all future political life and historical development.

To be sure, neither the Greeks nor the Romans knew anything of a Creator-God whose unrelated One-ness could serve
as the paradigmatic emblem for an absolute beginning. But
the Romans at least, who dated their history from the foundation of Rome in 753, seem to have been aware that the very
nature of this business demanded a transmundane principle.
Otherwise Cicero could not have held that "human excellence
nowhere so closely approaches the paths of the gods as in the
founding of new and the preserving of already founded communities."[131] For Cicero as for the Greeks, from whom he
derived his philosophy, the founders were not gods but divine
men, and the greatness of their deed was to have established a
law that became the font of authority, an immutable standard
against which all positive laws and decrees enacted by men
could be measured and from which they received their legiti-
macy.

Harking back to religious beliefs right in the middle of
the Age of Enlightenment might have sufficed if there had
been no more at stake than the authority of a new law; and
indeed it is striking to find explicit mentions of a "future state
of rewards and punishments" inserted into all American state
constitutions, although we find no allusion to a hereafter in the
Declaration of Independence or the Constitution of the United
States. The motives for such desperate attempts to hold fast to
a faith that in reality would be unable to survive the co-tem-
poraneous emancipation of the secular realm from the Church
were entirely pragmatic and highly practical. In his speech on
the Supreme Being and the immortality of the soul to the National Convention on May 7, 1794, Robespierre asks "*Quel
avantage trouves-tu à persuader l'homme qu'une force aveugle
préside à ses destins, et frappe au hasard le crime et la vertu?*"
("What advantage do you see in persuading men to believe
that a blind force presides over their destinies, striking crime
and virtue at random?"), and in the *Discourses on Davila*,
John Adams speaks in the same curiously rhetorical way of
"the most disconsolate of all creeds, that men are but fireflies,
and that this *all* is without a father . . . [which would] make

murder itself as indifferent as shooting a plover, and the extermination of the Rohilla nation as innocent as the swallowing of mites on a morsel of cheese."[132]

In brief, what we find here is a short-lived effort on the part of secular government to retain not the Hebrew-Christian faith but political instruments of rule that had been so very effective at protecting the medieval communities against criminality. In retrospect it may look almost like a tricky device of the educated few to persuade the many not to follow on the slippery road to enlightenment. In any case, the attempt totally failed (at the beginning of our century few indeed were left who still believed in "a future state of rewards and punishments") and was probably foredoomed to failure. Nevertheless the loss of belief and, with it, of a good deal of the old panic-stricken fear of death has certainly contributed to the massive invasion of criminality into the political life of highly civilized communities that our own century has witnessed. There is an odd built-in helplessness about the legal systems of entirely secularized communities; their capital punishment, the death penalty, only gives a date to and accelerates a fate all mortals are subject to.

In any event, wherever men of action, driven by the very momentum of the liberation process, began to prepare in earnest for an entirely new beginning, the *novus ordo seclorum*, instead of turning to the Bible ("In the beginning God created the heavens and the earth"), they ransacked the archives of Roman antiquity for "ancient prudence" to guide them in the establishment of a Republic, that is, of a government "of laws and not of men" (Harrington). What they needed was not only an acquaintance with a new form of government but also a lesson in the art of foundation, in how to overcome the perplexities inherent in every beginning. They were quite aware of course of the bewildering spontaneity of a free act. As they knew, an act can only be called free if it is not affected or caused by anything preceding it and yet, insofar as it immediately turns into a cause of whatever follows, it demands a justification which, if it is to be successful, will have to show the act as the continuation of a preceding series, that is, renege on the very experience of freedom and novelty.

The abyss of freedom and the novus ordo seclorum

And what Roman antiquity had to teach them in this respect was quite reassuring and consoling. We do not know
why the Romans, in the third century B.C. or perhaps even
earlier, decided to trace their descent not from Romulus but
from Aeneas, the man from Troy who had brought "Ilium and
her conquered household gods into Italy" and thus became
"the fount of the Roman race." But it is obvious that this fact
was of great importance not only to Virgil and his contemporaries in Augustus' time, but also to all those who, starting
with Machiavelli, had gone to Roman antiquity to learn how
to conduct human affairs without the help of a transcendent
God. What men of action were learning in the archives of
Roman antiquity was the original purport of a phenomenon
with which, curiously enough, Western civilization had been
acquainted ever since the end of the Roman empire and Christianity's definite triumph.

Far from being new, the phenomenon of re-birth or renaissance, from the fifteenth and sixteenth centuries onward, had
dominated the cultural development of Europe and had been
preceded by a whole series of minor renascences that terminated the few centuries of what really were "dark ages," between the sack of Rome and the Carolingian renaissance. Each
of these re-births, consisting in a Revival of Learning and
centering on Roman and to a lesser degree Greek antiquity,
had altered and revitalized only the rather restricted milieus of
the educated elite inside and outside monasteries. It was not
till the Age of Enlightenment—that is, in a now completely
secularized world—that the revival of antiquity ceased to be a
matter of erudition and responded to highly practical political
purposes. For that enterprise the only predecessor had been
the lonely figure, Machiavelli.

The problem men of action were being called upon to solve
was the perplexity inherent in the task of *foundation,* and
since for them the paradigmatic example of a successful
foundation was bound to be Rome, it was of the greatest
importance to them to find that even the foundation of Rome,
as the Romans themselves had understood it, was not an absolutely new beginning. According to Virgil, it was the resurgence of Troy and the re-establishment of a city-state that had

preceded Rome. Thus the thread of continuity and tradition, demanded by the very continuum of time and the faculty of memory (the innate lest-we-forget, which seems to belong to a temporal creature as much as the ability to form projects for the future) had never been broken. Seen in this light, the foundation of Rome was the re-birth of Troy, the first, as it were, of the series of re-nascences that have formed the history of European culture and civilization.

We need only recall Virgil's most famous political poem, the Fourth Eclogue, to understand how vital it was for the Roman view of their state to interpret constitution and foundation in terms of the re-establishment of a beginning which, as an absolute beginning, remains perpetually shrouded in mystery. For if in the reign of Augustus "the great cycle of periods is born anew" (as all standard modern-language translations render Virgil's great line *"Magnus ab integro saeclorum nascitur ordo"*), it is precisely because this "order of the ages" is not *new* but only the return of something antecedent. To Augustus, who in the *Aeneid* is supposed to start this re-birth, a promise is even given that he will lead the way still further back and "again establish the ages of gold in Latium over the fields that once were the realm of Saturn," i.e., the Italic land before the arrival of the Trojans.[133]

At any rate, the order invoked in the Fourth Eclogue is great by virtue of going back to and being inspired by an earlier beginning: "Now returns the Maid, returns the reign of Saturn." And yet the way *back*, seen from the viewpoint of those now living, is a true beginning: "now from high heaven a new generation is sent down."[134] This poem, no doubt, is a nativity hymn, a song in praise of a child's birth and the arrival of a *nova progenies*, a new generation. It has long been misunderstood as a prophecy of salvation through a *theos sōtēr,* a savior god, or at least as the expression of some pre-Christian religious yearning. But, far from predicting the arrival of a divine child, the poem is an affirmation of the divinity of birth as such; if one wishes to extract a general meaning from it, this could only be the poet's belief that the world's potential salvation lies in the very fact that the human species regenerates itself constantly and forever. But that meaning is not explicit:

all the poet himself says is that every child born into the continuity of Roman history must learn *"heroum laudes et facta parentis,"* "the glories of the heroes and the deeds of the fathers," so as to be able to do what all Roman boys were supposed to do—help "rule the world that his fathers' virtues have set at peace."[135]

In our context, what matters is that the notion of foundation, of counting time *ab urbe condita,* is at the very center of Roman historiography along with the no less profoundly Roman notion that all such foundations—taking place exclusively in the realm of human affairs, where men enact a tale to tell, to remember, and preserve—are re-establishments and re-constitutions, not absolute beginnings.

This becomes quite manifest if one reads Virgil's *Aeneid*— the story of the foundation of the city of Rome—side by side with the *Georgics,* the four poems in praise of husbandry, of "the tending of fields and flocks and trees," and of the "quiet earth" assigned to the care of "the circling toil of the husband-man, [which] returns even as the year rolls back on itself along the familiar track": "she abides unstirred, and outlives many children's children, and sees roll by her many genera-tions of men." This is Italy before Rome, the "land of Saturn, mighty of men"; he who lives in it, "who knows the gods of the country, Pan and old Silvanus and the Nymphs' sisterhood" and remains true to the love of "stream and woodland," is "lost to fame." "Him fasces of the people or purple of kings sway not . . . not the Roman state or realms destined to decay; nor may pity of the poor or envy of the rich cost him a pang. What fruits the . . . gracious fields bear of their own free will, these he gathers, and sees not the iron of justice or the mad forum and the archives of the people." This life "in sacred purity" was "life golden Saturn led on earth," and the only trouble is that in this world full of wonders and a superabundance of plants and beasts, "there is no *tale* of the manifold kinds or of the names they bear, nor truly were the tale worth reckoning out; whoso will know it, let him . . . learn likewise how many grains of sand eddy in the west wind on the plain of Libya, or count . . . how many waves come shoreward across Ionian seas."

Those who sing of the origin of this pre-Roman and pre-Trojan world, whose circling years produce no tales worth telling, while at the same time they produce all the wonders of nature that never cease to delight men, those who in Virgil praise "the realm of Saturn" and creation-myths (in the Sixth Eclogue or in the first book of the *Aeneid*) are chanting of a fairy-tale land and are themselves marginal figures. Dido's "long-haired" bard and Silenus, "his veins swollen as ever with yesterday's wine," entertain a youthful, playful audience with old tales of the "wandering moon and the sun's travail; whence is the human race and the brute, whence water and fire," "how throughout the vast void were gathered together the seeds of earth and air and sea, and withal of fluid fire, and how from these all the beginnings of things and the young orbed world itself grew together."

Still—and this is decisive—this utopian fairy-tale land outside of history is sempiternal and survives in the indestructibility of nature; husbandmen or shepherds who tend the fields and the flocks still testify, in the midst of Roman-Trojan history, to an Italic past when the natives were "Saturn's people whom no laws fettered to justice, upright of their own free will and the custom of the god of old."[136] Then no Roman ambition was charged "to rule the nations and ordain the law of peace" ("*regere imperio populos . . . pacisque imponere morem*"), and no Roman morality was necessary to "spare the conquered and beat the haughty down" ("*parcere suiectis et debellare superbos*").

I have dwelt on Virgil's poems at some length for several reasons. To sum up: men, when they emerged from the tutelage of the Church, turned to antiquity, and their first steps in a secularized world were guided by a revival of ancient learning. Confronted with the riddle of foundation—how to re-start time within an inexorable time continuum—they naturally turned to the story of the foundation of Rome and learned from Virgil that this starting-point of Occidental history had already been a re-vival, the resurgence of Troy. That could tell them no more than that the hope of founding a "new Rome" was an illusion: the most they could hope for was to repeat the primeval foundation and found "Rome anew." Whatever lay prior to this first foundation, itself the resurgence of some definite past, was situated outside history; it was nature, whose cyclical sempiternity might provide a refuge from the onward march of time, the vertical, rectilinear direction of history—a place of leisure, *otium*—when men tired of the busy-ness of citizenship (*nec-otium* by definition), but whose own origin was of no interest because it was beyond the scope of action.

To be sure, there is something puzzling in the fact that men of action, whose sole intent and purpose was to change the whole structure of the future world and create a *novus ordo seclorum*, should have to go to that distant past of antiquity, for they did not "deliberately [reverse] the time-axis and [bid] the young 'walk back into the pure radiance of the past' (Petrarch) because the classic past *is* the true future."[137] They looked for a paradigm for a new form of government in their own "enlightened" age and were hardly aware of the fact that they were looking backward. More puzzling, I think, than their actual ransacking of the archives of antiquity is that they did not rebel against antiquity when they discovered that the final and certainly profoundly Roman answer of "ancient prudence" was that salvation always comes from the past, that the ancestors were *maiores*, the "greater ones" by definition.

It is striking, besides, that the notion of the future—precisely a future pregnant with final salvation—bringing back a kind of initial Golden Age, should have become popular at a time when Progress had come to be the dominant concept to explain the movement of History. And the most striking example of the resilience of that very old dream is of course Marx's fantasy of a classless and warless "realm of freedom" as prefigured in "original communism," a realm that has a more than superficial resemblance to Saturn's aboriginal Italic rule, when no laws "fettered [men] to justice." In its original ancient form as the inception of history, the Golden Age is a melancholy thought; it is as though, thousands of years ago, our ancestors had a foreboding of the eventual discovery of the entropy principle in the midst of the progress-drunk nineteenth century—a discovery which, if it had gone unchallenged, would have deprived action of all meaning.[138] What actually disposed of the entropy principle for the men who made the revolutions of the nineteenth and twentieth centuries was less Engels' "scientific" refutation than Marx's turning—and, of course, Nietzsche's too—to a cyclical time concept where the prehistoric innocence of the beginning would finally return, no less triumphant than the Second Coming.

But this does not concern us here. When we directed our attention to men of action, hoping to find in them a notion of freedom purged of the perplexities caused for men's minds by the reflexivity of mental activities—the inevitable recoil on itself of the willing ego—we hoped for more than we finally achieved. The abyss of pure spontaneity, which in the foundation legends is bridged by the hiatus between liberation and the constitution of freedom, was covered up by the device, typical of the Occidental tradition (the only tradition where freedom has always been the *raison d'être* of all politics) of understanding the *new* as an improved re-statement of the old. In its original integrity, freedom survived in political theory —i.e., theory conceived for the purpose of political action— only in utopian and unfounded promises of a final "realm of freedom" that, in its Marxian version at any rate, would indeed spell "the end of all things," a sempiternal peace in which all specifically human activities would wither away.

No doubt to arrive at such a conclusion is frustrating, but I know of only one tentative alternative to it in our entire history of political thought. If, as Hegel believed, the philosopher's task is to catch the most elusive of all manifestations, the spirit of an age, in the net of reason's concepts, then Augustine, the Christian philosopher of the fifth century A.D., was the only philosopher the Romans ever had. He was a Roman by education rather than birth, and it was his learning that sent him back to the classical texts of Republican Rome of the first century B.C., which even then were alive only in the form of erudition. In his great work on the *City of God*, he mentions, but does not explicate, what could have become the ontological underpinning for a truly Roman or Virgilian philosophy of politics. According to him, as we know, God created man as a temporal creature, *homo temporalis;* time and man were created together, and this temporality was affirmed by the fact that each man owed his life not just to the multiplication of the species, but to birth, the entry of a novel creature who *as* something entirely new appears in the midst of the time continuum of the world. The purpose of the creation of man was to make possible a *beginning:* "That there be a beginning man was created, before whom nobody was"—"*Initium* . . . *ergo ut esset, creatus est homo, ante quem nullus fuit.*"[139] The very capacity for beginning is rooted in *natality,* and by no means in creativity, not in a gift but in the fact that human beings, new men, again and again appear in the world by virtue of birth.

I am quite aware that the argument even in the Augustinian version is somehow opaque, that it seems to tell us no more than that we are *doomed* to be free by virtue of being born, no matter whether we like freedom or abhor its arbitrariness, are "pleased" with it or prefer to escape its awesome responsibility by electing some form of fatalism. This impasse, if such it is, cannot be opened or solved except by an appeal to another mental faculty, no less mysterious than the faculty of beginning, the faculty of Judgment, an analysis of which at least may tell us what is involved in our pleasures and displeasures.

Notes

Chapter I

1. See *Sophist*, 253–254 and *Republic*, 517.
2. Hermann Diels and Walther Kranz, *Die Fragmente der Vorsokratiker*, Berlin, 1960, vol. I, frag. B4.
3. *Confessions*, bk. XI, chap. 13.
4. *La Pensée et le Mouvant* (1934), Paris, 1950, p. 170.
5. *Ibid.*, p. 26.
6. 1174b6 and 1177a20. See also Aristotle's objections to Plato's concept of pleasure, 1173a13–1173b7.
7. *Op. cit.*, p. 5.
8. For the following, see *Metaphysics*, bk. VII, chaps. 7–10.
9. *De Anima*, 433a30.
10. Bruno Snell, *The Discovery of the Mind*, New York, Evanston, 1960, pp. 182–183.
11. *The Spirit of Medieval Philosophy*, New York, 1940, p. 307.
12. "Whether whatsoever comes to pass proceed from *necessity*, or some things from *chance*, has been a question disputed amongst the old philosophers long before the incarnation of our Saviour. . . . But the third way of bringing things to pass . . . namely *freewill*, is a thing that never was mentioned amongst them, nor by the Christians in the beginning of Christianity. . . . But for some ages past, the doctors of the Roman Church have exempted from this dominion of God's will the will of man; and brought in a doctrine, that . . . [man's] will is free, and determined . . . by the power of the will itself." "The Question concerning *Liberty, Necessity and Chance*," *English Works*, London, 1841, vol. V, p. 1.
13. See *Nicomachean Ethics*, bk. V, chap. 8.
14. *Ibid.*, bk. 3, 1110a17.
15. Gilbert Ryle, *The Concept of Mind*, New York, 1949, p. 65.
16. Henry Herbert Williams, article on the Will in *Encyclopaedia Britannica*, 11th ed.

17. *De Generatione,* bk. I, chap. 3, 317b16–18.
18. *Ibid.,* 318a25–27 and 319a23–29; *The Basic Works of Aristotle,* ed. Richard McKeon, New York, 1941, p. 483.
19. *Meteorologica,* 339b27.
20. Bk. I, 1100a33–1100b18.
21. *De Caelo,* 283b26–31.
22. *The Will to Power,* ed. Walter Kaufmann, Vintage Books, New York, 1968, no. 617.
23. *De Civitate Dei,* bk. XII, chap. 20.
24. *Ibid.,* chap. 13.
25. Our present calendar, which takes the birth of Christ as the turning-point from which to count time both backward and forward, was introduced at the end of the eighteenth century. The textbooks present the reform as prompted by scholarly needs to facilitate the dating of events in ancient history without having to refer to a maze of different time reckonings. Hegel, as far as I know the only philosopher to ponder the sudden remarkable change, saw in it a clear sign of a truly Christian chronology because the birth of Christ now became the turning-point of world history. It seems more significant that in the new scheme we can count backward and forward in such a way that the past reaches back into an infinite past and the future likewise stretches out into an infinite future. This twofold infinity eliminates all notions of beginning and end, establishing mankind, as it were, in a potentially sempiternal reality on earth. Needless to add that nothing could be more alien to Christian thought than the notion of an earthly immortality of mankind and its world.
26. See the article on the Will in the *Encyclopaedia Britannica,* mentioned above, in n. 16.
27. See Dieter Nestle, *Eleutheria. Teil I: Studien zum Wesen der Freiheit bei den Griechen und im Neuen Testament,* Tübingen, 1967, pp. 6 ff. It seems to be noteworthy that modern etymology inclines to derive the word *"eleutheria"* from an Indo-Germanic root signifying *Volk* or *Stamm,* with the result that only those who belong to the same ethnic unity can be recognized as "free" by their fellow-ethnics. Does not this piece of erudition sound rather uncomfortably close to the notions of German scholarship during the nineteen-thirties, when it first saw the light of day?
28. *Critique of Pure Reason,* B476. For this and other citations, see Norman Kemp Smith's translation, *Immanuel Kant's*

Critique of Pure Reason, New York, 1963, which the author frequently relied on.

29. *Uber die ästhetische Erziehung des Menschen in einer Reihe von Briefen,* 1795, 19th letter.

30. *The World as Will and Idea* (1818), trans. R. B. Haldane and J. Kemp, vol. I, pp. 39 and 129. Quoted here from Konstantin Kolenda's Introduction to Arthur Schopenhauer, *Essay on the Freedom of the Will,* Library of Liberal Arts, Indianapolis, New York, 1960, p. viii.

31. *Of Human Freedom* (1809), trans. James Gutmann, Chicago, 1936, p. 24.

32. *Beyond Good and Evil* (1885), trans. Marianne Cowan, Chicago, 1955, sect. 18.

33. "Also Sprach Zarathustra," in *Ecce Homo* (1889), no. 1.

34. *Ibid.,* no. 3.

35. See Karl Jaspers, *Nietzsche: An Introduction to the Understanding of His Philosophical Activity* (1935), trans. Charles F. Wallraff and Frederick J. Schmitz, Tucson, 1965; and Martin Heidegger, *Nietzsche,* 2 vols., Pfullingen, 1961.

36. *Philosophy* (1932), trans. E. B. Ashton, Chicago, 1970, vol. 2, p. 167.

37. *"Das primäre Phänomen der ursprünglichen und eigentlichen Zeitlichkeit ist die Zukunft."* In *Sein und Zeit* (1926), Tübingen, 1949, p. 329; *Gelassenheit,* Pfullingen, 1959, English translation: *Discourse on Thinking,* trans. John M. Anderson and E. Hans Freund, New York, 1966.

38. Editor's note: we have been unable to find this reference.

39. *English Works,* vol. V, p. 55.

40. Letter to G. H. Schaller, dated October 1674. See Spinoza, *The Chief Works,* ed. R. H. M. Elwes, New York, 1951, vol. II, p. 390.

41. *Ethics,* pt. III, prop. II, note, in *ibid.,* vol. II, p. 134; Letter to Schaller, in *ibid.,* p. 392.

42. *Leviathan,* ed. Michael Oakeshott, Oxford, 1948, chap. 21.

43. *Essay on the Freedom of the Will,* p. 43.

44. *An Examination of Sir William Hamilton's Philosophy* (1867), chap. XXVI, quoted from *Free Will,* eds. Sidney Morgenbesser and James Walsh, Englewood Cliffs, 1962, p. 59.

45. See Martin Kähler, *Das Gewissen* (1878), Darmstadt, 1967, pp. 46 ff.

46. See *Laws,* bk. IX, 865e.

47. *Op. cit.*, pp. 63–64.
48. *Notebooks 1914–1916,* bilingual ed., trans. G. E. M. Anscombe, New York, 1961, entry under date of August 5, 1916, p. 80e; cf. also pp. 86e–88e.
49. Augustine, *On Free Choice of the Will (De Libero Arbitrio),* bk. III, sect. 3.
50. In the Reply to Objection XII against the First Meditation: "that the freedom of the will has been assumed without proof." See *The Philosophical Works of Descartes,* trans. Elizabeth S. Haldane and G. R. T. Ross, Cambridge, 1970, vol. II, pp. 74–75.
51. Meditation IV, in *ibid.,* 1972, vol. I, pp. 174–175. Author's translation.
52. *Principles of Philosophy,* in *ibid.,* pt. I, prin. XL, p. 235.
53. *Ibid.,* prin. XLI, p. 235.
54. *Critique of Pure Reason,* B751.
55. *Op. cit.,* pp. 98–99.
56. *Critique of Pure Reason,* B478.
57. See Hans Jonas, "Jewish and Christian Elements in Philosophy," in *Philosophical Essays: From Ancient Creed to Technological Man,* Englewood Cliffs, 1974.
58. Henri Bergson, *op. cit.,* p. 13.
59. *Ibid.,* p. 15.
60. Thus wrote Wilhelm Windelband in his famous *History of Philosophy* (1892), New York, 1960, p. 314. He also calls Duns Scotus "the greatest of the Scholastics" (p. 425).
61. John Duns Scotus, *Philosophical Writings: A Selection,* trans. Allan Wolter, Library of Liberal Arts, Indianapolis, New York, 1962, pp. 84 and 10.
62. Hans Jonas, *op. cit.,* p. 29.
63. *Op. cit.,* p. 10.
64. *Ibid.,* p. 33.
65. *Time and Free Will: An Essay on the Immediate Data of Consciousness* (1889), trans. F. L. Pogson, Harper Torchbooks, New York, 1960, p. 142.
66. *Ibid.,* pp. 240 and 167.
67. *Principles of Philosophy,* prin. XLI, in *The Philosophical Works of Descartes,* p. 235.
68. Reply to Objections to Meditation V, *op. cit.,* p. 225.
69. Duns Scotus, *op. cit.,* p. 171.
70. See his exhaustive examination of the fatalist argument, " 'It Was to Be,' " in *Dilemmas,* Cambridge, 1969, pp. 15–35.

71. *Ibid.,* p. 28.
72. *De Fato,* xiii, 30–14, 31.
73. *Ibid.,* V, 35.
74. As Chrysippus had already pointed out. See *ibid.,* xx, 48.
75. *Confessio Philosophi,* bilingual ed., ed. Otto Saame, Frankfurt, 1967, p. 66.
76. *Jenenser Logik, Metaphysik und Naturphilosophie,* Lasson ed., Leipzig, 1923, p. 204, in *"Naturphilosophie I A: Begriff der Bewegung."*
77. See Friedrich Nietzsche, *Thus Spoke Zarathustra,* pt. II, "On Redemption": "The will cannot will backwards. . . . That time does not run backwards, that is his wrath; 'that which was' is the name of the stone he cannot move," in *The Portable Nietzsche,* trans. Walter Kaufmann, New York, 1954, p. 251.
78. See chap. III, p. 142 and n. 89.
79. *Op. cit.,* p. 110.
80. *Ibid.,* p. 122.
81. *Ibid.,* pp. 42, 44, 76, 92, 98, 100.
82. Quoted by Walter Lehmann in his Introduction to an anthology of the German writings, *Meister Eckhart,* Göttingen, 1919, sent. 15, p. 16.
83. The essay is now available in *Etudes d'Histoire de la Pensée Philosophique,* Paris, 1961.
84. Now available in English: *Introduction to the Readings of Hegel,* ed. Allan Bloom, New York, 1969, p. 134.
85. *Op. cit.,* p. 177.
86. *Philosophy of Right,* Preface; *Encyclopedia,* no. 465 in 2nd ed.
87. *Op. cit., loc. cit.*
88. *Ibid.,* pp. 177 and 185, note.
89. *Ibid.,* p. 188.
90. *Jenenser Logik,* p. 204.
91. Koyré, *op. cit.,* p. 183, quoting Hegel, *Jenenser Realphilosophie,* ed. Johannes Hoffmeister, Leipzig, 1932, vol. II, pp. 10 ff.
92. Koyré, *op. cit.,* p. 177.
93. Plato, *Republic,* 329b–c.
94. Koyré, *op. cit.,* p. 166.
95. *Ibid.,* p. 174.
96. Koyré, "La terminologie hégélienne," in *op. cit.,* p. 213.
97. Martin Heidegger, *Sein und Zeit,* no. 65, p. 326.

98. Koyré, *op. cit.*, p. 188, quoting *Phänomenologie des Geistes.*
99. Koyré, *op. cit.*, p. 183, quoting *Jenenser Realphilosophie.*
100. Koyré, "Hegel à Iéna," in *op. cit.*, p. 188.
101. Koyré, *op. cit.*, p. 185, quoting *Jenenser Realphilosophie.*
102. The passage in Plotinus is a commentary on Plato's *Timaeus,* 37c–38b. It occurs in *Ennead,* III, 7, 11: "On Time and Eternity." I have used the translation by A. H. Armstrong in the Loeb Classical Library, London, 1967, and Emile Bréhier's translation into French in the bilingual edition of the *Ennéades,* Paris, 1924–38.
103. An excellent and detailed report of the literature about Hegel is now available in Michael Theunissen, *Die Verwirklichung der Vernunft. Zur Theorie-Praxis-Diskussion im Anschluss an Hegel,* Beiheft 6 of the *Philosophische Rundschau,* Tübingen, 1970. The main works for our context are: Franz Rosenzweig, *Hegel und der Staat,* 2 vols. (1920), Aalen, 1962; Joachim Ritter, *Hegel und die französische Revolution,* Frankfurt/ Main, 1965; Manfred Riedel, *Theorie und Praxis im Denken Hegels,* Stuttgart, 1965.
104. *The Philosophy of History,* trans. J. Sibree, New York, 1956, pp. 446, 447; *Philosophie der Weltgeschichte,* Hälfte II, "Die Germanische Welt," Lasson ed., Leipzig, 1923, p. 926.
105. In a letter to Schelling of April 16, 1795. *Briefe,* Leipzig, 1887, vol. I, p. 15.
106. Quoted from Theunissen, *op. cit.*
107. *The Philosophy of History,* p. 442.
108. *Ibid.,* p. 446.
109. *Ibid.,* pp. 30 and 36.
110. *Ibid.,* p. 442.
111. *Ibid.,* p. 443. Author's translation.
112. *Ibid.,* p. 36.
113. *Ibid.,* p. 79. Author's translation; cf. *Werke,* Berlin, 1840, vol. IX, p. 98.
114. *Op. cit.,* p. 189.
115. *The Phenomenology of Mind,* trans. J. B. Baillie (1910), New York, 1964, p. 803.
116. Koyré, *op. cit.,* p. 164, quoting *Encyclopedia,* no. 258.
117. Hegel, *The Phenomenology of Mind,* pp. 801, 807–808. Italics added.
118. *Ibid.,* p. 808.
119. "Uberwindung der Metaphysik," in *Vorträge und Aufsätze,* Pfullingen, 1954, vol. I, sect. xxii, p. 89.

120. Hegel, *Science of Logic,* trans. W. H. Johnston and L. G. Struthers, London, New York, 1966, vol. I, p. 118.
121. *Toward a Genealogy of Morals* (1887), no. 28.
122. Heidegger, "Uberwindung der Metaphysik," *op. cit.,* sect. xxiii, p. 89.
123. *Science of Logic,* vol. I, pp. 95, 97, 85.

Chapter II

1. *Concept of the Mind,* pp. 62 ff.
2. See the marvelously illuminating study by E. H. Gombrich, *Art and Illusion,* New York, 1960.
3. *De Anima,* 433a21–24 and *Nicomachean Ethics,* 1139a35.
4. For this and the following, see *De Anima,* bk. III, chaps. 9, 10.
5. *Meister Eckhart,* ed. Franz Pfeiffer, Göttingen, 1914, pp. 551–552.
6. Quoted from Werner Jaeger, *Aristotle,* London, 1962, p. 249. Jaeger also notices that "the third Book *On the Soul,*" from which I have quoted here, "stands out as peculiarly Platonic" (p. 332).
7. *Nicomachean Ethics,* 1168b6.
8. *Ibid.,* 1166b5–25.
9. See the last lines of *Antigone.*
10. *Nicomachean Ethics,* 1139b1–4.
11. Quoted from Andreas Graeser, *Plotinus and the Stoics,* Leiden, 1972, p. 119.
12. *Nicomachean Ethics,* 1139a31–33, 1139b4–5.
13. *Ibid.,* 1134a21.
14. *Ibid.,* 1112b12.
15. *Eudemian Ethics,* 1226a10.
16. *Ibid.,* 1223b10.
17. *Ibid.,* 1224a31–1224b15.
18. *Ibid.,* 1226b10.
19. *Ibid.,* 1226b11–12. Cf. *Nicomachean Ethics,* 1112b11–18.
20. For an excellent discussion of Will and Freedom in Kant, see Lewis White Beck, *A Commentary on Kant's Critique of Practical Reason,* Chicago, London, 1960, chap. XI.
21. *Op. cit.,* p. 551.
22. Hans Jonas, *Augustin und das paulinische Freiheitsproblem,* 2nd ed., Göttingen, 1965; see especially app. III, published as "Philosophical Meditation on the Seventh Chapter of

Paul's Epistle to the Romans" in *The Future of Our Religious Past,* ed. James M. Robinson, London, New York, 1971, pp. 333–350.

23. *Metamorphoses,* bk. VII, ll. 20–21: "*Video meliora proboque, / deteriora sequor.*"
24. Chagigah II, 1. Quoted from Hans Blumenberg, *Paradigmen zu einer Metaphorologie,* Bonn, 1960, p. 26, n. 38.
25. Bk. XI, chaps. xii and xxx.
26. See *Discourses,* bk. II, chap. xix.
27. *Fragments,* 23.
28. *The Manual,* 23 and 33.
29. *Discourses,* bk. II, chap. 16.
30. All the works we have, including the *Discourses,* are "apparently almost a stenographic record of his lectures and informal discussions taken down and compiled by one of his pupils, Arrian." See Whitney J. Oates, General Introduction to his *The Stoic and Epicurean Philosophers,* Modern Library, New York, 1940, whose translation I often follow.
31. *Discourses,* bk. I, chap. xv.
32. *Ibid.,* bk. II, chap. xviii.
33. *Ibid.,* bk. I, chap. xxvii.
34. *Ibid.,* bk. II, chap. i.
35. *Ibid.,* bk. II, chap. xvi.
36. *The Manual,* 23 and 33.
37. *Discourses,* bk. II, chap. xvi.
38. *Ibid.,* bk. I, chap. i.
39. *Ibid.*
40. *Ibid.,* bk. I, chap. xvii.
41. *Physics,* 188b30.
42. *Discourses,* bk. I, chap. xvii.
43. *Ibid.,* bk. II, chap. xi.
44. *Ibid.,* bk. II, chap. x.
45. *Ibid.,* bk. III, chap. xiv.
46. *The Manual,* 1.
47. *Fragments,* 1.
48. *Ibid.,* 8.
49. *Discourses,* bk. I, chap. i.
50. *The Manual,* 30.
51. *Discourses,* bk. I, chap. xxv.
52. *Ibid.,* bk. I, chap. ix.
53. *Ibid.,* bk. I, chap. xxv. Italics added.
54. *Le Mythe de Sisyphe,* Paris, 1942.

55. *De Trinitate*, bk. XIII, vii, 10.
56. *Ibid.*, viii, 11.
57. *Discourses*, bk. II, chap. x.
58. *Ibid.*, bk. II, chap, xvii.
59. *The Manual*, 8.
60. *Fragments*, 8.
61. In *De Libero Arbitrio*, bk. III, v–viii.
62. *Discourses*, bk. II, chap. xviii.
63. *Ibid.*, bk. II, chap. viii.
64. *The Manual*, 51, 48.
65. Frag. 149; *Enarrationes in Psalmos, Patrologiae Latina*, J.-P. Migne, Paris, 1854–66, vol. 37, CXXXIV, 16.
66. Paul Oskar Kristeller, a bit more cautiously, calls Augustine "probably the greatest Latin philosopher of classical antiquity." See *Renaissance Concepts of Man*, Harper Torchbooks, New York, 1972, p. 149.
67. *On the Trinity*, bk. 13, iv, 7: "*Beati certe, inquit* [Cicero] *omnes esse volumus.*"
68. "*O vitae philosophia dux,*" *Tusculanae Disputationes*, bk. V, chap. 2.
69. Quoted with approbation from a Roman writer (Varro) in *The City of God*, bk. XIX, i, 3: "*Nulla est homini causa philosophandi nisi ut beatus sit.*"
70. For the importance and depth of this question, see especially *On the Trinity*, bk. X, chaps iii and viii: "How the mind may seek and find itself is a remarkable question: whither does it go in order to seek, and whence does it come in order to find?"
71. *Confessions*, bk. XI, especially chaps. xiv and xxii.
72. Peter Brown, *Augustine of Hippo*, Berkeley and Los Angeles, 1967, p. 123.
73. *Ibid.*, p. 112.
74. *On Free Choice of the Will*, bk. I, chaps. i and ii.
75. *Ibid.*, chap. xvi, 117 and 118.
76. *Confessions*, bk. VIII, chap. v.
77. *Ibid.*, chap. viii.
78. A detailed explanation deriving *voluntas* from *velle* and *potestas* from *posse* occurs in *The Spirit and the Letter*, arts. 52–58, a late work, concerned with the question "Is faith itself placed in our power?" in Morgenbesser and Walsh, *op. cit.*, p. 22.
79. *On Free Choice of the Will*, bk. III, chap. iii, 27; cf. *ibid.*, bk. I, chap. xii, 86 and *Retractationes*, bk. I, chap. ix, 3.

80. *Epistolae*, 177, 5; *On Free Choice of the Will*, bk. III, chap. i, 8–10; chap. iii, 33.
81. See Etienne Gilson, *Jean Duns Scot: Introduction à ses positions fondamentales*, Paris, 1952, p. 657.
82. *On Free Choice of the Will*, bk. III, chap. xxv.
83. *Ibid.*, chap. xvii.
84. *On Grace and Free Will*, chap. xliv.
85. *Confessions*, bk. VIII, chap. iii, 6–8.
86. *On Free Choice of the Will*, bk. III, chaps. vi–viii; Lehmann, *op. cit.*, sent. 14, p. 16.
87. *On Free Choice of the Will*, bk. III, chap. v.
88. "Precious Five," *Collected Poems*, New York, 1976, p. 450.
89. *Confessions*, bk. VIII, chap. viii.
90. *Ibid.*, chap. ix.
91. *Ibid.*, chaps. ix and x.
92. *Ibid.*, chap. x.
93. *Epistolae*, 157, 2, 9; 55, 10, 18; *Confessions*, bk. XIII, chap. ix.
94. In *An Examination of Sir William Hamilton's Philosophy*, "On the Freedom of the Will" (1867), quoted from Morgenbesser and Walsh, *op. cit.*, pp. 57–69. Italics added.
95. *Confessions*, bk. III, chap. vi, 11.
96. Bk. IX, chap. iv.
97. Bk. XIII, chap. xi.
98. Bk. X, chap. xi, 18.
99. *Ibid.*, bk. XI, chap. iii, 6.
100. *Ibid.*, chap. ii, 2.
101. *Ibid.*, chap. iv, 7.
102. *Ibid.*, chap. v, 8.
103. *Ibid.*, bk. XII, chap. iii, 3.
104. Efrem Bettoni, *Duns Scotus: The Basic Principles of His Philosophy*, trans. Bernardine Bonansea, Washington, 1961, p. 158. Italics added.
105. *On the Trinity*, bk. XV, chap. xxi, 41.
106. *Ibid.*, bk. VIII, chap. x.
107. *Ibid.*, bk. X, chap. viii, 11.
108. *Ibid.*, bk. XI, chap. ii, 5.
109. *Ibid.*, bk. X, chap. v, 7. Italics added.
110. *Ibid.*, chap. xi, 17.
111. *Ibid.*, bk. XI, chap. v, 9.
112. *Ibid.*, bk. X, chap. v, 7.
113. *Ibid.*, chap. viii, 11.

114. *Ibid.,* chap. v, 7. Cf. bk. XII, chaps. xii, xiv, xv.
115. *Ibid.,* bk. XII, chap. xiv, 23.
116. *Ibid.,* bk. X, chap. xi, 18.
117. *Ibid.,* bk. XI, chap. xi, 18.
118. *The City of God,* bk. XI, chap. xxviii.
119. William H. Davis, *The Freewill Question,* The Hague, 1971, p. 29.
120. In its extreme form, as held by Augustine at the end of his life, the doctrine maintains that children are eternally damned if they die before receiving the sacrament of baptism. This cannot be justified by referring to Paul because these children cannot yet have known faith. Only after grace has materialized in a sacrament, dispensed by the Church, and when faith has been institutionalized, can this version of predestination be justified. Institutionalized grace is no longer a datum of consciousness—an experience of the inward man—and therefore not interesting for philosophy; nor is it a matter of faith, strictly speaking. No doubt, this is among the most important *political* factors in the Christian creed, with which we are not concerned here.
121. *The City of God,* bk. XI, chap. xxi.
122. *Confessions,* bk. XI, chap. xiv.
123. *Ibid.,* chaps. xx and xxviii.
124. *Ibid.,* chap. xxi.
125. *Ibid.,* chaps. xxiv, xxvi, and xxviii.
126. See especially bks. XI–XIII of *The City of God.*
127. *Ibid.,* bk. XII, chap. xiv.
128. *Ibid.,* bk. XI, chap. vi.
129. *Ibid.,* bk. XII, chap. xiv.
130. *Ibid.,* chaps. xxi and xx.
131. *Ibid.,* bk. XI, chap. xxxii.
132. *Ibid.,* bk. XII, chaps. xxi and xxii.
133. *Ibid.,* chap. vi.
134. *Ibid.,* bk. XIII, chap. x.
135. B478.

Chapter III

1. *The Spirit of Medieval Philosophy,* pp. 207 and 70.
2. *Summa Theologica,* I, qu. 82, a. 1.
3. *Ibid.,* qu. 81, a. 3, and qu. 83, a. 4.

4. Duns Scotus as quoted by Gilson, *The Spirit of Medieval Philosophy*, p. 52.
5. Gilson, *The Spirit of Medieval Philosophy*, p. 437.
6. In "What Is Authority" in *Between Past and Future*, I tried to show the importance of the past for any strictly Roman understanding of politics. See especially the explication of the Roman triad: *auctoritas, religio, traditio.*
7. *De Civitate Dei*, bk. XII, chap. xiv.
8. *Op. cit.*, I, qu. 5, a. 4.
9. *Ibid.*, I–II, qu. 15, a. 3.
10. *Ibid.*, I, qu. 5, a. 1, and I–II, qu. 18, a. 1.
11. *Ibid.*, I, qu. 48, a. 3.
12. *Ibid.*, qu. 5, a. 5; qu. 49, a. 3.
13. Quoted in *ibid.*, qu. 49, a. 3.
14. *History of Christian Philosophy in the Middle Ages*, New York, 1955, p. 375.
15. *Summa Theologica*, I, qu. 75, a. 6.
16. *Ibid.*, qu. 81, a. 3.
17. *Ibid.*, qu. 82, a. 4.
18. Gilson, *History of Christian Philosophy in the Middle Ages*, p. 766.
19. *Summa Theologica*, I, qu. 29, a. 3, Resp.
20. Augustine, *De Civitate Dei*, bk. XII, chap. xxi.
21. *Summa Theologica*, I, qu. 82, a. 4.
22. *Ibid.*, qu. 83, a. 3.
23. Raised by Thomas in the *Summa contra Gentiles*, III, 26.
24. Quoted from Wilhelm Kahl, *Die Lehre vom Primat des Willens bei Augustin, Duns Scotus und Descartes*, Strassburg, 1886, p. 61 n.
25. *The Divine Comedy*, Paradiso, Canto xviii, line 109 f., trans. Laurence Binyon, New York, 1949.
26. Quoted from Gustav Siewerth, *Thomas von Aquin, Die menschliche Willensfreiheit. Texte . . . ausgewählt & mit einer Einleitung versehen*, Düsseldorf, 1954, p. 62.
27. *Summa Theologica*, I, qu. 79, a. 2.
28. *Ibid.*, I–II, qu. 9, a. 1.
29. *Nicomachean Ethics*, bk. X, 1178b18–21; 1177b5–6.
30. *Summa Theologica*, I–II, qu. 10, a. 2; *Summa contra Gentiles*, loc. cit.
31. *Metaphysics*, 1072b3.
32. *Summa Theologica*, I–II, qu. 11, a. 3. Cf. *Commentary on St. Paul's Epistle to the Galatians*, chap. 5, lec. 3.

33. *Grundlegung zur Metaphysik des Sitten,* Akademie Ausgabe, vol. IV, 1911, p. 429.
34. See, for instance, sect. IV of the bilingual edition of Duns Scotus: *Philosophical Writings,* ed. and trans. Allan Wolter, Edinburgh, London, 1962, pp. 83 ff.
35. Quoted from Kahl, *op. cit.,* pp. 97 and 99.
36. See Efrem Bettoni, "The Originality of the Scotistic Synthesis," in John K. Ryan and Bernardine M. Bonansea, *John Duns Scotus, 1265–1965,* Washington, 1965, p. 34.
37. *Duns Scotus,* p. 191. In a different context, however, though in the same book (p. 144), Bettoni maintains that "to a great extent . . . the originality of the Scotistic demonstration [of the existence of God lies] in being a synthesis of St. Thomas and St. Anselm."
38. In addition to the items quoted above, I have used chiefly: Ernst Stadter, *Psychologie und Metaphysik der menschlichen Freiheit,* München, Paderborn, Wien, 1971; Ludwig Walter, *Das Glaubensverständnis bei Johannes Scotus,* München, Paderborn, Wien, 1968; Etienne Gilson, *Jean Duns Scot;* Johannes Auer, *Die menschliche Willensfreiheit im Lehrsystem des Thomas von Aquin und Johannes Duns Scotus,* München, 1938; Walter Hoeres, *Der Wille als reine Vollkommenheit nach Duns Scotus,* München, 1962; Robert Prentice, "The Voluntarism of Duns Scotus," in *Franciscan Studies,* vol. 28, Annual VI, 1968; Berard Vogt, "The Metaphysics of Human Liberty in Duns Scotus," in *Proceedings of the American Catholic Philosophical Association,* vol. XVI, 1940.
39. Quoted from Wolter, *op. cit.,* pp. 64, 73, and 57.
40. Quoted from Kristeller, *op. cit.,* p. 58.
41. Quoted from Wolter, *op. cit.,* p. 162. Author's translation.
42. *Ibid.,* p. 161. Author's translation.
43. *Ibid.,* n. 25 to sect. V, p. 184.
44. *Ibid.,* p. 73.
45. *Ibid.,* p. 75.
46. *Ibid.,* p. 72. Gilson holds that the very notion of the infinite is Christian in origin. "The Greeks prior to the Christian era never conceived infinity save as an imperfection." See *The Spirit of Medieval Philosophy,* p. 55.
47. See Walter, *op. cit.,* p. 130.
48. Quoted from Stadter, *op. cit.,* p. 315.
49. Quoted from Auer, *op. cit.,* p. 86.

50. Quoted from Vogt, *op. cit.*, p. 34.
51. *Ibid.*
52. Quoted from Kahl, *op. cit.*, pp. 86–87.
53. Bettoni, *Duns Scotus*, p. 76.
54. See Bernardine M. Bonansea, "Duns Scotus' Voluntarism," in Ryan and Bonansea, *op. cit.*, p. 92. *"Non possum velle esse miserum; . . . sed ex hoc non sequitur, ergo necessario volo beatitudinem, quia nullum velle necessario elicitur a voluntate,"* p. 93, n. 38.
55. See *ibid.*, pp. 89–90 and n. 28. Bonansea enumerates the passages "which seem to indicate the possibility for the will to seek evil as evil" (p. 89, n. 25).
56. Quoted from Vogt, *op. cit.*, p. 31.
57. Bonansea, *op. cit.*, p. 94, n. 44.
58. See Vogt, *op. cit.*, p. 29, and Bonansea, *op. cit.*, p. 86, n. 13: *"Voluntas naturalis non est voluntas, nec velle naturale est velle."*
59. Quoted from Hoeres, *op. cit.*, pp. 113–114.
60. *Ibid.*, p. 151. The quotation is from Auer, *op. cit.*, p. 149.
61. Hoeres, *op. cit.*, p. 120. So long as the definitive edition of Duns Scotus' works is not completed, a number of questions will remain open concerning his teachings on these matters.
62. Bettoni, *Duns Scotus*, p. 187.
63. *Ibid.*, p. 188.
64. See Stadter, *op. cit.*, especially the section on Petrus Johannes Olivi, pp. 144–167.
65. See Bettoni, *Duns Scotus*, p. 193. n.
66. Such phrases occur here and there. For a discussion of this sort of "introspection," see Béraud de Saint-Maurice, "The Contemporary Significance of Duns Scotus' Philosophy," in Ryan and Bonansea, *op. cit.*, p. 354, and Ephrem Longpré, "The Psychology of Duns Scotus and Its Modernity," in *The Franciscan Educational Conference*, vol. XII, 1931.
67. For the "proof" of contingency, Scotus invokes the authority of Avicenna, quoting from his *Metaphysics:* "Those who deny the first principle [i.e., "Some being is contingent"] should be flogged or burned until they admit that it is not the same thing to be burned and not burned, or whipped and not whipped." See Arthur Hyman and James J. Walsh, *Philosophy in the Middle Ages*, New York, 1967, p. 592.
68. Anybody who is acquainted with the medieval disputations between the schools is still struck by their contentious spirit,

a kind of "contentious learning" (Francis Bacon) that aimed at an ephemeral victory rather than at anything else. Erasmus' and Rabelais' satires as well as Francis Bacon's attacks testify to an atmosphere in the schools that must have been quite annoying to those who were doing philosophy in earnest. For Scotus, see Saint-Maurice in Ryan and Bonansea, *op. cit.*, pp. 354–358.

69. Quoted from Hyman and Walsh, *op. cit.*, p. 597.
70. Bonansea, *op. cit.*, p. 109, n. 90.
71. Hoeres, *op. cit.*, p. 121.
72. Bonansea, *op. cit.*, p. 89.
73. Stadter, *op. cit.*, p. 193.
74. *Ibid.*
75. Wolter, *op. cit.*, p. 80.
76. Aristotle, *Physics*, 256b10.
77. Auer, *op. cit.*, p. 169.
78. For the theory of "concurring causes," see Bonansea, *op. cit.*, pp. 109–110. The quotations are chiefly from P. Ch. Balie, "Une question inédite de J. Duns Scots sur la volonté," in *Recherches de théologie ancienne et médiévale*, vol. 3, 1931.
79. Wolter, *op. cit.*, p. 55.
80. Cf. Bergson's insight cited in chap. I of this volume, p. 31.
81. Quoted from Hoeres, *op. cit.*, p. 111, who unfortunately does not give any Latin original for the sentence: *"Denn alles Vergangene ist schlechthin notwendig."*
82. See Bonansea, *op. cit.*, p. 95.
83. Quoted from Hyman and Walsh, *op. cit.*, p. 596.
84. See Vogt, *op. cit.*, p. 29.
85. Auer, *op. cit.*, p. 152.
86. Bettoni, *Duns Scotus*, p. 158.
87. Wolter, *op. cit.*, pp. 57 and 177.
88. Hoeres, *op. cit.*, p. 191.
89. Stadter, *op. cit.*, pp. 288–289.
90. Quoted in Heidegger, *Was Heisst Denken?*, Tübingen, 1954, p. 41.
91. Quoted from Vogt, *op. cit.*, p. 93.
92. Hoeres, *op. cit.*, p. 197.
93. Bettoni, *Duns Scotus*, p. 122.
94. Bonansea, *op. cit.*, p. 120.
95. *Ibid.*, p. 119.
96. *Ibid.*, p. 120.
97. *On the Trinity*, bk. X, chap. viii, 11.

98. Bettoni, *Duns Scotus*, p. 40.
99. I have used for my interpretation the following Latin text from the *Opus Oxoniense* IV, dist. 49, qu. 4, nn. 5–9: "*Si enim accipiatur quietatio pro . . . consequente operationem perfectam, concedo quod illam quietationem praecedit perfecta consecutio finis; si autem accipiatur quietatio pro actu quietativo in fine, dico quod actus amandi, qui naturaliter praecedit delectationem, quietat illo modo, quia potentia operativa non quietatur in obiecto, nisi per operationem perfectam, per quam attingit obiectum.*"

I propose the following translation: "For if quietude is accepted as following upon the perfect operation, I admit that a perfect attainment of the end precedes this quietude; if, however, quietude is accepted for an act resting in its end, I say that the act of loving, which naturally precedes delight, brings quiet in such a way that the acting faculty does not come to rest in the object except through the perfect operation by which it attains the object."

100. B643–B645, Smith trans., pp. 515–516.

Chapter IV

1. Lewis White Beck, *op. cit.*, p. 41.
2. For Pascal, see *Pensées*, no. 81, Pantheon ed.; no. 438 [257], Pléiade ed.; and "Sayings Attributed to Pascal" in *Pensées*, Penguin ed., p. 356. For Donne, see "An Anatomy of the World; The First Anniversary."
3. *The Will to Power*, no. 487, p. 269.
4. *Ibid.*, no. 419, p. 225.
5. Heidegger, in "Uberwindung der Metaphysik," *op. cit.*, p. 83.
6. For this and the following, see especially Edgar Zilsel, "The Genesis of the Concept of Scientific Progress," in *Journal of the History of Ideas*, 1945, vol. VI, p. 3.
7. Zilsel thus finds the genesis of the Progress concept in the experience and "intellectual attitude" of "superior artisans."
8. *Préface pour le Traité du Vide*, Pléiade ed., p. 310.
9. VII, 803c.
10. See Kant, *Idea for a Universal History from a Cosmopolitan Point of View* (1784), Introduction, in *Kant on History*, ed. Lewis White Beck, Library of Liberal Arts, Indianapolis, New York, 1963, pp. 11–12.

11. *Ibid.*, Third Thesis. Author's translation.
12. Schelling, *Of Human Freedom*, p. 351.
13. *Ibid.*, p. 350.
14. Trans. F. D. Wieck and J. G. Gray, New York, Evanston, London, 1968, p. 91.
15. *Vorträge und Aufsätze*, p. 89.
16. *The Will to Power*, no. 419, pp. 225–226.
17. *Critique of Pure Reason*, B478.
18. *Human All Too Human*, no. 2, in *The Portable Nietzsche*, p. 51.
19. *The Will to Power*, no. 90, p. 55.
20. *Ibid.*, no. 1041, p. 536.
21. "An Anatomy of the World; The First Anniversary."
22. *The Will to Power*, no. 95, p. 59.
23. *Ibid.*, no. 84, p. 52.
24. *Ibid.*, no. 668, p. 353. Author's translation.
25. *Nietzsche*, vol. I, p. 70.
26. No. 19.
27. *Ibid.* Italics added.
28. *The Will to Power*, no. 693, p. 369.
29. *Ibid.*, no. 417, p. 224.
30. See chap. III, p. 142.
31. In *Aufzeichnung zum IV, Teil von* "Also Sprach Zarathustra," quoted from Heidegger, *Was Heisst Denken?*, p. 46.
32. *The Will to Power*, no. 667, p. 352. Author's translation.
33. *The Gay Science*, trans. Walter Kaufmann, Vintage Books, New York, 1974, bk. IV, no. 310, pp. 247–248.
34. See *Thinking*, chap. II, pp. 98–110.
35. *Toward a Genealogy of Morals*, no. 28.
36. *The Will to Power*, no. 689, p. 368.
37. *The Gay Science*, bk. IV, no. 341, pp. 273–274.
38. *The Will to Power*, no. 664, p. 350.
39. *Ibid.*, no. 666, pp. 351–352. Author's translation.
40. *Thus Spoke Zarathustra*, pt. II, "On Self-Overcoming," in *The Portable Nietzsche*, p. 227.
41. *The Will to Power*, no. 660, p. 349.
42. *Thus Spoke Zarathustra*, pt. II, "On Redemption," in *The Portable Nietzsche*, p. 251.
43. *The Will to Power*, no. 585 A, pp. 316–319.
44. *The Gay Science*, bk. IV, no. 324. Author's translation.
45. See chap. II, n. 11.
46. *The Will to Power*, no. 585 A, p. 318.

47. See *Twilight of the Idols,* especially "The Four Great Errors," in *The Portable Nietzsche,* pp. 500–501.
48. *Thus Spoke Zarathustra,* pt. II, in *The Portable Nietzsche,* p. 252.
49. *The Will to Power,* no. 708, pp. 377–378.
50. *The Gay Science,* bk. IV, no. 276, p. 223.
51. *Thus Spoke Zarathustra,* pt. III, "Before Sunrise," also "The Seven Seals (or: The Yes and Amen Song)," in *The Portable Nietzsche,* pp. 276–279 and 340–343.
52. See the excellent *Index* to Heidegger's whole work up to and including *Wegmarken* (1968) by Hildegard Feick, 2nd ed., Tübingen, 1968. Under *"Wille Wollen,"* the *Index* refers the reader to *"Sorge, Subjekt"* and quotes one sentence from *Sein und Zeit:* "*Wollen und Wünschen sind im Dasein als Sorge verwurzelt.*" I have mentioned that the modern emphasis on the future as the predominant tense showed itself in Heidegger's singling out Care as the dominating existential in his early analyses of human existence. If one rereads the corresponding sections in *Sein und Zeit* (especially no. 41), it is evident that he later used certain characteristics of Care for his analysis of the Will.
53. New York, 1971, p. 112.
54. First edition, Frankfurt, 1949, p. 17.
55. *Die Selbstbehauptung der deutschen Universität* (The Self-Assertion of the German University).
56. Mehta, *op. cit.,* p. 43.
57. "Brief über den 'Humanismus,'" *Platons Lehre von der Wahrheit,* Bern, 1947, p. 57; translation quoted from Mehta, *op. cit.,* p. 114.
58. "Brief über den 'Humanismus,'" p. 47.
59. Vol. II, p. 468.
60. "Brief über den 'Humanismus,'" p. 53; translation quoted from Mehta, *op. cit.,* p. 114.
61. "Brief über den 'Humanismus,'" pp. 46–47.
62. *Nietzsche,* vol. I, p. 624.
63. *The Will to Power,* no. 708. Author's translation.
64. *Nietzsche,* vol. II, p. 272. In Mehta, *op. cit.,* p. 179.
65. *Nietzsche,* vol. I, pp. 63–64.
66. *Ibid.,* p. 161.
67. *Ibid.,* vol. II, p. 462.
68. *Ibid.,* p. 265.
69. *Ibid.,* p. 267.

70. Pp. 92–93. Author's translation.
71. Gelassenheit, p. 33; Discourse on Thinking, p. 60.
72. Laws, I, 644.
73. The Will to Power, no. 90, p. 55.
74. Die Technik und die Kehre, Pfullingen, 1962, p. 40.
75. Quoted from Jean Beaufret, Dialogue avec Heidegger, Paris, 1974, vol. III, p. 204.
76. Valéry, Tel quel, in Oeuvres de Paul Valéry, Pléiade ed., Dijon, 1960, vol. II, p. 560.
77. Sein und Zeit, no. 57, pp. 276–277.
78. Ibid., no. 53, p. 261.
79. Vorträge und Aufsätze, pp. 177 and 256.
80. No. 54, p. 267.
81. Ibid., no. 41, p. 187, and no. 53, p. 263.
82. Bergson, Time and Free Will, pp. 128–130, 133.
83. Ibid., pp. 138–143; cf. p. 183.
84. Bergson, Creative Mind, trans. Mabelle L. Andison, New York, 1946, pp. 27 and 22.
85. Pp. 63–64.
86. No. 34, p. 162.
87. Pp. 329 and 470–471.
88. Nos. 54–59. See especially pp. 268 ff.
89. Ibid., no. 58, p. 287.
90. Ibid., p. 284.
91. Ibid., nos. 59–60, pp. 294–295.
92. Ibid., no. 60, p. 300.
93. Ibid., no. 34, p. 163.
94. Ibid., no. 59, p. 294.
95. Ibid., nos. 59–60, p. 295.
96. I use and quote throughout David Farrell Krell's translation, first published in Arion, New Series, vol. 1, no. 4, 1975, pp. 580–581.
97. The whole citation, from which I quote, in my own translation, reads as follows: "Wir leben . . . als ob wir pochend vor den Toren ständen, die noch geschlossen sind. Bis heute geschieht vielleicht im ganz Intimen, was so noch keine Welt begründet, sondern nur dem Einzelnen sich schenkt, was aber vielleicht eine Welt begründen wird, wenn es aus der Zerstreuung sich begegnet." I suppose that the speech at Geneva was published in the magazine Wandlung, but have drawn on the preface to Sechs Essays, Heidelberg, 1948, a collection of essays I wrote during the nineteen-forties.

98. "The Anaximander Fragment," *Arion*, p. 584.
99. *Ibid.*, p. 596.
100. "Brief über den 'Humanismus,'" now in *Wegmarken*, Frankfurt, 1967, p. 191.
101. "The Anaximander Fragment," *Arion*, p. 595.
102. Frag. 123.
103. P. 591.
104. *Ibid.*, p. 596.
105. *Ibid.*, p. 591.
106. *Ibid.*, p. 618.
107. *Ibid.*, p. 591.
108. *Ibid.*, p. 592.
109. *Ibid.*, p. 609.
110. *Ibid.*, p. 626.
111. Unpublished poem, written around 1950.
112. P. 611.
113. *Ibid.*, p. 609.
114. To avoid misunderstandings: both quotations are so well known that they are part of the German language. Every German-speaking person will spontaneously think along these lines without necessarily having been influenced by Goethe.
115. P. 623.
116. Heidegger, *Sein und Zeit*, no. 57.
117. Thomas Kuhn, *The Structure of Scientific Revolutions*, Chicago, 1962, p. 172.
118. *The Lives of a Cell*, New York, 1974.
119. See *Newsweek*, June 24, 1974, p. 89.
120. *Ibid.*
121. *Esprit des Lois*, bk. XII, chap. 2.
122. *Ibid.*, bk. XI, chap. 6.
123. Quoted from Franz Neumann's introduction to Montesquieu's *The Spirit of the Laws*, trans. Thomas Nugent, New York, 1949, p. xl.
124. *Esprit des Lois*, bk. XI, chap. 3.
125. *Ibid.*, bk. I, chap. 1, bk. XXVI, chaps. 1 and 2.
126. See, for instance, R. W. B. Lewis, "Homer and Virgil—The Double Themes," *Furioso*, Spring, 1950, p. 24; "The recurrent explicit references to the *Iliad* in those books [of the *Aeneid*] are there not in way of parallel, but in the way of reversal."
127. *Critique of Pure Reason*, B478.
128. *Aeneid*, bk. III, 1–12, in *Virgil's Works*, trans. William C. McDermott, Modern Library, New York, 1950, p. 44.

129. The Fourth Eclogue.
130. I borrowed this felicitous term for communities from the highly instructive essay "The Character of the Modern European State" in Michael Oakeshott's *On Human Conduct,* Oxford, 1975, p. 199.
131. *De Republica,* I, 7.
132. *Oeuvres,* ed. Laponneraye, 1840, vol. III, p. 623; *The Works of John Adams,* ed. Charles Francis Adams, Boston, 1850–1856, vol. VI, 1851, p. 281.
133. VI, 790–794.
134. The Fourth Eclogue.
135. There exists an enormous literature on this subject; quite instructive is *Die Aeneis und Homer* by Georg Nikolaus Knauer, Göttingen, 1964. Virgil's "*Homerauffassung scheint mir von der spezifisch römischen Denkform persönlicher Verpflichtung geprägt zu sein, die dem Römer auferlegte, nach dem aus der Vergangenheit überkommenen Vorbild der Ahnen Ruhm und Glanz der eigenen Familie und des Staates durch Verwirklichung im Heute für die Zukunft der Nachfahren zu bewahren,*" p. 357.
136. *Aeneid,* bk. VII, 206.
137. Quoted from George Steiner, *After Babel,* New York and London, 1975, p. 132.
138. R. J. E. Clausius (1822–1888), German mathematical physicist, who enunciated the second law of thermodynamics, introduced the entropy concept (energy unavailable for useful work in a thermodynamic system, represented by the symbol ϕ). "Postulating that the entropy of the universe is increasing continuously, he predicted that it would expire of 'heat death' when everything within it attained the same temperature." *Columbia Encyclopedia,* 3rd ed. (Ed.)
139. *De Civitate Dei,* bk. XII, chap. xx.

Editor's Postface

Hannah Arendt died suddenly on December 4, 1975. It was a Thursday evening; she was entertaining friends. The Saturday before, she had finished "Willing," the second section of *The Life of the Mind*. Like *The Human Condition*, its forerunner, the work was conceived in three parts. Where *The Human Condition*, subtitled *The Vita Activa*, had been divided into Labor, Work, and Action, *The Life of the Mind*, as planned, was divided into Thinking, Willing, and Judging, the three basic activities, as she saw it, of mental life. The distinction made by the Middle Ages between the active life of man in the world and the solitary *vita contemplativa* was of course present to her thought, although her own thinker, willer, and judger was not a contemplative, set apart by a monkish vocation, but everyman insofar as he exercised his specifically human capacity to withdraw from time to time into the invisible region of the mind.

Whether or not the life of the mind is superior to the so-called active life (as antiquity and the Middle Ages had considered) was an issue she never pronounced on in so many words. Yet it would not be too much to say that the last years of her life were consecrated to this work, which she treated as a task laid on her as a vigorously thinking being—the highest she had been called to. In the midst of her multifarious teaching and lecture commitments, her service on various round tables and panels and consultative boards (she was a constant recruit to the *vita activa* of the citizen and public figure, though seldom a volunteer), she remained immersed in *The Life of the Mind*, as though its completion would acquit her not so much of an obligation, which sounds too onerous, as of a

241

compact she had entered into. All roads, however secondary, on which chance or intention put her in her daily and professional existence, led back to that.

When an invitation came, in June 1972, to give the Gifford Lectures at the University of Aberdeen, she chose to use the occasion for a kind of try-out of the volumes already in preparation. The Gifford Lectures also served as a stimulus. Endowed in 1885 by Adam Gifford, a leading Scottish justice and law lord, "for the purpose of establishing in each of the four cities of Edinburgh, Glasgow, Aberdeen, and St. Andrews . . . a Chair . . . of Natural Theology, in the widest sense of that term," they had been given by Josiah Royce, William James, Bergson, J. G. Frazer, Whitehead, Eddington, John Dewey, Werner Jaeger, Karl Barth, Etienne Gilson, Gabriel Marcel, among others—an honor roll to which she was quite proud to accede. If she was normally superstitious, she must have seen them too as a *porta-fortuna: The Varieties of Religious Experience*, Whitehead's *Process and Reality*, Dewey's *The Quest for Certainty*, Marcel's *The Mystery of Being*, Gilson's *The Spirit of Medieval Philosophy* had first seen the light as Gifford Lectures. . . . Having accepted, she drove herself harder perhaps than she ought to have to get hers ready in the time available; she delivered the first series, on Thinking, in the spring of 1973. In the spring of 1974, she returned for the second series, on Willing, and was interrupted by a heart attack after she had given her first lecture. She was intending to go back, in the spring of 1976, to finish the series; meanwhile she had given most of Thinking and Willing to her classes at the New School for Social Research in New York. Judging, she had not started, though she had used material on Judgment in courses she gave at the University of Chicago and at the New School on Kant's political philosophy. After her death, a sheet of paper was found in her typewriter, blank except for the heading "Judging" and two epigraphs. Some time between the Saturday of finishing "Willing" and the Thursday of her death, she must have sat down to confront the final section.

Her plan was for a work in two volumes. Thinking, the

longest, was to occupy the first, and the second was to contain
Willing and Judging. As she told friends, she counted on
Judgment to be much shorter than the other two. She also
used to say that she expected it to be the easiest to handle.
The hardest had been the Will. The reason she gave for counting on Judgment to be short was the lack of source material: only Kant had written on the faculty, which before him
had been unnoticed by philosophers except in the field of
aesthetics, where it had been named Taste. As for ease, she
no doubt felt that her lectures on Kant's political philosophy,
with their careful analysis of *The Critique of Judgment,* had
pretty well prepared the ground to be covered. Still, one can
guess that Judging might have surprised her and ended by
taking up a whole volume to itself. In any case, to give the
reader some notion of what would have been in the concluding
section, an appendix has been joined to the second volume
containing extracts from her classroom lectures. Aside from a
seminar paper, not included here, on the Imagination, which
touches briefly on its role in the judging process, this is all
we now have of her thoughts on the subject (though something further may turn up in her correspondence, when that is
edited). Mournful that there is not more; anyone familiar
with her mind will feel sure that the contents of the appendix
do not exhaust the ideas that must already have been stirring
in her head as she inserted the fresh page in her typewriter.

About the editing. As far as I know, all of Hannah Arendt's
books and articles were edited before reaching print. Those
written in English, naturally. It was done by publishers' editors,
magazine editors (William Shawn on *The New Yorker,* Robert
Silvers on *The New York Review of Books,* Philip Rahv, in the
old days, on *Partisan Review*), and also by friends. Sometimes
several hands, unknown to each other, went to work on her
manuscripts, with her consent and usually, though not always,
with her collaboration; those she had learned to trust, she
tended to leave rather free with the blue pencil. She referred
to all this wryly as her "Englishing." She had taught herself to
write English as an exile, when she was over thirty-five, and
never felt as comfortable in it even as a spoken tongue as she

had once felt in French. She chafed against our language and its awesome, mysterious constraints. Though she had a natural gift, which would have made itself felt in Sioux or Sanskrit, for eloquent, forceful, sometimes pungent expression, her sentences were long, in the German way, and had to be unwound or broken up into two or three. Also, like anybody writing or speaking a foreign language, she had trouble with prepositions. And with what Fowler called "cast-iron idiom." And with finding the natural place for adverbs; for that in English there are no rules—only an unwritten law, which appears tyrannous and menacing to a foreigner because it can also, unpredictably, be broken. Besides, she was impatient. Her sentences could be unwieldy not only because her native language was German, with its affection for strings of modifiers and subordinate clauses encumbering the road to the awaited verb, but also because she tried to get too much in at once. The mixture of hurry and generosity was very characteristic.

Anyway, she was edited. I worked on several of her texts with her, sometimes after another editor, amateur or professional, had preceded me. We went over "On Violence" together one summer in the Café Flore, and then I took it home for further attention. We worked on "On Civil Disobedience" in a *pensione* in Switzerland for several days, and we put some finishing touches on her last published article, "Home to Roost," in an apartment she had been lent in Marbach (Schiller's birthplace), handy to the *Deutsche Literaturarchiv*, where she was sorting Jaspers' papers. I worked with her on the Thinking section of *The Life of the Mind* in Aberdeen; in the photostat of the original manuscript, I can make out my penciled changes. The next spring, when she was in a ward in the Aberdeen hospital, for some days under an oxygen tent, I went over bits of Willing by myself, at her request.

When she was alive, the editing was fun, because it was a collaboration and an exchange. On the whole she accepted correction with good grace, with relief when it came to prepositions, for instance, with interest when some point of usage came up that was new to her. Sometimes we argued and continued the argument by correspondence; this happened over her translation of Kant's *Verstand* as "intellect"; I thought it should be "understanding" as in the standard translations. But I never convinced her and I yielded. Now I think we were both right, because we were aiming at different things: she clung to the original sense of the word, and I was after audience comprehension. In the present text it is "intellect." Most of the disagreements we had were settled by compromise or by cutting. But in the process her natural impatience, sooner or later, would reassert itself. She did not like fussing over details. "*You* fix it," she would say, finally, starting to cover a yawn. If she was impatient, she was also indulgent; for her, I figured as a "perfectionist," and she was inclined to humor the tendency, provided no proselytization was in view.

In any case, we never had a substantive difference. If at times I questioned the thought in one of her manuscripts, it was only to point out what seemed to be a contradiction with another thought she had been putting forward several pages back. It would usually turn out that I had failed to perceive some underlying distinction or, conversely, that she had failed to perceive the reader's need for the *distinguo*. Strange as it may seem, our minds were in some respects very close—a fact she often remarked on when the same notion would occur to each of us independently, while an ocean—the Atlantic—lay between us. Or she read some text I had written and found there a thought she had been silently pondering. This convergence of cast of mind, she decided, must have something to do with the theology in my Catholic background, which had given me, she believed, an aptitude for philosophy. Actually I had made far from brilliant marks in the two college courses in philosophy I had taken, bumbling and lethargically taught, it must be added. Otherwise, though, our studies had not been so far apart. In Germany, she had done her doctoral thesis on the Concept of Love in St. Augustine; in America, I had read him in an undergraduate course in Medieval Latin and been exhilarated by *The City of God*—my favorite. Possibly my medieval and Renaissance studies in French, Latin, and English, plus years of classical Latin and later home reading of Plato, had joined with a Catholic girlhood to make up the deficiency in formal philosophical training. There is also the fact, which she did not consider, that in the course of years I had learned a great deal from her.

I mention these things now to cite my qualifications for editing *The Life of the Mind.* It was not a job I had applied for, and when, in January, 1974, she made me her literary executor, I doubt very much that she foresaw what was coming, i.e., that she would not live to finish those volumes and that it would be I, without benefit of her assistance, who would see them through the press. If finally she did foresee it, at least as a distinct possibility, after the heart attack a few months later in Aberdeen, she must have known how I would set about the work, with all my peculiarities and stringencies, and have accepted the inevitable in a philosophical spirit. Knowing me, she may even have foreseen the temptations that the new freedom from interference would dangle before me, freedom to do it "my" way, but if she read me as well as that, she would also have foreseen the resistance the mere glimmer of such temptations would muster in my still-Catholic conscience. . . . If she divined, in short, that there would be days when I would become a battlefield on which allegiance to the prose of my forefathers fought my sense of a duty to her, the picture of all that furious contention—the contest of the scruples and the temptations—so foreign to her own nature, would probably have amused her. I must assume that she trusted my judgment, had faith that in the end no damage would be done, that the manuscript would emerge unscarred from the fighting; lacking that basic confidence in *her* confidence, I would have soon had to throw in the sponge.

But whatever she foresaw, or failed to foresee, she is not here now to consult or appeal to. I have been forced to guess her reaction to every act of editorial interference. In most cases, previous experience has made that easy: if she knew me, I also knew her. But here and there problems have come up which in the past I would surely not have attempted to solve on my own, by guesswork. Whenever I was unsure, I would pepper a manuscript with question marks meaning "What do you want to say here?" "Can you clarify?" "Right word?" Today those points of interrogation ("What do you suppose

she means by that?" "Does she intend this repetition or not?")
are leveled at me. Yet not in my own person exactly; rather,
I put myself in her place, turn into a sort of mind-reader or
medium. With eyes closed, I am talking to a quite lively ghost.
She has haunted me, given pause to my pencil, caused erasures
and re-erasures. In practice, the new-found freedom has meant
that I feel less free with her typescript than I would have felt
if she were alive. Now and then I have caught myself leaning
over backwards for fear of some imagined objection and have
had to right myself with the reminder that in normal circumstances the page-long sentence staring at me would never have
been allowed to pass.

Or on the contrary it has happened that I have firmly
crossed out a phrase or sentence whose meaning was opaque
to me and substituted language that seemed to make better
sense; then, on a second reading, I have had misgivings,
gone back to consult the original text, seen that I had missed a
nuance, and restored the passage as written or else made a
fresh effort at paraphrase. Anybody who has done translating
will recognize the process—the repeated endeavors to read
through language into the mind of an author who is absent.
Here the fact that several years ago—and mainly, I suppose,
because of my friendship with her—I started taking German
lessons has turned out to be a benign stroke of fate. I know
enough of her native language now to make out the original
structure like a distant mountainous outline behind her English
phrasing; this has rendered many troublesome passages "trans-
latable": I simply put them into German, where they become
clear, and then do them back into English.

In any event, so far as I know, no change has been made
that in any way affects the thought. A few cuts, mostly small,
have been made, usually to eliminate repetitions, when I concluded that these were accidental rather than deliberate. In a
very few places, not more than two or three, I have added
something, for the sake of clarity, e.g., the words "Scotus was
a Franciscan" to a passage that otherwise would be obscure
to a reader lacking that information. But with these minor
exceptions, what has been done is just the habitual "Englishing" that all her texts underwent.

This does not apply to the material from her lectures printed in the appendix. These extracts are given verbatim, except for obvious typing mistakes, which have been corrected. It appeared to me that since the Kant lectures had never been intended for publication but to be delivered viva voce to a class of students, any editorial meddling would be inappropriate. It was not my business to tamper with history. Along with her other papers, the lectures from which the extracts have been taken are in the Library of Congress, where they can be consulted with permission from her executors.

I ought to mention one other group of changes. The manuscripts of both "Thinking" and "Willing" were still in lecture form, unchanged in that respect from the way they had been delivered in Aberdeen and New York, though in other respects much revised and added to (the last chapter of "Willing" was wholly new). Had she had time, obviously she would have altered that, turning listeners into readers, as she normally did when what had been given as a lecture came out in a book or magazine. In the present text, this has been done, except in the case of the general introduction, with its pleasant allusion to the Gifford Lectures. If something of the flavor of the spoken word nevertheless remains, that is all to the good.

A final remark about the Englishing should be interjected. Evidently personal taste plays a part in an editor's decisions. My own notion of acceptable written English is, like everybody's, idiosyncratic. I do not object, for instance, to ending a sentence with a preposition—in fact, I rather favor it—but I am squeamish when I see certain nouns, such as "shower" (in the sense of shower-bath) or "trigger," being used as verbs. So I could not let Hannah Arendt, whom I so greatly admired, say "trigger" when "cause" or "set in motion" would do. And "when the chips are down": I cannot say why the phrase grates on me, and particularly coming from her, who, I doubt, ever handled a poker chip. But I can see her (cigarette perched in holder) contemplating the roulette table or chemin de fer, so it is now "when the stakes are on the table"—more fitting, more in character. Would she have minded these small examples of interference with her freedom of expression? Did she set much store on "triggered"? I hope she would have indulged me in my prejudices. And though personal taste has occasionally marched in as arbiter (where once I would have sought to persuade), much care has been taken throughout to respect her characteristic tone. My own idiom has not been permitted to intrude; there is not a "Mary McCarthy word" in the text. In the one instance when, finding nothing better, I used such a word, it stuck out like a sore thumb from the galley proof and had to be hastily amputated. So that the text that the reader has been reading is hers; it *is* her, I hope, in the sense that the excisions and polishing reveal her, just as cutting away the superfluous marble from a quarried block lays bare the intrinsic form. Michelangelo said that about sculpture (as opposed to painting), and here at any rate there has been no hint of laying on or embellishment.

It has been a heavy job, which has kept going an imaginary dialogue with her, verging sometimes, as in life, on debate. Though in life it never came to that, now I reproach her, and vice versa. The work has gone on till late at night; then, in my dreams, pages of the manuscript are found all of a sudden to be missing or, on the contrary, turn up without warning, throwing everything, including the footnotes, out of kilter. But it has also been, if not fun, as in former days, rewarding. I have learned, for example, that I can understand the *Critique of Pure Reason,* which I had previously thought impenetrable by me. Searching for a truant reference, I have read some entire Platonic dialogues (the *Thaeatetus,* the *Sophist*) that I had never dipped into before. I have learned the difference between an electric ray and a sting ray. I have reread bits of Virgil's Bucolics and Georgics, which I had not looked at since college. Many of my old college textbooks have come down from their shelves, and not only mine but my husband's (he studied philosophy at Bowdoin) and my dear secretary's husband's (he had Rilke, some of the Aristotle we lacked, and more Virgil).

It has been a co-operative enterprise. My secretary, typing the manuscript, has gently interposed on behalf of commas and a sterner way with grammatical lapses: she is a Scruple, doing battle on the side of Temptation. Hannah Arendt's teaching assistant at the New School—Jerome Kohn—has hunted down dozens of references and, quite often, answering the appeal of those anxious question marks, been able to clarify, or else we have pooled our bewilderment and arrived at reasonable certainties. He has even (see the bad dream above) discovered a page that, unnoticed by us, was missing from the photostatted manuscript. Other friends, including my German teacher, have helped. Throughout this travail, there have been times of positive elation, a mixture of our school days revisited (those textbooks, late-night discussions of philosophic points), and the tonic effect of our dead friend's ideas, alive and generative of controversy as well as of surprised agreement. Though I have missed her in the course of these months—in fact more than a year now—of work, wished her back to clarify, object, reassure, compliment and be complimented, I do not think I shall truly miss her, feel the pain in the amputated limb, till it is over. I am aware that she is dead but I am simultaneously aware of her as a distinct presence in this room, listening to my words as I write, possibly assenting with her musing nod, possibly stifling a yawn.

A few explanations of practical matters. Since the manuscript, though finished in terms of content, was not in final shape, not every quotation and allusion in the text was accompanied by a footnote. Thanks to Jerome Kohn and to Roberta Leighton and her helpers at Harcourt Brace Jovanovich, many of these have been run down. But as I write, a few are still missing and if they cannot be found in time, the search will have to continue and the results be included in a future edition. Also, even where we do have references, a few of the footnotes are incomplete, chiefly because the page or volume number as given appears to be wrong and we have not yet been able to locate the right passage. This too, I hope, will eventually be rectified. We have been aided by having books from Hannah Arendt's library that were used by her for reference. But we do not have all the books she referred to.

It is clear that she often quoted from memory. Where her memory did not correspond with a cited text, this has been corrected. Except in the case of translations: here we have sometimes corrected, sometimes not. Again it has been a question of trying to read her mind. When she varied from a standard translation of a Greek or Latin or German or French original, did she do so on purpose or from a faulty recollection? Often one cannot be sure. As comparison shows, she did use standard translations: Norman Kemp Smith's of Kant, Walter Kaufmann's of Nietzsche, McKeon's Aristotle, the various translations of Plato in the Edith Hamilton–Huntington Cairns edition. But she knew all those languages well—a fact which prompted her to veer from the standard version when it suited her, that is, when she found Kemp Smith, for example, or Kaufmann imprecise, too far from the original, or for some other, purely literary reason. From an editorial point of view, this has created a rather chaotic situation. Do we credit Kemp Smith and Kaufmann in the footnotes when she has leaned heavily, but not entirely, on their versions? Not to do seems unfair, but in some eventualities the opposite could seem unfair too: Kaufmann, for instance, might not care to be credited with words and expressions that are not his. Kemp Smith is dead, like many of the Plato translators, but that does not mean that feeling for their feelings should die too.

Leaving the puzzles of credit aside for the moment, we have attacked the overall problem of translations in what may be a piecemeal, *ad hoc* way but which does meet the realities of the circumstance, for which no general and consistently applied rule seems to work. Where possible, each passage has been checked against the standard translation, often underlined or otherwise marked by her in the book she owned; when the variation is wide, we have gone back to the original language, and if Kemp Smith seems closer to Kant's German, we have used Kemp Smith. But when there is a shade of meaning overlooked in the standard translation that the Arendt translation brings out, we have used hers; also when the meaning is debatable. With practice, it soon becomes fairly easy to discern when a variant rendering corresponds to an intention on her part as opposed to inadvertence—a slip of memory or mistake in copying; differences in punctuation, for instance, we have treated as inadvertent.

Unfortunately, this common-sense solution does not meet

all contingencies. Unless the text cited was in her library, in English, we have no idea of what translation, if any, she used for reference. In the absence of further clues, I have assumed that she made her own translation and have felt free to alter it slightly, in the interests of English idiom or grammar, just as I would with her own text. (Once in a while, I have retranslated from the original myself. But I have lacked the effrontery to try that much with Heidegger, though I have dared with Master Eckhart.) In the case of classical authors, there is such a wealth of translations to choose among that one could hardly hope to find the one she might have been drawing on—a needle in a haystack. Once, by luck, I happened on a translation of Virgil which—it was apparent in a flash—she had used. My pencil moved (Eureka!) to indicate editor, date, and so on, in a footnote; then I looked again—no. Here, as so often, she had used a translation but had not stuck to it. And it is impossible to show in a footnote in which spots she diverged and which not.

Eventually we arrived at a policy, which has been to cite a translation only when it has been followed to the letter. Where no translator is named, it means that the version used is entirely or largely the author's or that we could not find the translation she drew on, if one exists. Yet even that policy requires qualification. The reader should know that some standard translations (McKeon, Kemp Smith, Kaufmann, the Hamilton-Cairns miscellany), even where not specifically mentioned, have served *grosso modo* as the author's guides.

The Bible has been a special problem. It seemed hard to tell at first whether she was using the King James version, the Revised Standard version, the Douai version, a German version which she then translated into English, or a mixture of all these. I even amused myself with the fond hypothesis that she had gone back to St. Jerome's Vulgate and done her own rendering from the Latin. My inclination was to use the King James version; aside from personal preference, there was the argument that the "thou shalt"s in the author's voice that appear repeatedly in the "Willing" volume should be matched by Biblical "thou" and "thee"s of the older version—otherwise it would sound peculiar. But Roberta Leighton has demonstrated to me that careful comparison shows that the manuscript is closest to the Revised Standard version; hence, that has been used, with a few exceptions, where the beauty of the King James language proved irresistible to us, as it evidently had to our author. At any rate, sticking on the whole to the Revised Standard has done away with one difficulty: the fact that the old version translates "love" (*agape*) as "charity." Since for modern ears, the word has a mainly tax-deductible connotation, or refers to "taking a charitable view" of something, it would have had to be changed to "love," in surrounding brackets, each time it occurred, which would have made awkward reading.

Such preoccupations with consistency and mirror-fidelity of reference will seem curious to the general reader. They are an occupational infirmity of editors and academics. Or they are the game-rules that scholarly writing agrees to and by their very strictness they add to the zest of the pursuit—a zest that cannot be shared by non-players. Hunting-the-slipper in the guise of an elusive footnote must be taken with dead seriousness, like any absorbing sport or game. Yet if it matters only to a few, mainly those engaged in it, where is the sense? What difference does it make whether God is "He" on one page and "he" on the next? Maybe the author just changed her attitude, which is her right. Why seek to divine her underlying preference and lock her, a free spirit, into a uniform "He" or "he"? Well, it is "He." And the will is "Will" when it is a concept and "will" when it is acting in a human subject.

I apologize to the general reader for mentioning these details of footnotes, capitalization, brackets, and so on, as devoid of interest to an outsider as a sportsman's pondered choice of trout-fly when a worm will catch the fish. That the fish is the point tends to be lost sight of by specialists, as Hannah Arendt would be the first to agree. She cared for the general reader, who for her remained a student in adult form. That was why she especially loved Socrates. Still, being a teacher and scholar, she knew about the game-rules and by and large accepted them, though more in the spirit of tolerance one brings to children's pastimes than with the zeal of a true participant. Anyhow, in the course of these months with the manuscript, my well-sharpened pencils have turned into stubs. And now I have talked enough shop-talk. It is time to leave the manuscript to itself.

Appendix: Judging

Excerpts from Lectures on
Kant's Political Philosophy

. . . We know from Kant's own testimony that the turning-point of his life was the discovery of the human mind's cognitive faculties and their limitations (in 1770), which took him more than 10 years to elaborate and publish as *Critique of Pure Reason*. We also know from his letters what this immense labor of so many years signified for his other plans and ideas. He writes of this "main subject" that it kept back and obstructed like "a dam" all the other matters which he had hoped to finish and publish, that it was like "a stone in his way" on which he could only proceed after its removal. . . . Prior to the event of 1770, he had intended to write and publish soon the *Metaphysics of Morals* which was then written and published nearly 30 years later. But at this early date, the book was announced under the title of *Critique of Moral Taste*. When Kant turned finally to the third *Critique*, he still called it to begin with Critique of Taste. Thus two things happened: Behind taste, a favored topic of the whole eighteenth century, he had discovered an entirely new human faculty, namely, judgment. But at the same time, he withdrew moral propositions from the competence of the new faculty. In other words: It now is more than taste that will decide about the beautiful and the ugly; but the [moral] question of right and wrong is to be decided neither by taste nor judgment but by reason alone.

Appendix: Judging

. . . . . .

The links between [the] two parts [of *The Critique of Judgment*] . . . are closer connected with the political than with anything in the other Critiques. The most important of these links are *first* that in neither of the two parts Kant speaks of man as an intelligible or cognitive being. The word truth does not occur. The first part speaks of men in the plural . . . as they live in societies, the second speaks of the human species. . . . The most decisive difference between the *Critique of Practical Reason* and the *Critique of Judgment* is that the moral laws of the former are valid for all intelligible beings whereas the rules of the latter are strictly limited in their validity to human beings on earth. And the 2nd link lies in that the faculty of judgment deals with particulars which "as such, contain something contingent in respect to the universal" which normally is what thought is dealing with. These particulars . . . are of two kinds; *the first part* of the *Critique of Judgment* deals with objects of judgment properly speaking, such as an object which we call "beautiful" without being able to subsume it under a general category. (If you say, What a beautiful rose! you don't arrive at this judgment by first saying, all roses are beautiful, this flower is a rose, hence it is beautiful.) The other kind, dealt with in *the second part,* is the impossibility to derive any particular product of nature from general causes: "Absolutely no human reason (in fact no finite reason like ours in quality, however much it may surpass it in degree) can hope to understand the production of even a blade of grass by mere mechanical causes." (Mechanical in Kant's terminology means natural causes; its opposite is "technical," by which he means artificial, i.e. something fabricated with a purpose.) The accent here is on "understand": How can I understand (and not just explain) why there is grass at all and then this particular blade of grass.

. . . . . .

Judgment of the particular—*this* is beautiful, this is ugly, this is right, this is wrong—has no place in Kant's moral philosophy. Judgment is not practical reason; practical reason "reasons" and tells me what to do and what not to do; it lays down the law and is identical with the will, and the will utters commands; it speaks in imperatives. Judgment, on the contrary, arises from "a merely contemplative pleasure or inactive delight [*untätiges Wohlgefallen*]." This "feeling of contemplative pleasure is called taste," and the *Critique of Judgment* was originally called Critique of Taste. "If practical philosophy speaks of contemplative pleasure at all it mentions it only in passing, and not as if the concept were indigenous to it." Doesn't that sound plausible? How could "contemplative pleasure and inactive delight" have anything to do with practice? Doesn't that conclusively prove that Kant . . . had decided that his concern with the particular and the contingent was a thing of the past and had been a somewhat marginal affair? And yet, we shall see that his final position on the French Revolution, an event which played a central role in his old age when he waited with great impatience every day for the newspapers, was decided by this attitude of the mere spectators, of those "who are not engaged in the game themselves," only follow it with "wishful," "passionate participation," which . . . arose from mere "contemplative pleasure and inactive delight."

. . . . . .

The "enlargement of the mind" plays a crucial role in the *Critique of Judgment.* It is accomplished by "comparing our judgment with the possible rather than the actual judgment of others, and by putting ourselves in the place of any other man." The faculty which makes this possible is called imagination. . . . Critical thinking is possible only where the standpoints of all others are open to inspection. Hence, critical thinking while still a solitary business has not cut itself off from "all others." . . . [By] force of imagination it makes the others present and thus moves potentially in a space which is public, open to all sides; in other words, it adopts the position of Kant's world citizen. To think with the enlarged mentality—that means you train your imagination to go visiting. . . .

I must warn you here of a very common and easy misunderstanding. The trick of critical thinking does not consist in an enormously enlarged empathy through which I could know what actually goes on in the mind of all others. To think, according to Kant's understanding of enlightenment, means

Appendix: Judging

Selbstdenken, to think for oneself, "which is the maxim of a never-passive reason. To be given to such passivity is called prejudice," and enlightenment is first of all liberation from prejudice. To accept what goes on in the minds of those whose "standpoint" (actually, the place where they stand, the conditions they are subject to, always different from one individual to the next, one class or group as compared to another) is not my own would mean no more than to accept passively their thought, that is, to exchange their prejudices for the prejudices proper to my own station. "Enlarged thought" is the result of first "abstracting from the limitations which contingently attach to our own judgment," of "disregarding its private subjective conditions . . . by which so many are limited," that is, of disregarding what we usually call self-interest and which according to Kant is not enlightened or capable of enlightenment but is in fact limiting. . . . [The] larger the realm in which the enlightened individual is able to move, from standpoint to standpoint, the more "general" will be his thinking. . . . This generality, however, is not the generality of concept—of the concept "house" under which you then can subsume all concrete buildings. It is on the contrary closely connected with particulars, the particular conditions of the standpoints you have to go through in order to arrive at your own "general standpoint." This general standpoint we mentioned before as impartiality; it is a viewpoint from which to look upon, to watch, to form judgments, or, as Kant himself says, to reflect upon human affairs. It does not tell you how *to act.* . . .

In Kant himself this perplexity comes to the fore in the seemingly contradictory attitude in his last years of almost boundless admiration for the French Revolution, on one side, and his equally almost boundless opposition to any revolutionary undertaking from the side of the citizens, on the other. . . .

Kant's reaction at first and even at second glance is by no means equivocal. . . . He never wavered in his estimation of the grandeur of what he called the "recent event," and he hardly ever wavered in his condemnation of all those who prepare such an event.

This event consists neither in momentous deeds nor misdeeds committed by men whereby what was great among men is made small or what was small is made great, nor in ancient splendid political structures which vanish as if by magic while others come forth in their place as if from the depths of the earth. No, nothing of the sort. It is simply the mode of thinking of the spectators which reveals itself publicly in this great game of transformations. . . .

The revolution of a gifted people which we have seen unfolding in our day may succeed or miscarry; it may be filled with misery and atrocities to the point that a sensible man, were he boldly to hope to execute it successfully the second time, would never resolve to make the experiment at such cost—this revolution, I say, nonetheless finds in the hearts of all spectators (who are not engaged in this game themselves) a wishful participation that borders closely on enthusiasm . . . with what exaltation the uninvolved public looking on sympathized then without the least intention of assisting.

. . . Without this sympathetic participation, the "meaning" of the occurrence would be altogether different, or simply nonexistent. For this sympathy is what inspires hope:

the hope that after many revolutions, with all their transforming effects, the highest purpose of nature, a *cosmopolitan existence*, will at last be realized within which all the original capacities of the human race may be developed.

From which, however, one should not conclude that Kant sided in the least with future men of revolutions.

These rights . . . always remain an idea which can be fulfilled only on condition that the means employed to do so are compatible with morality. This limiting condition must not be overstepped by the people, who may not therefore pursue their rights by revolution, which is at all times unjust.

. . . And:

If a violent revolution, engendered by a bad constitution, introduces by illegal means a more legal constitution, to lead the people back to the earlier constitution would not be permitted but, while the revolution lasted, each person who openly or covertly shared in it would have justly incurred the punishment due to those who rebel.

. . . What you see here clearly is the clash between the principle according to which you act and the principle according to which you judge. . . . Kant more than once stated his *opinion* on war . . . and nowhere more emphatically than in the *Critique of Judgment* where he discusses the topic, characteristically enough, in the section on the Sublime:

What is it which is, even to the savage, an object of the greatest admiration? It is a man who shrinks from nothing, who fears nothing, and therefore does not yield to danger. . . . Even in the most highly civilized state this peculiar veneration for the soldier remains . . . because even by these it is recognized that his mind is unsubdued by danger. Hence . . . in the comparison of a statesman and a general, the aesthetical judgment decides for the latter. War itself . . . has something sublime in it. . . . On the other hand, a long peace generally brings about a predominant commercial spirit and, along with it, low selfishness, cowardice, and effeminacy, and debases the disposition of the people.

This is the judgment of the spectator (i.e., aesthetical). . . . Yet, not only can war, "an unintended enterprise . . . stirred up by men's unbridled passions," actually serve because of its very meaninglessness as a preparation for the eventual cosmopolitan peace—eventually sheer exhaustion will impose what neither reason nor good will have been able to achieve—but

In spite of the dreadful afflictions with which it visits the human race, and the perhaps greater afflictions with which the constant preparation for it in time of peace oppresses them, yet is it . . . a motive for developing all talents serviceable for culture to the highest pitch.

. . . These insights of aesthetic and reflective judgment have no practical consequences for action. As far as action is concerned, there is no doubt that

moral-practical reason within us pronounces the following irresistible veto: *There shall be no war.* . . . Thus it is no longer a question of whether perpetual peace is possible or not, or whether we are not perhaps mistaken in our theoretical judgment if we assume that it is. On the contrary, we must simply act as if it could really come about . . . even if the fulfillment of this pacific intention were forever to remain a pious hope . . . for it is our duty to do so.

But these maxims for action do not nullify the aesthetic and reflective judgment. In other words: Even though Kant would always have acted for peace, he knew and kept in mind his judgment. Had he acted on the knowledge gained as a spectator, he would in his own mind have been a criminal. Had he forgotten because of this "moral duty" his insights as a spectator, he would have become what so many good men, involved and engaged in public affairs, tend to be—an idealistic fool.

. . . . . .

Since Kant did not write his political philosophy, the best way to find out what he thought about this matter is to turn to his *Critique of Aesthetic Judgment* where, in discussing the production of art works in their relations to taste which judges and decides about them, he confronts a similar, analogous problem. We . . . are inclined to think that in order to judge a spectacle you must first have the spectacle, that the spectator is secondary to the actor—without considering that no one in his right mind would ever put on a spectacle without being sure of having spectators to watch it. Kant is convinced that the world without man would be a desert, and a world without man meant for him: without spectator. In the discussion of aesthetic judgment, the distinction is between genius which is required for the production of art works, while for judging them, and deciding whether or not they are beautiful objects, "no more" (we would say, but not Kant) is required than taste. "For judging of beautiful objects *taste* is required . . . for their production *genius* is required." Genius according to Kant is a matter of productive imagination and originality, taste a . . . matter of judgment. He raises the question, which of the two is the "more noble" faculty, which is the condition sine qua non "to which one has to look in the judging of art as beautiful art?"—assuming of course that though most of the judges of beauty have not the faculty of productive imagination which is called genius, the few endowed with genius, lack not the faculty of taste. And the answer is:

Abundance and originality of ideas are less necessary to beauty than the accordance of the imagination in its freedom with the conformity to law of the understanding [which is called taste]. For all the abundance of the former produces . . . in lawless freedom nothing but nonsense; on the other hand, the judgment is the faculty by which it is adjusted to the understanding.

Appendix: Judging

Taste, like the judgment in general, is the discipline (or training) of genius; it clips its wings . . . gives guidance, brings clearness and order . . . into the thoughts [of genius], it makes the ideas susceptible of being permanently and generally assented to, and capable of being followed by others, and of an ever progressing culture. If, then, in the conflict of these two properties in a product something must be sacrificed, it should be rather on the side of genius—without which nothing for judgment to judge would exist.

But Kant says explicitly that "for beautiful art . . . *imagination, intellect, spirit,* and *taste* are required" and adds in a note that "the three former faculties are united by means of the fourth," that is, by taste—i.e., by judgment. Spirit, moreover, a special faculty apart from reason, intellect, and imagination, enables the genius to find an expression for the ideas "by means of which the subjective state of mind brought about by them . . . can be communicated to others." Spirit, in other words, namely, that which inspires the genius and only him and which "no science can teach and no industry can learn," consists in expressing "the ineffable element in the state of mind [*Gemütszustand*]" which certain representations arouse in all of us but for which we have no words and could therefore, without the help of genius, not communicate them to each other; it is the proper task of genius to make this state of mind "generally communicable." The faculty that guides this communicability is taste, and taste or judgment is not the privilege of genius. The condition sine qua non for the existence of beautiful objects is communicability; the judgment of the spectator creates the space without which no such objects could appear at all. The public realm is constituted by the critics and the spectators and not by the actors or the makers. And this critic and spectator sits in every actor and fabricator; without this critical, judging faculty the doer or maker would be so isolated from the spectator that he would not even be perceived. Or to put it another way, still in Kantian terms: The very originality of the artist (or the very novelty of the actor) depends on his making himself understood by those who are not artists (or actors). And while you can speak of genius in the singular because of his originality, you can never speak . . . in the same way of *the* spectator: spectators exist only in the plural. The spectator is not involved in the act, but he is always involved with his fellow-spectators. He does not share the faculty of genius, originality, with the maker, or the faculty of novelty with the actor; the faculty that they have in common is the faculty of judgment.

As far as making is concerned, this insight is at least as old as Latin (as distinguished from Greek) antiquity. We find it expressed for the first time in Cicero's *On the Orator:*

> For everybody discriminates [*diiudicare*], distinguishes between right and wrong in matters of art and proportion by some silent sense without any knowledge of art and proportion: and while they can do this in the case of pictures and statues [and] in other such works for whose understanding nature has given them less equipment, they display this discrimination much more in judging the rhythms and pronunciations of words, since these are rooted [*infixa*] in common senses and of such things nature has willed that no one should be altogether unable to sense and experience them [*expertus*].

And he goes on to notice that it is truly marvellous and remarkable

> how little difference there is between the learned and the ignorant in judging while there is the greatest difference in making.

Kant quite in the same vein remarks in his *Anthropology* that insanity consists in having lost this common sense which enables us to judge as spectators; and the opposite of it is a *sensus privatus,* a private sense which he also calls: "logical *Eigensinn*," implying that our logical faculty, the faculty which enables us to draw conclusions from premises, could indeed function without communication—except that then, namely, if insanity has caused the loss of common sense, it would lead to insane results precisely because it has separated itself from that experience which can be valid and validated only by the presence of others.

The most surprising aspect of this business is that common sense, the faculty of judgment and of discriminating between right and wrong, should be based on the sense of taste. Of our five senses, three give us clearly objects of the external world and therefore are easily communicable. Sight, hearing, touching deal directly and, as it were, objectively, with objects; smell and taste give inner sensations which are entirely private and incommunicable; what I taste and what I smell cannot be

Appendix: Judging

expressed in words at all. They seem to be the private senses by definition. Moreover, the three objective senses have in common that they are capable of *re*presentation—to have something present which is absent; I can recall a building, a melody, the touch of velvet. This faculty is called in Kant: Imagination—of which neither taste nor smell are capable. On the other hand, they are quite clearly the discriminatory senses: You can withhold judgment from what you see and, though less easily, you can withhold judgment from what you hear or touch. But in the matters of taste or smell, the it-pleases or displeases me is immediate and overwhelming. And pleasure or displeasure again are entirely private. Why then should taste—not only with Kant but since Gracian—be elevated to and become the vehicle of the mental faculty of judgment? And judgment in turn, that is, judgment that is not simply cognitive and residing on the senses which give us the objects which we have in common with all living things that have the same sensual equipment, but judgment between right and wrong, why should it be based on this private sense? Is it not true that about matters of taste we can so little communicate that we cannot even dispute about them—*de gustibus non disputandum est?*

. . . . . .

. . . We mentioned that taste and smell are the most private of the senses, that is, those senses where not an object but a sensation is sensed, where this sensation is not object-bound and cannot be recollected. You may recognize the smell of a rose or the taste of a dish if you sense it again, but you cannot have it present as you can have present any sight you ever saw or any melody you heard. . . . At the same time, we saw why taste rather than any of the other senses, became the vehicle for judgment; only taste and smell are discriminatory in their very nature *and* only these senses relate to the particular qua particular: all objects given to the objective senses share their properties with other objects; they are not unique. Moreover, the it-pleases or displeases me is overwhelmingly present in taste and smell. It is immediate, nonmediated by any thought or reflection. . . . And the it-pleases or displeases is almost identical with an it-agrees or disagrees with me. The point of the matter is: I am directly affected. For this very reason, there can be no dispute about right or wrong here. . . . No argument can persuade me to like oysters if I do not like them. In other words, the disturbing thing about matters of taste is that they are not communicable.

The solution of these riddles can be indicated by the names of two other faculties—imagination and common sense. 1) Imagination . . . transforms an object into something with which I do not have to be directly confronted but which in some sense I have internalized, so that I now can be affected by it as though it were given to me by a nonobjective sense. Kant says: "That is beautiful which pleases in the mere act of judging it." That is: It is not important whether or not it pleases in perception; what pleases merely in perception is gratifying but not beautiful. It pleases in representation: The imagination has prepared it so that I now can reflect on it: "the operation of reflection." Only what touches, affects, you in representation, when you can no longer be affected by immediate presence—uninvolved as the spectator is uninvolved in the actual doings during the French Revolution—can then be judged to be right or wrong, important or irrelevant, beautiful or ugly or something in-between. You then call it judgment and no longer taste because, though it still affects you like a matter of taste, you have now, by means of representation, established the proper distance, the remoteness or uninvolvedness or disinterestedness requisite for approbation and disapprobation, or for evaluating something at its proper worth. By removing the object, you have established the condition for impartiality.

And 2) *common sense:* Kant was very early aware that there was something non-subjective in what seems to be the most private and subjective sense; this awareness is expressed as follows: There is the fact that matters of taste, "the beautiful, interests only in *society.* . . . A man abandoned by himself on a desert island would adorn neither his hut nor his person. . . . [Man] is not contented with an object if he cannot feel satisfaction in it in common with others," whereas we despise ourselves when we cheat at play, but are ashamed only when we get caught. Or: "In matters of taste we must renounce ourselves in favor of others" or in order to please others (*Wir müssen uns gleichsam anderen zu gefallen*

Appendix: Judging

entsagen). Finally, and most radically: "In Taste egoism is overcome," we are considerate in the original meaning of the word. We must overcome our special subjective conditions for the sake of others. In other words, the non-subjective element in the non-objective senses is intersubjectivity. (You must be alone in order to think; you need company to enjoy a meal.)

Judgment, and especially judgments of taste, always reflect upon others and . . . take their possible judgments into account. This is necessary because I am human and cannot live outside the company of men. . . . The basic other-directedness of judgment and taste seems to stand in the greatest possible opposition to the very nature, the absolutely idiosyncratic nature of the sense itself. Hence, we may be tempted to conclude that the faculty of judgment is wrongly derived from this sense. Kant, being very aware of all the implications of this derivation, remains convinced that it is a correct one. And the most plausible phenomenon in his favor is his observation, entirely correct, that the true opposite to the Beautiful is not the Ugly but "that which excites *disgust*." And do not forget that Kant originally planned to write a Critique of Moral Taste. . . .

. . . The operation of the imagination: you judge objects that are no longer present . . . and no longer affect you directly. Yet while the object is removed from your outward senses, it now becomes an object for your inward senses. When you represent something to you that is absent, you close as it were those senses by which objects in their objectivity are given to you. The sense of taste is a sense in which it is as though you sense yourself, like an inner sense. . . . This operation of imagination prepares the object for "the operation of reflection." And this operation of reflection is the actual activity of judging something.

. . . By closing your eyes you become an impartial, not directly affected, spectator of visible things. The blind poet. Also: By making what your external senses perceived an object for your inner sense, you compress and condense the manifold of the sensually given, you are in a position to "see" by the eyes of your mind, i.e., to see the whole that gives meaning to particulars. . . .

The question that now arises is: What are the standards of the operation of reflection? . . . It [the inner sense] is called taste because, like taste, it *chooses*. But this choice itself is once more subject to another choice: You can approve or disapprove of the very fact of *pleasing*, it is subject to "approbation or disapprobation." Kant gives examples: "The joy of a needy but well-meaning man at becoming the heir of an affectionate but penurious father"; or, conversely, "a deep grief may satisfy the person experiencing it (the sorrow of a widow at the death of her excellent husband; or . . . a gratification can in addition please (as in the sciences that we pursue); or a grief (e.g., hatred, envy, revenge) can moreover displease." All these approbations and disapprobations are after-thoughts; while you are doing scientific research you may be vaguely aware that you are happy doing it, but only in reflecting on it later . . . will you be able to have this additional "pleasure"—of approving it. In this additional pleasure, it is no longer the object that pleases but that we judge it pleasing: If you relate this to the whole of nature or the world, you can say: We are pleased that the world of nature pleases us. The very act of approbation pleases, the very act of disapprobation displeases. Hence the question: How do you choose between approbation and disapprobation? One criterion you may guess if you consider the examples: the criterion is communicability or publicness. You will not be over-eager to announce your joy at the death of your father or your feelings of hatred and envy; you will on the other hand have no compunctions to tell that you enjoy doing scientific work and you will not hide your grief at the death of an excellent husband.

The criterion is communicability, and the standard of deciding about it is Common Sense.

On the Communicability of a Sensation.

It is true that the sensation of the senses is "generally communicable because we can assume that everyone has senses like our own. But this cannot be presupposed of any single sensation." These sensations are private, also no judgment is involved: we are merely passive, we react, we are not spontaneous as we are when we at will imagine something or reflect on it.

At the opposite pole we find moral judgments: these, according to Kant, are necessary; they are dictated by practical reason . . . even if they could not [be communicated] they would remain valid.

We have, third, judgments or pleasure in the beautiful: "this pleasure accompanies the ordinary apprehension [*Auffassung*, not perception] of an object by the imagination . . . by means of a procedure of the judgment which it must also exercise on behalf of the commonest experience." Some such judgment is in every experience we have with the world. This judgment is based on "that common and sound intellect [*gemeiner* and *gesunder Verstand*] which we have to presuppose in everyone." How does this "common sense" distinguish itself from the other senses which we also have in common and which nevertheless do not guarantee agreement of sensations?

Taste as a Kind of Sensus Communis.

The term is changed. The one, common sense, meant a sense like our other senses—the same for everybody in his very privacy. By using the Latin term, Kant indicates that he means something different: He means an extra sense—like an extra mental capability (the German: Menschen*verstand*)—which fits us into a community. The "common understanding of men . . . is the very least to be expected from anyone claiming the name of man." . . .

The *sensus communis* is the specifically human sense because communication, i.e., speech, depends on it. . . . "The only general symptom of insanity is the loss of the *sensus communis* and the logical stubbornness in insisting on one's own (*sensus privatus*). . . ."

Under the *sensus communis* we must include the idea of a sense *common to all*, i.e. of a faculty of judgment which, in its reflection, takes account (*a priori*) of the mode of representation of all other men in thought, in order, as it were, to compare its judgment with the collective reason of humanity. . . . This is done by comparing our judgment with the possible rather than the actual judgment of others, and by putting ourselves in the place of any other man, by abstracting from the limitations which contingently attach to our own judgment. . . . Now this operation of reflection seems perhaps too artificial to be attributed to the faculty called *common sense*, but it only appears so when expressed in abstract formulae.

In itself there is nothing more natural than to abstract from charm or emotion if we are seeking a judgment that is to serve as a universal rule.

After this follow the maxims of this *sensus communis:* To think for oneself (the maxim of enlightenment); to put ourselves in thought in the place of everyone else (the maxim of the enlarged mentality); and the maxim of consistency (to be in agreement with oneself, *mit sich selbst einstimmig denken*).

These are not matters of cognition; truth compels you, you do not need any "maxims." Maxims apply and are needed only for matter of opinions and in judgments. And just as in moral matters your maxim of conduct testifies to the quality of your Will, so the maxims of judgment testify to your "turn of thought" (*Denkungsart*) in the worldly matters which are ruled by the community sense.

However small may be the area or the degree to which a man's natural gifts reach, yet it indicates a man of *enlarged thought* if he disregards the subjective private conditions of his own judgment, by which so many others are confined, and reflects upon it from a *general standpoint* (which he can only determine by placing himself at the standpoint of others).

. . . Taste is this "community sense" (*gemeinschaftlicher Sinn*) and sense means here "the effect of a reflection upon the mind." This reflection affects me as though it were a sensation. . . . "We could even define taste as the faculty of judging of that which makes generally communicable, without the mediation of a concept, our feeling [like sensation] in a given representation [not perception]."

If we could assume that the mere general communicability of a feeling must carry in itself an interest for us with it . . . we should be able to explain why the feeling in the judgment of taste comes to be imputed to everyone, so to speak, as a duty.

. . . The validity of these judgments never [has] the validity of cognitive or scientific propositions, which are not judgments, properly speaking. (If you say, the sky is blue or two and two are four, you do not "judge"; you say what is, compelled by the evidence either of your senses or your mind.) In this way, you can never compel anybody to agree with your judgments—this is beautiful, this is wrong (Kant however does not believe that moral judgments are the product of reflection and imagination, hence they are not judgments strictly speaking)—you can only "woo, court" the agreement of everybody else. And in this persuasive activity you actually appeal to the "community sense." . . . The less idiosyncratic your taste is the better can it be communicated; communicability again is the touchstone. Impartiality in Kant is called "disinterestedness," the disinterested delight in the Beautiful. . . . If, therefore, #41 [in the *Critique of Judgment*] speaks of an "Interest in the Beautiful," it actually speaks of having an "interest" in disinterestedness. . . . Because we can call something beautiful, we have a *"pleasure in its existence"* and that is "wherein all interest consists." (In one of his reflections in the notebooks, Kant remarks that the Beautiful teaches us to love without self-interest [*ohne Eigennutz*].) And the peculiar characteristic of this interest is that it "interests only in society."

. . . Kant stresses that at least one of our mental faculties, the faculty of judgment, presupposes the presence of others. And not just what we terminologically call judgment; bound up with it is . . . our whole soul apparatus, so to speak. . . . By communicating your feelings, your pleasures and disinterested delights, you tell your *choices* and you choose your company. "I'd rather be wrong with Plato than right with the Pythagoreans" [Cicero].

Finally, the larger the scope of men to whom you could communicate, the greater the worth of the object:

Although the pleasure which everyone has in such an object is inconsiderable [that is, so long as he does not share it] and in itself without any marked interest, yet the idea of its general communicability increases its worth in an almost infinite degree.

At this point, the *Critique of Judgment* joins effortlessly Kant's deliberation about a united mankind, living in eternal peace. . . . If

everyone expects and requires from everyone else this reference to general communication [of pleasure, of disinterested delight, then we have reached a point where it is as though there existed] an original compact dictated by mankind itself.

. . . It is by virtue of this idea of mankind, present in every single man, that men are human, and they can be called civilized or humane to the extent that this idea becomes the principle of their actions as well as their judgments. It is at this point that actor and spectator become united; the maxim of the actor and the maxim, the "standard," according to which the spectator judges the spectacle of the world become one. The, as it were, categorical imperative for action could read as follows: Always act on the maxim through which this original compact can be actualized into a general law.

In conclusion, I shall try to clear up some of the difficulties: The chief difficulty in judgment is that it is "the faculty of thinking the particular"; but to *think* means to generalize, hence it is the faculty of mysteriously combining the particular and the general. This is relatively easy if the general is given—as a rule, a principle, a law—so that the judgment merely subsumes the particular under it. The difficulty becomes great "if only the particular be given for which the general has to be found." For the standard cannot be borrowed from experience and cannot be derived from outside. I cannot judge one particular by another particular; in order to determine its worth I need a *tertium quid* or a *tertium comparationis,* something related to the two particulars and yet distinct from both. In Kant we find actually two altogether different solutions of this difficulty:

As a real *tertium comparationis* two ideas appear in Kant on which you must reflect in order to arrive at judgments: This is *either,* in the political writings and, occasionally, also in the *Critique of Judgment,* the idea of an original compact of mankind as a whole and derived from this idea the notion of humanity, of what actually constitutes the humanness of human beings, living and dying in this world, on this earth that is a globe, which they inhabit in common, share in common, in the succession of generations. In the *Critique of Judgment* you also find the idea of purposiveness: Every object, says Kant, as a particular, needing and containing the ground of its actuality in itself, has a purpose. The only objects that seem purposeless are aesthetic objects, on one side, and men, on the other. You cannot ask *quem ad finem*—for what purpose?—since they are good for nothing. But . . . purposeless art objects as well as the seemingly purposeless variety of nature have the "purpose" of pleasing men, making them feel at home in the world. This can never be proved; but Purposiveness is an idea to regulate your reflections in your reflective judgments.

Or Kant's second and I think by far more valuable solution is the following. It is *exemplary validity.* ("Examples are the go-cart of judgments.") Let us see what that is: Every particular object, for instance a table, has a corresponding concept by which we recognize the table as a table. This you can conceive of as a Platonic "idea" or Kantian schema, that is, you have before the eyes of your mind a schematic or merely *formal table shape* to which every table somehow must conform. Or: if you proceed conversely from the many tables which you have seen in your life, strip off them all secondary qualities and the remainder is a table in general, containing the minimum properties common to all tables. *The abstract table.* You have one more possibility left, and this enters into judgments which are not cognitions: You may meet or think of some table which you judge to be the best possible table and take this table as the example of how tables actually should be—*the exemplary table.* (Example from *eximere*, to single out some particular.) This is and remains a particular which in its very particularity reveals the generality which otherwise could not be defined. Courage is like Achilles. Etc.

We were talking here about the partiality of the actor who, because he is involved, never sees the meaning of the whole. . . . The same is not true for the beautiful or for any deed in itself. The beautiful is, in Kantian terms, an end in itself because all its possible meaning is contained within itself, without reference to others, without linkage, as it were, to other beautiful things. In Kant himself, there is this contradiction: Infinite Progress is the law of the human species; at the same time man's dignity demands that he is seen, every single one . . . in his particularity, reflecting as such, but without any comparison and independent of time, mankind in general. In other words the very idea of progress—if it is more than a mere change of circumstances and an improvement of the world—contradicts Kant's notion of man's dignity.

Index

273

Index